Alfonso Gálvez

Meditations at Sunset

New Jersey
U.S.A. - 2024

Meditations at Sunset by Alfonso Gálvez. Copyright © 2024 by Shoreless Lake Press. American edition published with permission. All rights reserved. No part of this book may be reproduced, stored in retrieval system, or transmitted, in any form or by any means, electronic, mechanical, photocopying, recording or otherwise, without written permission of the Society of Jesus Christ the Priest, P.O. Box 157, Stewartsville, New Jersey 08886.

CATALOGING DATA

Author: Gálvez, Alfonso, 1932–2022
Title: Meditations at Sunset
Library of Congress Control Number: 2024916545

ISBN: 978-1-953170-43-9 (hardcover)
978-1-953170-44-6 (e-book)

Published by
Shoreless Lake Press
P.O. Box 157
Stewartsville, New Jersey 08886

PROLOGUE

Among the various works of Alfonso Gálvez, this one undoubtedly possesses a character of its own. Though it might seem to the reader nothing more than a random selection of lectures or homilies, united merely by their being published in the same volume, it will soon become clear that it is, in fact, **a book with a true *leitmotiv*, an individual soul, and a very specific content**: This book is a profound theological meditation on the greatest problems facing the Church today, taking into special account what the author has dubbed *The Great Change*, in reference to the events surrounding the Second Vatican Council and which have caused the Bride of Christ to suffer "perhaps the greatest crisis she has ever faced..."[1]

Each one of the book's nine chapters has, to my understanding, a main topic from which several others, closely related to the first, are then drawn out. In this way, important problems are brought successively to our attention, namely:

- A certain *horizontalizing* of Church views: a change in emphasis of its shepherds' concerns from the supernatural to the natural and human plane. Forgetting about the authentically grave and agonizing problems of the People of God, they focus instead on trivial and meaningless issues (Chapter 1).

---

[1] Cf. page 112; cf. also pages 13; 229–231; 304; etc.

- A *lack in both the number and quality of the shepherds of today's Church*, explained in part by a total disregard for the hierarchical structure of the Church and for the qualities that define a true Catholic shepherd (Chapter 2).

- The *kenosis or absence of the Lord* in the present–day Church (Chapter 3).

- The *crisis of current vocational campaigns*, and how to properly recruit and educate candidates for the priesthood (Chapter 4). This topic will also be discussed, and in greater depth, in the final chapter of the book.

- The current problem of a *pastoral ministry that both is lukewarm and requires no true commitment*, leading many shepherds to choose easy but misguided answers to the challenges of our time. In stark contrast to this, the author expounds on both the role of the true Catholic in the midst of a Church suffering from a profound crisis and on the greatness of the true Christian Priesthood, despite the terrible crisis it has suffered in recent years (Chapter 5).

- The *infiltration of democratically hued ideological tendencies* in the Church, resulting in the "*de jure*" blurring and "*de facto*" minimizing of her hierarchical structure, as well as the devaluing of Christ as Head of the Church. These have been used as methods of manipulation, infiltration, and dissemination of neo–modernist ideologies. The true subjects of Christ the King, the true members of the Church, have always been the meek, the poor, the children of heart: those, in short, who have fallen in love with God. That this has been forgotten serves to explain how sectors within the Church have granted excessive importance to the annihilation of poverty or to social justice issues (Chapter 6).

- The *omission of the concept of "person"* in the Church of our time. A greater emphasis (in certain sectors of the Church) is now placed on the "structure" to the detriment of the "person." There is also an attempt to make Christianity both easier for the human mind to grasp and more acceptable in the eyes of the World (as the gnostic heresy would have it). This venture has led to a total misconception of the reality of love and its demands, a falsification of the priestly ideal, and a crisis in vocations (Chapter 7).

- The *profound changes* that have taken place in the Church in recent decades brought about in the hope of finding the "Springtime" of the Church, the actual results of these changes, and the lack of vision they entail. The author stresses, in light of these sea changes, the need to be faithful to the Bride of Christ (despite the label of being "officially condemned" that many who are faithful will receive) as well as the necessity of a true and profound reform of the Church (Chapter 8).

- The *great crisis of the priesthood and of vocations in general* which plagues the Church of our time, what has caused it, and how some would like it to end with the complete destruction of the Catholic priesthood itself. The only solution to this problem is to inspire young men with an idea of the priesthood that is based on their falling in love with Christ. This will allow them to face both the hardships present in their own lives and the countless difficulties of these very unstable times with courage and strength of character. Deep below the surface of this chapter lies not only the ultimate reason for the present crisis in the Church, but also the key to how we must act on a personal level in such times. This chapter is the great finale which brings the author's work to a close with a nostalgic song of hope: a virtue which, as will be pointed out further on, permeates this entire volume (Chapter 9).

By developing the topics aforementioned, the author essentially takes an "x–ray" of the present situation in the Church, revealing: the horizontalizing of views; the misguided youth ministry; the crisis of the priesthood and the failure to recruit vocations; strange phenomena such as homilies preached by children, and altar–girls; feminism within the Church; the *modus operandi* and pastoral criteria used by current bishops; the role of the Bishop's Conferences; permanent deacons; a crisis within the orthodox teaching of the Church; the absence of any type of Magisterium; the crisis of faith in many; the guidelines employed in the election of parish priests, bishops, and cardinals; the blurring of the relationship between the priest and his bishop; the *de facto* acceptance of divorce; the sad state of modern–day seminaries; disasters in the liturgical realm; a false ecumenism; the advancement/promotion of the laity; the crisis affecting the Catholic family; youth catechesis that is completely devoid of content; a crisis within those called to the religious life, etc., etc.

We cannot but highlight the love and veneration that the author professes for the priesthood. Not only has he studied the causes that have brought about its current state of desolation (and which happens to be one of the keys to understanding the crisis that the Church is now facing), but he has also given us answers as to how to foster priestly vocations in these historically trying times: Candidates to the priesthood must be educated to become men fully belonging to God, and at the same time fully adapted to living in that very real world in which their vocations will blossom.[2] This is a concern of the author that is present in many of this book's chapters, and which finds its ultimate explanation at the end.

I would also point out as useful and illuminating the courageous unmasking and demolishing by the author of certain topics and false efforts to either explain the current "status" of the Church or to justify the type of theology that sustains it.

Of all the chapters of the book, I would highlight the fifth, the eighth, and the ninth as the backbone of the author's purpose in writing it. With that in mind, I heartily suggest a careful rereading of said chapters, once the contents of the entire work have been seen.

This is a work that denotes maturity, and in two different ways. In the first place, because the author is already an elderly priest who writes about what he has lived and suffered, what he knows from personal experience. If, as Saint Francis of Assisi has said, one only knows what one has undergone, it can be said without a doubt that the author has truly mastered the subject matter of which he writes. For he has experienced, suffered, and shed many tears prior to writing each one of these pages and before personally facing the problems he himself describes. Here are paragraphs which have been born of sweat and blood and written heart–in–hand. Each new blight on the Church pains him deeply. For this reason, in reading the profound chapters of this volume, we will encounter not so much the cold reasoning of an academic discourse, but rather the product of a beating heart worn out for love of Christ and His Church. We can hear throughout these pages the sorrowful cry of one who has suffered to the utmost degree while living out a long

---

[2]This is a recurring topic, for the most part, in all the earlier works of the author. Cf. especially, A. Gálvez: *Notes on the Spirituality of the Society of Jesus Christ the Priest,* New Jersey, USA, 1994, pgs. 41, 44 and *passim.*

and faithful priesthood in service of the Bride of Christ. Years of serious challenges, trials, upheavals, crises, and revolutions which have put the faith and loyalty of so many Catholics to the test.

It is also a work of maturity in another sense: Beneath the surface of these pages lies the author's entire spiritual and theological framework which, though methodically explained in earlier books, emerges again and again as the key to understanding the problems that are being dealt with here. This is perhaps the reason for the depth of the author's ability to analyze problems and provide suitable solutions, since, as the reader will discover, the root of the matter in each topic is solidly reached. That is why this book, beyond what may appear to the superficial reader, is in fact a difficult one, a work of profound meditation.

This book is also about hope, a true and lasting Hope that is rooted in God; a Hope that shines out all the brighter when every merely human expectation has disappeared. As Saint Paul said: *Spes contra spem* (Rom 4:18). In this we find the ultimate reason behind Lucan's entreaty to the god Jupiter: *Liceat sperari timenti*.[3] That is why each of the chapters ends with a song of joy, full of trust in God. As in all of his earlier works, the author never limits himself to simply highlighting a list of problems. He provides us with solid solutions to the problems he points out, imitating the style and spirit of the Gospel itself. In my opinion, there are three great pillars upon which the author's ideas stand, and which make their appearance in different ways throughout the book:

---

[3]Lucan, *Pharsalia*, II, 12–15, cit. by É. Gilson, *Heloise and Abelard*, Pamplona, Eunsa, 2004, pg. 87.

- The importance of living the reality of Love, which is the very essence of God and of the entire Catholic Faith, and to draw from this concept every possible implication.[4]

- The Church's urgent need to focus once more on the supernatural in all her activities, grounding herself firmly on the authentic teachings of the New Testament.

- The importance of once more placing a loyal and passionate love for Christ in the forefront of our lives and at the heart of all ecclesiastical affairs.

In this sense, the present book will undoubtedly bring light and comfort to all those who find themselves overwhelmed by the present upheavals plaguing the Church of our time. Those who read it will feel fresh air filling their hearts with life, and their thirst for truth sated by pure and crystalline waters.

Is this a book for the masses? Unfortunately, at the present time, I think not. Few are willing to listen to the "unsettlers" of today. The entire world (including a great number of people within the Church herself) seems to have cut itself off from the love of truth (Cf. 2 Thess 2: 10–12),[5] taking great interest in silencing (or ignoring) any who attempt to point it out if previous persecution and unjustified hate have been unable to accomplish the job beforehand.

---

[4] The author's very original theory on the nature of human–divine Love, which has not as yet been the subject of deep and serious study, may be found above all in his *Commentaries on the Song of Songs*, 2 vols., New Jersey, 1995 and 2006. It may also be helpful to read the thoughts on this subject given by Father Faustino Ruiz in his treatise: *El Estatuto Ontológico del Alma Después de la Muerte: un estudio a Través de Platón y Santo Tomás de Aquino*, Santiago de Chile, 2002.

[5] The author's thought about truth can be found mainly in *The Importunate Friend*, Shoreless Lake Press, New Jersey, 1998, Chapter II: "Love for the Truth," pgs. 60–107.

To once again paraphrase Saint Francis, we could say that if it is true that Lady Poverty wandered about lonely and abandoned since Her First Husband died on the Cross, it is even more true that, with the deicide which took place on Golgotha, the world has decided to crucify Truth Itself.

However, I am convinced that in the near future it will become a book sought by many, for several reasons. Firstly, because truth and love always conquer in the end (1 Jn 5:4; Jn 16:33; 1 Cor 13:8; Sg 8:7). Secondly, because it is evident that as time goes by, Catholics will feel more and more confused, more and more lost; and perhaps then, in their search for meaning, they will chance to stop by an old bookstore or hidden library and will discover that One Book that will speak to them of the current situation and how to face it; that will tell them of the wonders of true love; and that will confirm in their hearts the great and consoling truths that Our Lord has bestowed upon us. Thirdly, because a book which has been born amidst so much pain and suffering must needs bear fruit. Not idly did Bernanos say, through the mouth of the Priest of Torcy, in his famous book *Diary of a Country Priest:* "...when the Lord draws from me, by chance, a word that is useful to others, I know it by the pain it causes me."[6]

Is this perhaps the reason why, while reading this book, I never fail to perceive in the background, like a soft and far away whisper, the feelings that are evoked by that poem which the author composed in his youth, and which now in his old age has come to fruition?[7]

---

[6] G. Bernanos: *Obras*, Barcelona, 1959, pg. 60. Indeed, anyone who wishes to follow Christ must experience what it means to suffer for the sake of His Body, the Church (cf. Col 1:24).

[7] With the suggestive title of "While I am singing of my sorrow". One may also read his deeply emotional poem *Desde las altas cimas* which appears on page 165.

Prologue

> *The sun, just starting to shine,*
> *With soft rose–colored hues makes its way slowly*
> *Down the hill's gentle incline,*
> *Waking the sleepy valley*
> *While I speak of woes which greatly burden me.*
>
> *Songs of birds in distant hills,*
> *Dawn's chariot as it rises peacefully,*
> *Softly, with a thousand trills*
> *Now filling up the valley*
> *While I speak of woes that greatly burden me.*
>
> *He keeps searching down the long slopes and steep sides*
> *Of the mountains, forming gullies in long strides,*
> *The great river falls and pounds,*
> *And soon a soft murmuring echo resounds;*
> *But hearing no one answer*
> *His song; greatly saddened, his road now longer,*
> *With a course more sinuous,*
> *Weary and sad, lazy, and more languorous,*
> *He keeps searching for the sea*
> *While I speak of woes which greatly burden me.*

Finally, this is a **book on deep love and fidelity to the Church**. *You weep for that which you loved...,* said the poet Lucan. So too does the author weep; and the pages to follow, born of an adamantine faithfulness to the Church, will help us to understand her and to love her not only as She is now, but also how She should be, once conformed to the will of her Husband.

By choosing to remain thus faithful, the author avoids walking down one of three mistaken paths which, during these times of profound crisis in the Church, appear deceptively at the feet of any man of God: first, the path of false adulation or blind flattery, which serve as poor disguises for either one's need to self–justify or one's desire to advance; second, that of rebellion and complete separation from the Church, which serves only to worsen the situation, as so many "false reforms" of the past have shown; and third, that of trying to resurrect purely formal structures which, though successful in their time, are now obsolete. None doubt the good intention behind this last option; however, it ends up being nothing more than a desire to live a nostalgic dream, highlighted not only by its good wishes, but also (and more importantly) by its anachronisms and its blatant ignorance in evaluating reality. I consider the challenge to be a far more difficult and demanding one, as it requires from us both a total obedience to the true Magisterium of the Church (and therefore to her true Shepherds), as well as an unshakable adherence to truth and reality. If both walk hand in hand with a passionate love for Christ and for His Bride the Church, all the dangers, falsehoods, and ambiguities of our time will be clearly unmasked; and the cry for a deep and lasting reform, *in capite et in membris*, in the bosom of She who is in constant need of it (*Ecclesia semper reformanda*), will surely be heard. Needless to say, such an approach will attract criticism, misunderstanding, "labeling," and perhaps even persecution from others who defend opposing standpoints. However, this has always been the path of those who truly wished to reform the Church,[8] and has therefore been laid out in these pages as the key to facing the current crisis.[9]

---

[8] For instance, let us remember the stance taken by Saint Paul with respect to Saint Peter (Gal 2: 11–14), or that of Saint Francis of Assisi or of Saint Catherine of Siena, to name a few more examples. The author delights in recalling the quote by Bernanos, who said that it is heroic to suffer at the hands of the Church, and not just for the Church.

[9] This is Position C described by the author in the fifth chapter and to which he returns at the end of the eighth and ninth. His final statements on the subject are in his work *Notes...*, pgs. 87–89.

Two concluding observations: Firstly, the meditations of this collection have come to us from two different sources; some have been taken down just as the words were spoken (with the obvious polishing and cleaning–up in terms of style that is usual in these cases), while others (very few) have been written "*ex profeso*" for this book. A keen reader of the text will no doubt distinguish easily between them.

Secondly, I do not know exactly why the author chose the title "Meditations at Sunset" for this book. Perhaps it is because these meditations have been composed and written in the latter years of his life; or maybe because they all have to do with the ultimate theme of Love, a topic to which the author tirelessly returns in all of his talks and writings. Present before him always are the words of Saint John of the Cross, who told us that it is in the evening of our lives (at sunset, if you will) when we will be examined by Love.

Juan Andrés de Jorge García–Reyes
Santiago de Chile, November of 2004

INTRODUCTION

This book is a small collection of meditations, reflections, sermons, or whatever you would like to call it; any name meaning an appeal to those who wish to meditate on the Gospel. Some of these were originally talks or conferences that someone had enough curiosity to record, using the means that modern technology has placed at our disposal. This done, it was only necessary then to add the small task of cleansing the style and eliminating repetitions, something which will surprise no one who is familiar with the burdens to which oral language is subjected. Others, however, have been written *ex profeso* for the publication of this book, with the intended purpose of endowing it with a certain consistency and doctrinal unity.

The purpose of bringing them all together is not hard to explain. It must remain clear, however, that one of the main objectives of the author has been to lay bare his love for the Church. A deep love that has, notwithstanding, found itself to be overwhelmed by a grief no less profound. The author has no intention to teach anyone with these considerations, much less to be seen as possessing unshakeable truths. Mistaken or not —whether it be in every aspect, in part, or not at all— he is convinced that the Church is immersed in a crisis the extent of which (as well as its possible solution) is known only to God. The Church has, to all appearances, surrendered in the face of certain alleged values (purely human ones) and has moved her true supernatural mission to the background. It is as if she had let herself be invaded by the anthropocentric spirit of the modern world and had allowed, at the same time, the *salt to lose its flavor*. The Church, however, was not founded to promote values which could better man's life in this world, but rather to lead him to that real and ultimate world for which he is destined.

Throughout these considerations, the reader will find here and there what someone might flippantly dub "criticisms" of the Church. To be both precise and fair, and taking into account that the Church is essentially Holy, it would be better to call them criticisms of modern-day Christians. After all, we ourselves are her current members. This collection of writings does not mean to be a catalog of the problems the Church is now facing. The grievous situations that we mention here, taking both their number and their seriousness into consideration, are but the tip of the iceberg.[1]

On the other hand, the lack of means with which one may comfortably express oneself is another of the obstacles that the System, always ready to guard its own interests, uses to silence those who oppose it. Despite the fact that today there is widespread talk of man's freedoms and rights, the hard truth proves to us every day that honesty (no matter how respectful and well intentioned it may be) can be a cause of grief to those who practice it.

Bearing this in mind, we could not but feel nostalgia for bygone days. Days in which Christians were allowed to think and express themselves as children of God without fear of reprisal and without suffering punitive measures except those which were the consequence of truly criminal behavior. Even if we were to consider the reprimand

---

[1] Strange as it may seem, the bibliography on this subject is quite scarce. The best and most exhaustive work one may consult is Romano Amerio's book *Iota Unum: A Study of Changes in the Catholic Church in the XXth Century*, Sarto House, Kansas City, 2002. The original version was published in Italian in the year 1985. This book is very hard to find.

Introduction 15

made by Saint Paul to the Apostle Saint Peter as very far off in time, it is not too rare a thing to find certain saints (throughout the tempestuous History of the Church) who would dare to scold the Popes on account of their conduct. This being almost as worthy as the fact that the Popes would accept these corrections, plainly, objectively, and serenely. For instance, the freedom and confidence with which Dante, in his *Divine Comedy*, denounces both the blameworthy conduct of the Popes as well as a myriad of other ills of the Church of His time, is truly admirable.[2] Yet no one has ever doubted the Divine Poet's deep Christian identity or his fidelity to the Church. In the same vein, no historian has dared at any time to question Emperor Charles V's Catholicism, despite political differences and occasional scuffles with the Pope.

Only God knows what may happen to the Church in the times ahead, be it in the near or not–so–near future. From a merely human perspective, the prospects are not encouraging. From the standpoint of the New Testament prophecies concerning the end times... worse still. There is something in them that remains abundantly clear, the reality of which seems to be stubbornly confirmed even by current events: that, as the end times draw near, the Church will be reduced to its minimal expression, and that God will shorten the length of these times expressly *out of love for the elect*. The promise Our Lord made concerning the ultimate defeat of the *Gates of Hell* in their battle against the Church, removes nothing from what we have just said.

---

[2] As a matter of interest, the following passages of the *Divine Comedy* may be consulted, among others: Inf., 15, 112; 3,60; Par., 27, 19–45; 21, 127–135; Pg., 16, 106–111; 3, 133–135; Par.,18, 127–129; Inf., 19 (the entire canto); Par., 18, 122–123; 27, 52–54; Inf., 19, 57; 19, 100–114; Par., 9, 142; Pg., 32, 142–160; Par., 27,66; Inf 23, 58 ff; Inf., 7, 46–48; Par.,11, 118–139. See also, for example, *Monarchia*, 3,3. Etc., etc.

As always, supernatural Hope is our last resort. It is She who leads us to be firmly convinced that God looks after His Church (through the ever-mysterious ways of His Providence) and that He loves those of us who are His children, those for whom He gave His life in Jesus Christ: *Fear not, little flock.* But here we see it once again: it will always be a little flock.

The difficult age in which we live is undoubtedly an age for saints. These dark times happen to be also the most appropriate, the precise, and exact moment, for all those with heart to go bravely forth into the streets and town squares, making Our Lord's motto a reality: *You are the light of the world.*

Lastly, if anyone reads thoroughly and with the ability to summarize, they will soon hit upon the underlying idea of all that is being said in these considerations. Which is none other than that of the priesthood, as well as the generosity of love leading up to it. For, as we have already stated, committing oneself to the priesthood at the present time is a decision that is as generous as it is heroic and sublime.

Everyone knows, however, that the priesthood is the only profession available to men which is either exercised with authenticity to its final consequences —The Good Shepherd— or else it is no priesthood at all —The Mercenary, who works for hire and because of this has no love for the sheep—. That is why it would be useless to gain access to such a high honor, indeed it would be a waste of time to even speak of it, if one does not truly know what Love is. Trying to *relive* the existence of Him Who came into the world to bring us Love, without being completely in love with Him in turn, would make no sense. And the priesthood is precisely the situation, which, more than any other, demands perfect love. Hence, as the poet once said:

To speak of it and not live it is sadness,
To live it and not speak of it is sublime,
Guardian of my dreams, come and tell me in time
How to attain this beautiful existence.

THE HEALING OF THE MAN BORN BLIND

MEDITATION

(March 10th, 2002. Jn 9:1 ff.)

If you are faithful to the will of God concerning your own lives, and therefore faithful also to your vocation, it goes without saying that most of you will reach the priesthood. Then you will understand —as those of us who are already priests know well by experience— that both the task of preaching and that of confessing are burdens quite heavy to bear. In the Sacrament of Confession, for instance, it is not simply about hearing the sins and imparting the corresponding penances; rather, it is also necessary to take upon oneself, in a way, the sins of the penitent. After all, the priest is *another Christ;* and if He took our infirmities upon Himself, carried the weight of our wretchedness, and became sin for us..., given that our mission is a continuation and an extension of His own —we might say that it is indeed the very same mission: *As the Father sent me so I send you*—, the priest takes the sins of the people upon himself to such an extent that, in a certain way, he makes them his own. In this way do the sufferings and the misery of his brothers fall upon him, and hence my mentioning it as a burden both heavy and difficult to bear.

As for the task of preaching..., it seems more like a joke that God plays upon us than anything else. A fairly annoying joke, since by it He hands over to us the no lesser task than that of conveying His Word. Or put in another way: the task of reaching the hearts of others and filling them, being ourselves empty; of igniting them with the fire of God's love, when in reality we do not possess it ourselves. To such an extent does God impose this duty on us that we can truly say, together with Saint Paul: *Woe to me, should I not preach!* However, this burdensome and nearly unbearable task may become, and indeed does become, something wonderful and sublime. For truly the thoughts of God are not our thoughts, and His plans are not our plans; and even that which we might consider, perhaps, as something wretched, God sees however as something glorious and indescribable.

In fact, that is exactly what God has desired for us. To the extent that —as I have repeated to you so many times— if a priest were convinced of the effectiveness of his own strengths and possibilities, he would find himself in a situation where his apostolate would be useless. He will only bear fruit in as much as he is conscious of his shortcomings, *and even by the very fact of the shortcomings themselves.* On account of this the Apostle said: *For see your vocation, brethren, that there are not many wise according to the flesh, not many mighty, not many noble; but the foolish things of the world hath God chosen, that he may confound the wise; and the weak things of the world hath God chosen, that he may confound the strong. And the base things of the world, and the things that are contemptible, hath God chosen, and things that are not, that he might bring to naught things that are. That no flesh should glory in his sight. But of him are you in Christ Jesus, who of God is made unto us wisdom, and justice, and sanctification, and redemption: That, as it is written: He that glorieth, may glory in the Lord."*[1] This is our vocation, and this is our destiny.

The virtue of Poverty reaches its peak and maximum expression in Our Lord Jesus Christ. Who, *being rich, became poor for our sake.*[2] Who deprived Himself of everything to the point of *emptying himself* (Phil 2:7), and of *becoming sin for us* (2 Cor 5:21). Hence the need for us also to be poor and to make ourselves as nothing. To the extent that only inasmuch as we live according to the instructions of Saint Paul will we be assured of the fruitfulness of a ministry that would otherwise be ineffective.

The Lord said this to us in many ways: *If the grain of wheat does not fall to the ground and die, it does not bear fruit,*[3] for instance. And rightly so; for if anyone wishes to live life to the fullest, he must be willing to lose his own, in order to obtain the Master's life in exchange: *I live, yet it is no longer I, but Christ living in me,* Saint Paul said.[4]

The text from today's Gospel reading recounts, in a very wordy fashion —despite the schematic nature of the Gospel— the episode of the healing of the man born blind. A man whom the Apostles found as they were travelling, and about whom they wished to ask the Lord; for this was a beggar whose miserable life had been spent imploring alms and whose state of blindness had existed from the moment of his birth. So, did he find himself in this state on account of his own sins, or perhaps those of his parents? Our habit of

---

[1] 1 Cor 1: 26–31.
[2] 2 Cor 8:9.
[3] Jn 12:24.
[4] Gal 2:20.

misinterpreting events, or of trying to explain them by causes that have little or nothing to do with them, is well known. The very thing is happening in our time. The assessments made concerning many of the problems presented to us by modern society are enough sometimes to make one laugh, or most certainly cry. Why, for instance, do the young people of today get so brutally drunk, causing uproars and disturbances which make it impossible for law-abiding citizens to lead a tranquil life? Sociologists and other experts point to a series of explanations that, despite making us laugh, are no less miserable in their falsehood on that account: municipal laws which have not been properly adapted, the local or municipal police not working efficiently..., or others; without ever reaching the crux of the issue, namely: the fact that modern society is rotten to its very core; that parents are currently incapable of properly educating and handling their children; the destruction and disappearance of the family; etc... to continue would not be worth it. Currently in Spain, for example, no other solution to the tremendous problem of the decrease in birth rate has been found —we happen to be, in fact, the country with the lowest birth rate in the world— except to turn a blind eye to the issue of immigration. And if an uncontrolled flow of immigrants will later on cause new and more serious problems, a solution is sure to be found on the fly: but always, I repeat, without reaching the root of the problem. No one ever speaks of the need for marriages to be generous when it comes to having children, and therefore about the earnestness with which the divine laws must be respected; nor does anyone mention that children are a blessing from God, or that parents are the educators of their children and those firstly responsible for them (and the virtue of generosity is precisely one of the first things that they should be transmitting to them). Something similar to what happens when one speaks about drugs, or of violence in all its forms; it is said that the fault lies in not respecting Human Rights, or in disregarding the Constitution. Because this much at least is clear: once we take the Constitution into full consideration, all our problems will be solved. And as for the youth in general... Ah, the youth! They must learn to take the content of the Declaration of Human Rights, or the United Nations Charter, or the Constitution of the United States and make it the objective of their existence. Once that is done, it is evident that justice will be established throughout the world, peace will reign, etc. And all this being affirmed even by serious people, or those who are at least considered to be intelligent, leads us to a clear conclusion: either the world has gone mad, or we have.

I am reminded at this moment of a Mafalda comic strip, as funny and deep as it always is, and which fits in perfectly with what we are saying. We see Mafalda speaking with Susanita (her best friend whose only desire is to get married and have children), and they both decide to play mom. *I will pretend to be my mom* —Susanita says— *and you, Mafalda, pretend to be yours; and let's talk like they do.* Meanwhile, Mafalda's mother is hiding in the next room and listening carefully. Until Mafalda says: *Okay then: so, which one of us should be the first to say something silly?* Disappointment and dismay for the eavesdropping mother. And rightly so, for too many are the silly things one always hears everywhere.

And his disciples asked him: Rabbi, who hath sinned, this man, or his parents, that he should be born blind? Jesus answered: Neither hath this man sinned, nor his parents; but that the works of God should be made manifest in him. When he had said these things, he spat on the ground, and made clay of the spittle, and spread the clay on his eyes, and said to him: Go, wash in the pool of Siloe, which is interpreted, Sent. He went therefore, and washed, and he came seeing. It is truly a disgrace that our assessments or interpretations of the facts are wrong on so many occasions. And it is because, aside from the fact that our comprehension is weak enough as it is, we also happen to be immersed in a world of lies and manipulation. A world which has made its free choice for falsehood, and about which I advise you all to read *La Metafísica de la Opción Intelectual* (The Metaphysics of Intellectual Choice), that book by Carlos Cardona which is quite interesting and already a classic.

The Lord then adds to this a few words which remain somewhat mysterious. In reality, His words are always profound, though they are also sometimes difficult to understand: *I must work the works of him that sent me, whilst it is day: the night cometh, when no man can work. As long as I am in the world, I am the light of the world.* What do these statements really mean? As you all know, Saint John likes to contrast light and darkness in his writings. In this particular text, in which he speaks of giving sight to the blind man, the contrast between light and darkness may be referencing the contrast between good and evil, truth and falsehood, kindness and malice.

When Jesus says that it is fitting to do the works of God while it is still day, for afterwards the night comes, when no one is able to work, only to add immediately after: *I am the light of the world...*, perhaps He wanted to say to us: Carry out the works of God while I am with you; because when the night comes and you find yourselves submerged in darkness, when I am no longer with you and you have need of Me, you will not be able to do anything. For *without me you can do nothing.*[5] Which means that if we are with Him and He comes to be our very life, transforming us, if anything, into other Christs; then, and only then, will we have the power to do anything.

---

[5] Jn 15:5.

Unfortunately, modern–day Catholicism, indeed Christianity as a whole, has lost so much of its identity that it has become a message of concern for social projects, social welfare, the establishment of justice or Democracy throughout the world, the elimination of the oppressed classes, the struggle for peace, etc. Though we must point out that, as far as peace goes, our current Pastoral ministry often understands it in its purely human sense and not in the sense of that peace spoken of by Jesus. The reality is that the Person of Our Lord has been displaced in favor of an ensemble of marginal affairs. They may be as fitting and as important as you like, but at the same time they are nothing more —at least many of them— than utopias and uchronias. We, the poor and the weak who live in the world, know very well that there will never be absolute peace here on earth, nor will all injustice disappear. Everywhere and at all times, *those who wish to live according to Christ will suffer persecution.*[6] We Christians, though we must never fall into pessimism, are fully aware that manipulation, the abuse of those in power against the weak, and the reign of Falsehood will always be there. When God expelled Adam and Eve from Paradise, He set an angel with a flaming sword at the gate; which may perhaps suggest that on earth there would never again be an Earthly Paradise (no matter how much Marx would speak to the contrary). Such a place would only be seen again at the end of History, when there will be *new heavens and a new earth.*[7]

What I am trying to say to you with all this is that the only really important thing, the only thing that counts, is to allow Jesus Christ to permeate your lives. Add afterwards anything you like to this: the concern for the marginalized and the oppressed, social

---

[6] 2 Tim 3:12.
[7] Is 65:17.

justice and peace throughout the world... But only as long as Christ, in the words of Saint Paul, is your life. Let your daily activities and toils, your objectives, hopes, and plans be always directed towards inserting in others the life of Christ —that life that you will already be living. This task you will have to carry out with true heroism. And why with heroism? Because we are well aware that, when leading others to Christ, we must do so knowing fully well that we ourselves are not filled with Him yet; and that we must strengthen them when we know ourselves to be weak, and enlighten them when we know all too well our own ignorance.

Therefore, it is safe to say that the role of the priest and minister of Christ, carried out in these times in which we live, is both heroic and super–human. A wonderful challenge, both thrilling and exciting. And it is fantastic to think that, despite the current state of things, God has nevertheless desired to place His trust in us: choosing the foolish according to the world to confound the wise according to the world. Making it clear, once again, that God is able make His plans using a system of measurement that, all too often, seems laughable to us.

In any case, the blind man, obeying Jesus, went to the pool of Siloe and returned healed. Which became the cause —we humans make things so difficult— of a great uproar and a terrible argument within the Synagogue. The leaders among the Jews, the Pharisee well–wishers, were scandalized to the utmost degree because the healing had taken place on the Sabbath. Once again, we see trifles getting in the way of man's puny understanding, keeping him from seeing what is truly important. Trees get in the way of our seeing the forest. What do we see happening, for example, to the Church as a whole, or specifically the Church in the United States? To be frank, the situation of the Church in the USA, at these moments, is horribly grave (though it could not be said that Europe is doing any better).

And yet, despite the existence in the Church of a rather distressing situation, we see many Shepherds concerned with trivial and insignificant matters, having forsaken all else. For example, in the United States we are angrily accused of not supporting the idea that *altar girls* should serve in our Masses. In the first place, I must say that there is no regulation in Canon Law which lays upon us the obligation to use *altar girls* in acts of worship. At least, we have never been ordered to do so by anyone. I remember that on a certain occasion Bishop Hughes of Metuchen (NJ, USA), a wonderful person and a good friend of mine, made me an offer in which I had to choose: he would offer us a parish under the condition that we should accept in it the implementation of *altar girls*. But the offer came merely in the form of a choice, as the bishop was unwilling, at any time, to force this parish upon us.

Of course, I thanked the bishop for his offer, but did not wish to accept the parish, as I felt there were good reasons for not doing so. Firstly, because it is a time–tested fact that when girls get involved in the liturgy they tend to oust the boys (who say that, since the service at the altar is now a girl thing, they wish to have nothing to do with it). Whereby, lacking the age–old institution of the *altar–boys*, we have deprived ourselves of a source of priestly vocations that was also age–old.

Aside from this, there is also the danger of undermining certain things. You will see that I am not about to start an argument, which moreover would be useless and pointless, concerning which of the two sexes is more important; if man is more important, or if perhaps woman is. I believe that both are equally important and that, within the Church and society itself, each has been assigned peculiar tasks, both specific and necessary; albeit different. For more than twenty centuries there have been saints in the Church both male and female, and all have completed their mission regardless of their sex. But there is a possibility, if certain new trends that have appeared succeed, that obstacles and impediments will be placed in the way of tasks that men and women —each on their part— are called to perform within the Church and society: some of which are meant to be carried out only by men, while others are called to be undertaken by women alone.

It is likely that many will think that women are playing a great part when they distribute Holy Communion in Eucharistic celebrations, when they read the liturgical texts, or even when they preach. I, for one, do not believe this is so. One of our priests told me recently about a nun who had come to his parish with the purpose of spreading a certain type of propaganda, of missionary ilk or something like that. The nun expressed her desire to preach during the Eucharistic liturgy. Our priest kindly thanked her while offering her his firmest refusal: I am sorry, Sister, but I will be the one —so he said kindly to the nun— to preach the homily, just like I am supposed to.

It is clear that if we were to establish as a custom that women be the ones to distribute the Holy Eucharist, preach the homilies, take care of the liturgical readings, etc., there is a serious danger of them forgetting and neglecting those tasks and duties which do belong to them —and which are moreover, indispensable— as members of society and of the Church: their role as mothers, and most importantly, as educators of their children; the care they give to the sick, the poor, and the helpless; or the job of comforting their husbands and teaching them be strong in the face of suffering, pain, or illness (for it is without doubt that the well–known label of *gentle sex* is nothing more than a fabrication of man). Women can play a very important role in catechism, to say nothing about their capabilities in the realm of prayer and contemplation. God alone knows the work that has been carried out by women, throughout twenty centuries of the Church, in cloistered convents, hospitals, and houses of mercy.

In both the United States and Spain, the Church is currently facing problems of even greater severity. It is abundantly clear that neither deliberations, nor the profusion of *altar girls* or of permanent deacons are going to solve anything. Regarding the latter (permanent deacons), I believe that their institution —or better yet, their re–institution— is something that falls under the exclusive authority of the Church, and it is logical to suppose that she will take into consideration all the circumstances concerning this case. If they happen to be necessary in some places, they should be welcome, since it is for that reason they have been established; however, to increase their number just for the sake of it seems pointless as well as harmful (I know parishes in the United States in which there are *more than one hundred Eucharistic ministers!*) in the sense that it might aggravate the problem of our priest–shortage (all the greater as time goes by). Though I have my own personal opinions about this, for I harbor the suspicion that some individuals have the elimination of priestly celibacy in mind (once all the priests have disappeared, it's obvious that these deacons —who in general will be married— will have to be ordained to the priesthood).

In any case, and all the while, the serious and fundamental problems remain, and no one seems to be paying them too much attention: the moral destruction of the clergy; the spiritual misery suffered by its members (ever since the Shepherds began dedicating themselves to promoting the laity), and their abandonment by so many Bishops (who have forgotten their duties as Fathers and Shepherds, dedicating, instead, so much of their energies to far and wide meetings as well as to complex and unending bureaucratic, administrative, and even political, projects); the scarcity of vocations —both to secular and religious life—, the destruction of the family; the desertion of our youth; the hedonizing and paganizing of society; a lack of genuine reform in the organization, formation, and teaching within the priestly Seminaries; the acceptance and implementation of divorce and euthanasia everywhere; widespread abortion; the manipulation and muddying of nearly all the media... *and meanwhile the greyhounds arrived and caught the two rabbits alive,* as the fable says.

Well then, and though it may seem incredible: How could a man be from God who heals on the Sabbath? Thus did the Synagogue and all the self–righteous speak. He has healed on the Sabbath; therefore he is a sinner. And we all know the ensuing violent dialogue with the ex-blind man and the resulting uproar immediately after.

—*How can a sinful man perform such miracles?* And they were unable to come to any sort of agreement. Until it occurred to them to ask the one who was the very cause of the scandal:

—*What do you say of him, since he has opened your eyes?* And the poor beggar answered plainly and courageously:

—*He is a prophet.*

Then, desirous to not believe in any way, they turned to the parents of the blind man who had been healed. They were terrified, logically, and managed to turn the course of the interrogation back towards the ex–blind man. So, the Jews called him again and resumed their assault, with results that were more than unexpected:

—*Give glory to God. We know that this man is a sinner.*

And the surprising answer:

—*I know not whether he is a sinner; the only thing I know is that I was blind and now I see... I have told you already and you would not listen. Do you want to become his disciples yourselves?*

Fierce exasperation from the Jews:

—*Be thou his disciple; but we are the disciples of Moses. We know that God spoke to Moses: but as to this man, we know not from whence he is.*

The only thing missing was for them to say: nor do we wish to know. Until the moment comes in which Jesus Himself arranges to be met by the ex-blind man and puts everything in its proper place. And as usual He goes straight to the heart and indeed to the very root of the matter. It is no longer an issue of whether the healing took place on Saturday or not. This problem is secondary and purely marginal. Nor is it about the disavowal, concerning His Person, upon which the Jews had previously decided against all evidence. Jesus now simply stands face to face with the wretched man. For often it is precisely the unfortunate and the wretched who are the most capable of opening their hearts to the truth. For this reason, He asks him now the key and decisive question:

—*Dost thou believe in the Son of Man?*

And the ex-blind man answers:

—*Who is he, Lord, that I may believe in him?*

—*Thou hast both seen him; and it is he that talketh with thee,* answered Jesus.

A question from Our Lord which was so striking and so intense since for the Jews the expression Son of Man had a meaning that was all too clear. It was a direct reference to the divinity of the Messiah, according to the well-known prophecy of Daniel. One of the ancient prophecies that was most full of mystery and that was most shrouded in that poetic beauty and that undefined veil of obscurity proper to this type of oracles. Obscurity and a direct hit to the heart all at once: *I beheld therefore in the vision of the night, and lo, one like the son of man came with the clouds of heaven, and he came even to the Ancient of days: and they presented him before him. And he gave him power, and glory, and a kingdom: and all peoples, tribes and tongues shall serve him: his power is an everlasting power that shall not be taken away.*

That is why Our Lord says to him:

—*Dost thou believe in the Son of Man?*

The ex–blind man understood all too well the meaning of the question, and because of this he answers:

—*Who is he, Lord, that I may believe in him?*

—*It is I. He who speaketh with you.* And it is then that the beggar, without further consideration, kneels down and adores Him, acknowledging Him as God. Our Lord's final words contain the same tremendous relevance as ever:

—*For judgment I am come into this world; that they who see not, may see; and they who see, may become blind.*

For to acknowledge Jesus as Messiah and as God one needs the will and the sense which emanates from a good and simple heart. Either way —by admission or denial— this is how it becomes possible for those who do not see, to see; and for those who can see, to become blind.

It is curious to note exactly what is made evident in this episode. In it, on the one hand, you have those who are officially good and religious, the Pharisees, the well–wishers, the scribes, the acknowledged institutions, the Synagogue... On the other hand we find the poor, the wretched, the weak, the abandoned, and those who are not acknowledged by the world..., precisely those whose heart is truly open to receiving God. And it is not that the Lord rejects institutions, by any stretch.

Jesus neither speaks nor acts in any way against the Synagogue. He even enters into it on the Sabbath days, to preach and even sometimes to carry out diverse forms of healing. All too well did Our Lord know the needs of the synagogues, the scribes, institutions like the Sanhedrin... Just as His Church was necessary then and continues to be necessary now; a Church which is both holy and sinful at the same time. The Lord knew that it would be precisely within the boundaries of that Church which is divine, even though it is, at the same time, so *human*, that the small and hapless ones of this world would find the road to salvation, which is none other than that of finding Him. For it is only in this Church that Jesus can be found. As for us, we are Her children and could never do away with her, even knowing that often she will not understand us. Pope Pius XII himself said in one of his addresses to priests that they should expect from the Church neither reward nor understanding in this world.

It is in this context where one clearly appreciates the condition of trifles that characterizes certain issues when compared with those that are truly fundamental, namely: Whether one should heal or not on the Sabbath, whether one agrees or not to the use of *altar girls* in worship..., and so many other mini–issues that so frequently draw the attention of the Shepherds and which lead nowhere.

The only precious Jewel is Jesus Christ and our life in Him. It is true enough that the most wonderful jewels are often hidden in cases or reliquaries of little or no value. Though it is no less true that it is precisely that case which makes the care and conservation of the jewel possible, and which makes easy the task of carrying it from one place to another so that it may be admired by all.

Having reached this point, let us go back to what I said to you at the beginning of this talk: I wish that the Lord would be your life! May your littleness and your weakness not stop you on your quest, nor may you ever draw back before the wonderful and sublime mission to which God has called you —which, indeed, will surpass your strengths and conquer your weaknesses. The Country Priest of Bernanos was truly convinced of his weaknesses and of the apparent futility of his life; despite the fact that it was precisely that weakness which brought about the conversion of others. Because of this, it is at the moment of his death when he finally realizes, as did the Apostle, that it was precisely that weakness which has facilitated the strength and intervention of God: *All is grace*, he tells us in his last and synoptic message as he dies.

I admit that I have always been strongly moved by certain words of Our Lord concerning what will happen at the end of our lives: *Well done, good and faithful servant, because thou hast been faithful over a few things, I will place thee over many things.* As if Our Lord, acknowledging and beginning with our weakness, had decided to build a great deal on it. In resemblance to Himself, Who made Himself as nothing out of love for us. For the thoughts of God have little to do with the thoughts of men.

God has issued to us the challenge of reaching holiness; a call to a veritable combat of love: *And the banner which he has raised over me is a banner of love.* When you do not fully understand the ways of the terrestrial Church, and this may happen to you often, follow them faithfully nevertheless. As did the Virgin at the foot of the Cross; who, though without understanding at all the designs of the Father, obeyed entirely with that fidelity that only true love can bestow.

THE GOOD SHEPHERD

MEDITATION

(April 21st, 2002. Jn 10:1 ff.)

I was saying to you yesterday in the homily that, even though it may seem that some of Our Lord's words affect us more than others, that such and such words possess a certain peculiarity or distinctive feature, in reality all of them are profound and essential: *The words that I have spoken to you are Spirit and Life.*[1] Though it must be acknowledged that among the statements or words of Our Lord which most draw our attention, we must name the parable or allegory of the Good Shepherd, which the Church puts forward today as the reading in her liturgy, on the feast day or Sunday of the Good Shepherd. The text belongs to the 10th chapter of the Gospel according to Saint John:

Amen, amen I say to you: He that entereth not by the door into the sheepfold, but climbeth up another way, the same is a thief and a robber. But he that entereth in by the door is the shepherd of the sheep. To him the porter openeth; and the sheep hear his voice: and

---

[1] Jn 6:64.

he calleth his own sheep by name, and leadeth them out. And when he hath let out his own sheep, he goeth before them: and the sheep follow him, because they know his voice. But a stranger they follow not, but fly from him, because they know not the voice of strangers.

The text goes on to say that Jesus spoke this parable which, of course, His disciples did not understand. Then He continued saying to them:

Amen, amen I say to you, I am the door of the sheep. All others, as many as have come, are thieves and robbers: and the sheep heard them not. I am the door. By me, if any man enter in, he shall be saved: and he shall go in, and go out, and shall find pastures. The thief cometh not, but for to steal, and to kill, and to destroy. I am come that they may have life, and may have it more abundantly.

This parable presents us with a subject of enormous importance and significance. We all know that Jesus Christ, the founder of the Church, established within her two classes of faithful: the so-called simple faithful and the Shepherds. The latter have been entrusted with the mission of leading the sheep of the flock; and both, Shepherds and the simple faithful, are to be led by Jesus Christ, the Supreme Shepherd of the sheep and Head of the entire organism: His Mystical Body which is the Church. The Church, therefore, possesses a hierarchical structure in accordance with the desires and plans of her Founder. Consequently, there are in her two kinds of faithful perfectly differentiated in degree as well as in quality: the simple faithful and the Shepherds, as we have said before.

This extremely important issue has to do with the very establishment of the Church herself, which none can now alter. Therefore, it has a profound bearing on some of the more serious problems with which the Church is now grappling: the lack of Shepherds, on the one hand, and the earnest moral and spiritual crisis that the clergy in general is currently suffering, on the other.

If there is a group of sciences which deserves to be termed as exact sciences (all sciences are sciences in as much as they are exact), we might well say that Mathematics is the exact science par excellence. But this science of numbers, so necessary when it comes to solving the theoretical/practical problems of everyday life, also requires for its proper functioning the correct exposition of those very problems and an accurate depiction of the data. Without this one would reach absurd and nonsensical conclusions. That is why, when it comes down to it, Mathematics is pure logic, which is to say a clear and simple exposition of the truth.

If we apply what has been said about Mathematics to the two just–mentioned problems of the Church, everything seems to point to the fact that the issue of the Shepherds, as it has been laid out today in the Church, has no solution. It would have one if the data brought to bear in this case were exact and correctly explained. There are, perhaps, not many who are willing to speak up about this issue, even though it is a topic which is already on everyone's mind: a large part of the Christian People live bereft of Shepherds, or with Shepherds that are such in name only.

However, the approach commonly made to such a grave issue is far from being the right one, and the final assessment tends to be worse still. Using medical terms, one could say that if the medical diagnosis of a patient were incorrect, the least of the patient's worries would be an indefinite lengthening of the illness.

In today's gospel (and throughout the entire Chapter ten of Saint John's Gospel), Our Lord speaks to us about this problem, its correct approach, and how to fix it. But quite often His voice is not listened to, unfortunately.

One can easily suppose that the Lord would have foreseen this problem and worried a great deal over what was going to happen to the Shepherds of His Church. It would be insane to think that Jesus was not going to address this topic or that He would not have provided us with the appropriate means to solve the problem.

Perhaps you think that I am beating too much around the bush. I am even afraid that, young as you are, you do not realize the tremendous importance of what we are dealing with here. Let me beg you first to make a small effort to understand, in some way at least, what I am clumsily trying to tell you; and secondly, to ponder all this in your prayer time so that, by the light of the Holy Spirit's inspirations, you may come to grasp the depth of this problem and the solutions which Our Lord provides.

It is surprising to see how reluctant we, and in general a great number of Christians, are to embrace Our Lord's analysis of the problem. And even more surprising still is our attitude of indifference towards the solutions He points out to us.

Amen, amen, I say to you... It is well known that, when Jesus begins His statements with this phrase, He does it to sharply call our attention to the importance of what He is going to say next (though it is very true that modern translations of biblical texts soften the phrase too much). *Amen, amen I say to you: He that entereth not by the door into the sheepfold, but climbeth up another way, the same is a thief and a robber.*

The first condition, then, according to the Lord, for someone not to be considered a thief or a robber —or, to put it another way, in order to be a good Shepherd of the sheep— is *to enter by the door*. But then, what exactly does the phrase *enter by the door* mean? It is a metaphor, undoubtedly, but one that does not impose upon us the need to torment our brain in figuring it out, for it is the Lord Himself who explains it quite clearly. In dealing with issues so tremendously vital, Our Lord did not wish to leave us plunged in darkness or defenseless against ambiguity. He does indeed use a metaphor, but He takes great care in quickly and clearly explaining to us, a little further on, that He is the door: *I am the door*. Which means, in all certainty, that whoever does not try seriously to imitate Christ, shall never be a good Shepherd; in fact, he will not be a Shepherd at all, but nothing other —in Jesus Christ's own words— than a thief and a robber.

But, why do I speak about a *serious attempt*? Because no one can claim that his identification with Christ's life and Person is so great as to be able to say with Saint Paul: *And I live, now not I; but Christ liveth in me.*[2] As for ourselves, we know all too well that we are weak and sinful; we would be lying if we were to say otherwise. But we can indeed ascertain, with the greatest determination, our desire to be good. And we could even speak of our nostalgia for holiness, and of our sincere and earnest desires to be like Christ — in some way at least, though it be far–off. Which is ultimately to what he who claims to be a good Shepherd to the sheep can aspire. If He is the Door, the meaning is very clear: whoever wishes to be a Shepherd of the flock will have to strive to live according to the very life that Jesus, the true Master and Lord, lived.

I am greatly astounded by the solutions brought forth in light of the severity of the problem of the shortage of vocations to the religious or priestly life, the spiritual and moral misery of the clergy and the religious, and the depth of the crisis we are suffering. Almost all the remedies proposed are programs based on sociology and lacking in supernatural content. Programs manufactured in pastoral alchemy laboratories of the Diocesan Curia which lead nowhere; for

---

[2] Gal 2:20.

instance, the idea of carrying out polls among the people to know everyone's opinion about the crisis. I wonder about what might happen when the priest of rural parish "X", following the instructions of the experts, requests the opinion of his own farmers and asks them for solutions —we could say the same about any town, and indeed, any parish. What the parishioners of any given place think, what they desire, and what they need is to see that their priest is a man of God; that he speaks to them of Jesus Christ, of true Love and of that which can destroy it —i.e., sin— and at the same time, that he is a man who likes to *mind the things that are above, not the things that are upon the earth.*[3]

So, apparently, it would seem that there are other ways to enter the sheepfold, aside from using the door. There may be cracks, gaps, or holes; or perhaps it is not difficult to climb the wall. I have already mentioned that, concerning the problem of which we speak, here and there an infinite number of solutions are brought forth. Though almost all of them lack supernatural content and are therefore mistaken. Here also it is often forgotten that problems of a supernatural order require solutions of a supernatural order: everyone knows that the means must be proportional to the ends.

It goes without saying that entering by the door —our identification with Christ— is not exactly an easy task. One of the basic principles of Christian life is that the disciple of Christ must die to himself, and this becomes all the more momentous and urgent in the case of a Shepherd. A pastoral ministry of a sociological and purely human nature, which does not commit to anything, is something far easier to do than taking the need for personal holiness seriously. Let us give an example that is easy to understand: The modern and renowned *children's homilies*, to mention a current practice. Priest

---

[3] Col 3:2.

X gathers the children of his parish every Sunday for a special Mass, which is obviously something fashionable, sounds up–to–date, and is well–considered. Let us add, as a parenthesis, that up till now no one has been able to discover why we need a *special Mass* for children or why it would be convenient; we have always believed in the importance of integrating them into parish and Church life. Well then, the time for the homily having arrived (shouting, din, games, children running about, the priest yelling himself hoarse trying to reestablish order, etc.), our Priest X asks one of the children:

—*Okay Pepito: What do you think about today's Gospel?*

And one could easily imagine what Pepito, who is probably somewhere between ten and twelve years old, might think about the Gospel reading of the day. You can forget about the biblical commentaries of Saint Thomas or of the Fathers of the Church, *which are completely out of date.* And here it might be added, also as a parenthesis, that Priest X has never read Saint Thomas, much less the Fathers of the Church. Despite the fact that, according to the Bible, from the mouths of children we will hear truths, it is evident that in this case, the only thing we will hear is a *true* bit of nonsense which our pastoral priest enthusiastically embraces, and even asks the other children to give a loud round of applause for the impromptu and childish exegesis (thunderous applause ensues, a heavy increase in the racket, shouting and laughter here and there, and anything else you can think of). Of course, all of this is extremely advantageous, at least for someone (every cloud has a silver lining): after all, Priest X has no need to rack his brain in preparing the corresponding homily, or to take it to prayer and struggle with it, or... etc. So in general, Priest X enjoys good standing among his parishioners as a modern pastoralist and as an expert who is *up–to–date* (except for the parish pharmacist, a man well known for being a traditionalist, a conservative, and averse to progress, God forgive him; who is convinced that our good clergyman, aside from not being very intelligent, is quite lazy and not very spiritual).

But the porter opens the door to him who enters by it, and the sheep hear his voice. For he calls them by their name and then leads them out. It is clear that if he calls them individually by name it is because he knows each one of them. Which supposes that between the Shepherd and each sheep —you see I use the singular— there is an intimate relationship, with personal knowledge and friendship. Highlighting moreover that the text calls them *his own sheep*, meaning that the Shepherd considers them as belonging to Him; not in the sense of being His property, of course; as if he were to use them to his own advantage: *Even as the Son of man is not come to be ministered unto, but to minister, and to give his life.*[4] Something similar to when we use expressions like *my heart belongs to him and he belongs to me;* or, *this person is my life*, or even *my life belongs to you*, etc.

The good Shepherd does not seek to profit from His sheep, but rather that the sheep may profit from Him. He does not seek to fatten Himself with the fruits that they provide, but rather he seeks to pour out His life for them, inasmuch as they have been assigned to Him.

And He *leadeth them out,* for He cannot keep them isolated and locked up in the sheepfold. He must guide them so that they benefit from the pure air and the grasses of the meadows..., though at the same time they must face the ensuing dangers that will arise there: *I pray not, O Father, that thou shouldst take them out of the world, but that thou shouldst keep them from the Evil One.*[5] For our specific

---

[4] Mt 20:28.
[5] Jn 17:15.

vocation demands that we should sanctify ourselves in the midst of the world, walking by that narrow path which leads to life and which is chosen by so few. It is by way of this environment —clean air, good grasses, and also dangers— that the good Shepherd will arrive, together with His sheep, to the end of the journey. Together with them, of course, just as Gandalf said: *For it will be better to ride back three together than one alone.* And the Poet, on his end, said also the same thing in a different way, speaking of our journey on this Earth:

> *As you walk towards the hills above*
> *Allow me to walk with you, Pilgrim, my friend*
> *And see if he whom I love*
> *Gives us his wine to drink of*
> *In reaching together our long journey's end.*

Furthermore, the good Shepherd always goeth *before his sheep*. For He cannot imagine that they would follow the way if He were not to go before them to show it; which is to say, so that they might follow in His footsteps, in order that they might know what they must do and where they should go. In other words, He must lead by example. I would never have been crazy enough to think that, if I did not honor the virtues of Christian life. I know myself well enough to be aware of the fact that I am far from seriously living virtues such as poverty, obedience, humility, purity of heart, generosity, righteousness and integrity of life, courage, the spirit of sacrifice and prayer, self-denial, and a love of the Cross, etc. And despite all this, however, the good Shepherd has no other path before him than that of trying to live them.

The text also adds something exceedingly interesting. The sheep follow the good Shepherd *because they hear and know his voice.* Two things, therefore: to hear the voice of the Shepherd and to know it. Which means that between the Shepherd and his sheep there must be communication through dialogue. The sheep hear and recognize the voice of their Shepherd; and at the same time the Shepherd hears and knows his sheep, *for he calls each of them by name.* Hence we can interpret this lesson in the sense that the Shepherd, while living and practicing the spirit of prayer, must teach his sheep to do the same. Though it is important to note that, if the Shepherd knows how to converse lovingly with his sheep —and, indeed, is there any true dialogue that is not loving?— it is because *he has first conversed directly with God* and has therefore learnt about the Holy Spirit, or He Who is the *Eternal Loving Dialogue between the Father and the Son.*

It is evident that whoever has not learned to get along with God shall never learn to get along with men either. Which is the real reason why men, who have never spoken as much about *Dialogue* as they do now, have nevertheless found themselves once again building the Tower of Babel, in which no one understands anyone else, and in which no one agrees on anything. We must never forget that the Shepherd of the sheep, or the priest, is a *Pontifex* —a Bridge— destined to obtain the intercommunication between God and men. Like all bridges, therefore, his task is to join two extremes, which in this case are God and man: He speaks to God of things concerning men and intercedes for them, and at the same time speaks to his brothers about God. If either of the two extremes fails, the bridge ceases to fulfill its purpose and is good for nothing.

Let us consider, as an example, the case of Bishops, being as they are the primary and genuine Shepherds of the Church. It is evident that one cannot consider managing the assets of a Diocese to be the main task of a Bishop. Neither has he been set up to intervene or collaborate, via his activities or opinions, with *purely political* issues which correspond exclusively to the world of the laity. He would be wasting his time —and perhaps something more— if his greatest concerns were geared toward obtaining job positions of greater relevance and renown. It would be highly convenient, indeed even desirable, that he be a member of the fewest number of Bishops Conference Committees possible; and the same goes for the Subcommittees. His sheep would surely feel delighted if he spent the greater part of his time in his own diocese. His priests —his dearest children in the Lord— would give thanks to God to be able to find their Father and Shepherd at all times and anywhere, ready to hear their problems and attend to their needs; and if by chance this were to happen without the indispensable and famous requisite of the *prior appointment*, it is more than likely that the happiness of those poor priests would reach a height similar to that which is attained in Heaven. And regarding this, I cannot hold back from telling you what happened to a good friend of mine, a priest.

The good man found himself facing a serious problem which worried him greatly; and which, according to him, only the Bishop could help him solve. So, he made a phone call to his Excellency's personal secretary to arrange a meeting:

—*Please, then, might I speak today, or perhaps tomorrow, with the Bishop, given the urgency and severity of this issue?*

The secretary's answer was disheartening:

—*Impossible. Today his schedule is already all taken up with interviews. And tomorrow, of course, he must attend the meeting with the Government Committee.*

A sigh of bitterness and disappointment from the poor priest.

—*Goodness gracious! What about the day after?*

—Not possible either. He has a meeting with the Economic Committee.

—Ok, ok, I get it. So, any day next week..., insisted the poor priest as he began to feel more and more miserable.

—It is by no means possible. The entire week is taken up by a pilgrimage to Lourdes which he is leading.

—Of course, ok; I understand. Then, we will have to leave the interview for the following week.

And while my poor friend the priest pressed on with determination in his despair, the zealous secretary continued unmoved in the answers that duty called him to relate:

—It cannot be. As I am sure you know —here one should actually interpret: as I am sure you *must* know— a meeting of the Bishops' Conference has already been scheduled for that week.

Here now in answer came the shy and distraught voice of my friend:

—Of course, that is especially important. Then...?

—No, no, impossible. Once the Assembly of the Bishops' Conference is over, he has here in his agenda a very important trip, already scheduled, to Rome. And before you ask me, let me warn you that, upon his return, he will have to assist at the Board of Education meetings, of which the Bishops' Conference has named him President. But you may be lucky, because I can write down your request for an interview for a little over a month and a half from now. Although, that will always depend on confirmation from the Bishop, which is never certain.

And my unfortunate friend, now at the height of his holocaust:

—That's alright, never mind... It's not worth it. Do not bother the Bishop.

One would certainly think that a Bishop should be, above all, a man of prayer. Which, should such a happy occurrence take place, would render totally unnecessary certain pastoral plans of rather sociological content, developed by the DLPA (Diocesan Laboratories of Pastoral Alchemy), as well as other plans of a similar nature used to attract vocations (the infallible recipe/remedy for which, precisely because it was drawn out by the Lord Himself, we already know: *Pray ye therefore the Lord of the harvest, that he send labourers, etc.*[6]).

I ask you, however, to imagine a strange dream. One that is as beautiful as it is strange.

Has anyone ever thought what might happen if a certain Bishop were to celebrate Mass every Sunday in his Cathedral...? And if, on top of that, he were to preach! (Which after all, is his main area of expertise). Immediately after which —continues our dream— he takes his place in the confessional to hear confessions. And, as if that were not enough, he also spends long hours seated in his office, calmly listening to his priests; so that he can encourage and comfort them, lend them assistance with their problems, stimulating and guiding the spiritual life and pastoral activities of his most cherished children. It is well known that the priest is also a human being, which means that he too finds himself beset by problems, just like everyone else: And to whom will he go to solve them if not to the Bishop, who is his Father and Shepherd? But there is more: keep on supposing what would happen if this sensational Bishop were to frequently come to his various parishes; to celebrate Mass in them, preaching and confessing, visiting the sick... Not to mention how wonderful it would be if by chance, instead of naming Vicars or episcopal Delegates to administer the Sacrament of Confirmation, he

---

[6] Lk 10:2.

were to confer it himself; something which would help him to stay in touch with his remaining children, the faithful of Jesus Christ, who would greatly appreciate an episcopal presence of such favorable results for the fostering of their Christian life.

Unfortunately, things do not always turn out this way. I know the case of a Bishop —there is no need for me to speak of a name or a place, though I vouch for the veracity of the fact— who, during the speech he gave when taking possession of his diocese, shortly after being consecrated bishop, said to his priests (with the good intention, no doubt, of encouraging them):

—*Do not neglect prayer. I, for one, have been praying since I became a Bishop.*

A good piece of advice dictated, undoubtedly, by good will. One can only hope that the priests did not take into account, at that moment, the many years the aforementioned Bishop had been a parish priest.

But let us continue and make an end. So, our text from the Gospel says that *this parable Jesus spoke to them. But they understood not what he spoke to them.* As it occurs with us, no more and no less. Or at least, as occurs when it becomes very difficult for us to put Jesus' instructions, so clear and profound, into practice.

When we talk about how the Good Shepherd provides his sheep with good pastures, we are referring undoubtedly —among other things— to his preaching ministry, to the urgent need that the Shepherd has of preaching the Gospel to his sheep: Above all else, and more than anything else, the Gospel! But currently, a situation frequently repeats itself, to which the words of Jesus contained in this very text from Saint John may be applied, and which are, without doubt, some of the saddest and harshest words of the Gospel: *But the hireling, he that is not the shepherd, whose own the sheep are not, seeth the wolf coming, and leaveth the sheep: and the wolf catcheth, and scattereth the sheep. Because the hireling hath no care for the sheep.*

But therein lies the power of your prayer and the strength of your hope. The true and foremost Shepherd of the sheep, the good Christ Jesus, will not cease to send good Shepherds to His flock; Shepherds who will not mind giving up their lives for the sheep; for it is certain that they will love them, *and no one shows greater love than he who gives his life...*[7] But let us leave it here.

---

[7] Jn 15:13.

THE RESURRECTION OF LAZARUS

MEDITATION

(March 17th, 2002. Jn 11: 1–44)

On this last Sunday in Lent the Church presents for our consideration Chapter 11 of the Gospel of Saint John, in which is narrated the episode of the resurrection of Lazarus, the brother of Martha and Mary.

I remember how pleasant it was, in the years of my youth, to preach about this episode. Young priests have always been fond of topics that contain an abundance of material and a wealth of ideas to be used when speaking to the faithful. As for the ones that are herein contained, they seemed to me to be as beautiful as they were thrilling; and that is why they so easily inflamed my imagination and excited my rookie–preacher zeal. Truly, this chapter of the Gospel of Saint John, with its spectacular miracle of the resurrection of Lazarus and adjacent topics, grants a wonderful opportunity for deep and savory commentaries.

Though I must confess to you that, at the moment in life in which I find myself and given my age, I no longer feel capable of imagining and linking together flourishes. So, I will try to speak to you as best I can, with the help of God. And I advise you nevertheless to read this gospel passage often, slowly, and with devotion.

The gospel text begins by telling us that there was a sick man, Lazarus of Bethany, who was apparently someone well known and loved by Our Lord. Bethany was the place where this sick man lived, together with his sisters Martha and Mary, whom you already know. Martha was the woman who was so busy that she had forgotten that *only one thing is necessary*; Mary, on the other hand, was the one who had known how to *choose the better part* and was sitting at the feet of Jesus listening to his words.[1]

The two sisters sent someone to Jesus to make a touching plea on their behalf: *Lord, behold, he whom thou lovest is sick...!* For the Lord was indeed a friend of the three siblings. Though He did not understand friendship the same way we tend to live it, but rather in its total depth of feeling: another perfect way in which true love makes itself known. That is why He could say later on that *greater love than this no man hath, that a man lay down his life for his friends.*[2] And He added on that same occasion, addressing His disciples: *I will not now call you servants: for the servant knoweth not what his lord doth. But I have called you friends: because all things whatsoever I have heard of my Father, I have made known to you.*[3] For true friends keep no secret among themselves, but rather tell each other everything and hand over everything to each other: what they are, what they have, and indeed their very lives. Jesus understood friendship in this way because that is exactly what true friendship is.

---

[1] Lk 10:41.
[2] Jn 15:13.
[3] Jn 15:15.

—Lord, behold, he whom thou lovest is sick...!

Such was the message sent to Jesus by the sisters of Lazarus. To Jesus, Who was far away, *because if He had been there, Lazarus would have not died.* And that is precisely what seems to happen to us when our heart suffers to the point of becoming ill; something which undoubtedly happens as soon as Jesus is no longer there, with us. *Or is it for that very reason that our heart becomes ill...?* And why is He not here? Is it that He has left our side, or are we the ones, perhaps, who have drifted away from Him? However things may be, the result is the same. For His absence is the reason we become ill on account of love; and when this occurs, does it really matter whether it was our fault or not?

> *Stay me up with flowers,*
> *compass me about with apples:*
> *because I languish with love.*[4]

As the bride from the *Song* says, sobbing with pain on account of the Bridegroom's absence.

On occasion, I too use the words of the sisters of Lazarus to address the Lord in prayer. I feel a great need to do so, but modifying them so that they may be pronounced in the past tense: *Lord, he whom thou once loved is ill...!* For it is strange and painful to me to think that the Lord still loves me, even after having seen (both He and I) the state of my life. And at the same time, I am overwhelmed with the doubt, otherwise quite disturbing, that I am perhaps committing an offense against Our Lord by doubting His love. To think that Jesus cannot love me on account of the mediocrity of my life

---

[4] Song 2:5.

would mean to forget His words, repeated over and over again, according to which *He had come not to call the just, but sinners;*[5] or those in which He stated that *they who are whole, need not the physician, but they who are sick.*[6] To these we must add those other words according to which *He came not to judge the world;*[7] nor did He come *to be ministered unto, but to minister and to give His life as redemption for many.*[8] To doubt a friend's love is to offend that friend, and to question the affection of One Whom we know loves us with Perfect Love is to be completely ignorant of true Love, which never gives up on account of defects in the beloved person. If its fire is not yet appeased by a reciprocal and total correspondence, as would be expected from the other party, then it will forever stand vigilant; but without allowing anyone or anything to extinguish it. As the *Song* puts it:

> *For love is strong as death,*
> *jealousy as hard as hell...*
> *Many waters cannot quench charity,*
> *neither can the floods drown it.*[9]

In any case, whether you say it as I do, or whether you express it as it appears in the Gospel, the expression is always as tender as it is beautiful and consoling: *Lord, behold, he whom thou lovest is ill...!* It is always reassuring to know that the Lover is aware of the sickness of the beloved; for it is true that, *had he been there, the beloved would not have died.*

---

[5] Lk 5:32.
[6] Lk 5:31.
[7] Jn 12:47.
[8] Mt 20:28.
[9] Song 8: 6–7.

Let's face it: we will never throughout our whole lives see the abolishment of our sins, our weaknesses, or our failures in being generous... at least as long as we count only on our own strengths. That is why, in my case, I also often say to the Lord, paraphrasing an expression of the lepers in the Gospel: *If thou wilt, thou canst make me clean....!*[10] Or perhaps that of the blind man on the road to Jericho, or that of other wretches who approached Jesus and stammered in answer to his query: *Rabboni, that I may see!*[11]

Lord, behold, he whom thou lovest is ill...! And for a trust that was enamored, that was all it took. Does the Lover really need to know anything else other than that the beloved needs Him? This is the trust that grants us the assurance and the certainty that only He can cure the illness —in Latin, the word *infirmitas* means, above all, weakness— of our soul. And he will undoubtedly do it, of course.

We make a great mistake when we allow our weaknesses to overwhelm us. Or when we adopt a dolefully passive attitude when faced with the weight of our faults and our lack of generosity. For perhaps these things are not always as bad as we imagine them to be.

After all *this illness is not unto death, but for the glory of God, so that through it His Son will be glorified...* An answer similar to the one the Apostles received when they asked the Master about the illness of the man born blind: if he perhaps was so because of his own sins, or those of his parents. Whatever the case, we come here face to face with one more of those worthy pearls contained in the Gospel, and which has much to do with the state of our souls. For, according to this, the weak, the small, and the flawed, *can be used for the grandeurs of God.* And if this is true, why then do we let these things sadden us? If we were not sinners or full of

---

[10] Mk 1:40.
[11] Mk 10:51.

weaknesses, we would never give the Lord the chance to raise us up from the ground and press us lovingly against His heart; just as the father did with the prodigal son from the parable. And could we ever imagine God as not fully exercising His mercy? Has there ever been a father who has never had to forgive his children? Or as the *Letter to the Hebrews* states, addressing offspring: *For what son is there, whom the father doth not correct?*[12] And it is worthy of note that for God, correction is but one of the many ways in which He practices His fatherly love. A father shows his quality in the most beautiful and peculiar way precisely when he demonstrates his mercy, his goodness, his forgiveness, and his understanding...!

Looking back on my feelings as a child, I do not think I ever felt a greater love toward my parents than when I misbehaved. Precise because I was naughty very frequently, I offered my parents plenty of opportunities to flaunt their goodness and generosity towards me. And I must admit, despite all this, that my parents lacked neither the necessary disposition nor the sense of responsibility to punish me whenever they had to; fortunately for me, that is. But they always knew how to be parents.

I have told you about the time when I became intoxicated at the age of fourteen. Quite a drinking binge, to be sure, though perhaps it is only fair to add that it was the only time in my life. My father had a great deal to do with that, as would become clear soon after. I remember that my friends brought me home, for I was in no position to accomplish such a difficult task. Shortly before arriving at my home, I could glimpse the figure of my father —blurred and foggy— waiting at the door (I have never been able to discover the ways by which news travel so fast in small towns). Over the years I have relived that memory many times; and always the image of the

---

[12]Heb 12:7.

angel with the flaming sword, who guarded the Gates of Paradise so that men could not enter, comes to my mind. In fact, my father appeared before me in that moment as the terrible visage of Justice (distributive and restorative; but above all, retributive).

To this day I do not know how I found the strength to babble in a run–down voice:

—*Dad, heeeere I am; it tuuurns out, turns out that I got dru-uuunk... But don't worry; because I promise it will never happen again...*

As if it came from far away, I could still hear my father's thundering and avenging voice:

Of course it won't. Because as to this never happening again, I will be taking care of that.

And I think I was brought to my bed. The next morning, being in full possession of my faculties and lying down, fear gripped me even before I got up. A fitting lecture and an immediate punishment were as inevitable as my daily school attendance. My father was no licensed scholar —he had not even finished Middle School— but he was a gentleman with great common sense; and above all he was a good Christian and a great father. To my enormous surprise, and growing anxiety, the hours passed by that day and the dreaded storm did not break. Even days and weeks passed, and my father continued to utter not a single word, or make a single gesture, about my behavior; as if it had never happened, though I knew full well that none of it had left him indifferent. The years passed, I became a priest, my father passed away, and I am still waiting for the paternal reprimand. Or a maternal one, for that matter, since it seemed that my mother also *forgot* about the incident.

Throughout my life, when recalling this moment, I have never doubted that it was all a very well–thought–out fatherly tactic. Not once did I believe my father so weak as to never dare to punish or correct me. But he knew me well enough to know that his conduct in this case —his calculated silence and his magnanimous understanding towards a deed which was after all quite isolated and accompanied by signs of remorse— was going to work greater and better results in me than any other type of activity. And so it was, indeed, for this incident never happened again.

—*Lord, behold, he whom thou lovest is ill...!*

Here we have the most surprising thing of all. For Jesus simply clarifies that this illness was not unto death, but for the greater glory of God.

Indeed, we often get carried away by the tendency to consider things as evil or unfortunate when they are not. Or at least, they are not, in God's eyes, the only vantage point in which we can always and at all times place our trust. How easily do we forget the wonderful advice that the Apostle gives to the Christians in Rome when he tells them that *to them that love God, all things work together unto good!*[13] It is hard for us to confidently accept our weaknesses without understanding that, on no small number of occasions, they are far from being an evil for us; in fact, they may even serve as the instrument by which and through which the glory and greatness of God shine forth and are made manifest. Saint Paul asked God to free him from some sort of stimulus or sting of the flesh that ashamed him; but he only received in turn a very unexpected answer: *My grace is sufficient for thee. For power is made perfect in infirmity.*[14] Hence we know that human weakness can be an opportunity for God to show His strength. This is true to such an extent that, inasmuch as that weakness should disappear, or that

---

[13] Rom 8:28.
[14] 2 Cor 12:9.

someone were to think that they got rid of it, to that same degree the strength of God would also cease to manifest itself. And we could consider the specific case of the Christian preacher who is not convinced of his own uselessness in transmitting the Word of God and could never expect any fruits to be harvested from the faithful who are listening to him. *For see your vocation, brethren,* —says the Apostle— *that there are not many wise according to the flesh, not many mighty, not many noble. But the foolish things of the world hath God chosen, that he may confound the wise; and the weak things of the world God hath chosen, that he may confound the strong. And the base things of the world, and the things that are contemptible, hath God chosen, and things that are not, that he might bring to naught things that are.*[15] Perhaps he was echoing another set of his Master's words which dwelled on the same thought: *I confess to thee, O Father, Lord of heaven and earth, because thou hast hid these things from the wise and prudent, and hast revealed them to the little ones. Yea, Father; for so hath it seemed good in thy sight.*[16]

The bottom line is —let us admit it— that almost everything that God does seems strange to us. And not at all because it actually is strange, but rather because our weak minds are incapable of more depth. His ways are not our ways, and His thoughts are not our thoughts. Hence the feeling we get —of strangeness more than amazement— as we continue to recall the events that took place surrounding the death of Lazarus.

According to the Gospel narrative, once Jesus had found out that His friend Lazarus had fallen ill, He did not hurry to make His way to Bethany in haste. Quite the contrary. For the Master reacted calmly to the news, and in fact everything indicated that He had

---

[15] 1 Cor 1: 26–28.
[16] Mt 11: 25–26.

reacted too calmly: *Though He had heard therefore that he was sick, He still remained in the same place two days.* The estrangement we often feel when God takes His time in coming to our aid is something to behold; and even more so when it is not simply a matter of delay, but of His total absence. We do not understand the triumph of those who do evil or the constant persecution suffered by those who do good; nor do we find a satisfactory explanation for the fact that the world always agrees with those who are wrong; or that it proclaims as right and just what is but injustice and depravity. All this, it would seem, with God's permission. And on top of that —so we are told— allowed for the good of the elect, namely: in order that the little ones be littler still and the weak be weaker still... *Though He had heard therefore that he was sick, He still remained in the same place two days.* It is undeniable that this adversative conjunction —*though*— has a far greater importance in this instance than it would seem.

We will surely be happy when we understand that our weakness and our smallness is what opens the door to the heart of God, which then bursts in on us with His love and wisdom. For that is how His roads are made clear and His designs known. Actually, we are dealing here, once again, with the unfathomable wisdom of God and its paradoxical setting of smallness and human weakness against the pride, also human, of sin.

Jesus therefore lets two full days go by and then says to His disciples: *Let us go into Judea again.* The Apostles feel dismayed, and they warn Him of the dangers He faces in that province, where only recently He had been on the verge of being stoned. A dialogue then takes place in which Jesus, by way of an explanation, justifies before His friends the need for making this journey:

—Lazarus our friend sleepeth; but I go that I may awake him out of sleep.

The answer of the apostles seems to proceed, we must acknowledge, from an abundant dosage of the most deeply human common sense:

—Lord, if he sleep, he shall do well (or *"he shall wake,"* which is the obvious meaning of the text).

Any of us would have answered in the same way had we been in the same situation. And it would not be out of place here to take note that Jesus' words —which are spirit and life, according to His own statement—, despite what it might sometimes seem, never come forth as puzzles or riddles, but rather as possessing various layers of depths as to their meaning. This way of proceeding is pleasing to the Lord, and He uses it often (remember, for example, His conversation with Nicodemus). One might even think that the Master enjoyed using play on words (and there was often some of this in His way of speaking), when in reality it is all about the best possible way in which the Word made Flesh addresses men, with a view to being understood. It could even be that the longed–for understanding of His words be put off on purpose for a later time, more or less far away; as Jesus Himself warned Peter on one solemn occasion: *What I do thou knowest not now; but thou shalt know hereafter.*[17] Thus, Jesus adapts Himself to human nature's way of being, which progresses and understands always *per aspera ad astra*, or from the visible to the invisible, and by no other way. On the other hand, take into account that proceeding in this way was the normal way for the prophets to speak, who, by default, never expected their words to be fully understood *there and then*.

---

[17] Jn 13:7.

But when faced with the crude simplicity of His disciples, and given the importance of the moment, Jesus realizes that He must speak with greater clarity. He must ascend to more superficial layers of language, and of lesser depth.

—*Lazarus is dead. And I am glad, for your sakes, that I was not there, that you may believe.*

The disciples hear Him, dumbfounded, overwhelmed by a kind of stupor... which reaches all the way to us. Lazarus has died... and Jesus is glad to not have been there. Why?

Perhaps the reason may not be so hard to understand. Had He been present, His heart would have forced Him to not allow the death of such a dear friend. Up to this point there is no problem whatsoever, though the difficulties in understanding the event in depth may appear later. Someone, for example, might ask: And why would the Son of God have prevented the death of His friend had He been present, and not done it from afar, being absent? (Remember the well–known episode: *Lord, I am not worthy that you should enter under my roof, and there is no need even for you to go there...*).[18]

First of all and for starters, we must highlight an important issue which, although very well known, never ceases to amaze. Jesus, being a true Man, is therefore Someone with a heart full of emotions. And emotions of such a nature that *they are capable of prevailing at times upon His own Person*. It is thrilling to grasp that something so akin to human nature as the *struggle* that so often takes place between reason and the heart, was not something alien to Jesus Christ as Man. Had He been present, His heart would have driven Him to prevent His friend's death; He could, however, *bear it and consent to it from a distance which kept Him from seeing it.*

It is always striking to discover that God has a heart like ours and that He can be found so near to us. And if this is so, for

---

[18] Mt 8:8.

Him it is no longer a matter of *understanding* our problems, but of *participating* in them by taking them upon Himself, and what all that means for us.

So often we tend to imagine the relationship of love between God and us as being stationary. Something which lacks vitality, unforeseen events and moments of shock, joys and sufferings, absence and presence, triumph and failure, happiness and tears, generosity and stinginess, hopes and dismay... forgetting that the human/divine relationship of love is found within the realm of the historical. Which is precisely what makes it something so thrilling so as to be truly human and really divine!

The love story narrated in *The Song of Songs* is not a stationary situation of human/divine relationships in which God appears as God, the creature as a creature, and that is the end of it. Nothing would happen in such a situation and everything would develop according to a pre–established logic in which no variants are to be expected. Which would be anything but a love story:

> *Shew me, O thou whom my soul loveth,*
> *Where thou feedest, where thou liest in the midday,*
> *Lest I begin to wander*
> *After the flocks of thy companions.*[19]

> ....

> *He brought me into the cellar of wine,*
> *He set in order charity in me.*[20]

> ....

---

[19] Song 1:7.
[20] Song 2:4.

> *I will rise, and will go about the city:*
> *In the streets and the broad ways*
> *I will seek him whom my soul loveth:*
> *I sought him, and I found him not.*[21]
>
> ....
>
> *I opened the bolt of my door to my beloved:*
> *But he had turned aside, and was gone.*
> *My soul melted when he spoke:*
> *I sought him, and found him not:*
> *I called, and he did not answer me.*[22]

Or as Saint John of the Cross exclaimed:

> *Where have You hidden Yourself,*
> *And abandoned me in my groaning, O my Beloved?*
> *You have fled like the hart,*
> *Having wounded me.*
> *I ran after you, crying; but You were gone.*

There is no doubt that now it is easy to get closer to this Jesus as Man, Who partakes in our own feelings in such a way. For God loves man in His own way, which is none other than the divine way; but in order that the concordance and reciprocity of love should be real and perfect, it was also necessary for man to love in his own way, which is none other than the human way (the grace of elevation does not strip human love of its own nature). For this reason God became Man.

---

[21] Song 3: 2–3.
[22] Song 5:6.

However, among the issues still to be discussed, there are a few more of no small importance.

Jesus could suffer the death of His friend Lazarus, according to His own words, *because he was not present in that situation.* Not withstanding the obvious fact that the Master *knew* that the death of Lazarus was real and not a mere dream, as can be drawn also from the gospel text with the greatest clarity. He knew it, therefore, but was not present and that is why death could take place. According to this, what exactly does this mode of absence mean?

Christ the true Man is also Christ the true God. Being God, He therefore possesses the divine attribute of omnipresence (God is present in all beings). To say that His divine nature is not an entelechy is to affirm with the same truth and certainty that His human nature, beyond all doubt, is not an illusion either. When we speak, therefore, about Christ the Man we are affirming emphatically His condition as true Man.

And here is probably where a certain notion that the Fathers called *kenosis* (veiling, abasement, dwindling, humiliation, lack of presence or absence, etc.) comes into play. For it seems that, come what may of it, the situation of Our Lord's absence —of not being present— described in today's Gospel text, is no mere metaphor. For it is undeniable that Jesus was not there.

But the actions of Jesus Christ recorded in the Gospels can never be referred to situations that were merely incidental or circumstantial. What He did in any given time or place was always the best and the most perfect thing that could and should have been done: *Omnia bene fecit.*[23] That is why His actions were always a model or standard of behavior. And standards of behavior, by definition, are made to be upheld; or if you prefer, to be copied.

---

[23] Mk 7:37.

Which brings us to the conclusion that the *kenosis*, or absence, of the Lord in the case of Lazarus could be repeated in other circumstances, and even —as it appears to occur— in reference to His presence in the Church at certain moments in time. And specifically, the moments we are living through now.

I said to you earlier that the fact that God seems to sometimes hide His presence is commonplace; we see this as much in Holy Scripture as we do throughout the whole of the History of the Church or in Christian Spirituality (the *Nights*, for example, that the mystics speak to us of).

Unfortunately, in this case we are not dealing with a *Night of the spirit* belonging to this or that particular soul who happens to be walking the path of aesthetics, or perhaps that of mysticism. We now truly face *the apparent absence of the Lord in reference to His Church.* A statement which has all the trappings of being too severe; but which, if we do away with triumphalist propaganda and refuse to close our eyes, even if just for a moment, it might not seem so far-fetched after all.

The Sacraments have ceased to be signs that contain what they represent and have become mere symbols which simply represent what they represent.

This is much more serious in the case of the Eucharist. Having ruled out the Real Presence, it is no longer necessary to receive the Eucharist with a clean soul. Now it is just one more rite of the many that make up the Mass, and hence the faithful who assist at the Celebration receive it *massively,* having no concern for the state of their soul. Something quite normal, after all, since the very notion of sin has been banished and, therefore, the Sacrament of Penance is no longer considered necessary. This is not yet the worst of it all. Having been stripped of its content (the Real Presence), we are left in the temples with a frigid and dreary environment denoting the absence of the Lord. Now we can say, and with even greater feeling than Saint Peter: *Lord, where shall we go?*

In classes taught by many Catholic Faculties of Theology, the divinity of Jesus Christ is questioned, if not openly rejected. And no one seems to be scandalized by this at all.

Divorce has finally been allowed by Catholicism. Of course, it is not called by that name, just as abortion is not called abortion (now we say, interruption of a pregnancy), nor are the lame called lame (handicapped, rather). Modern post–Christian society has certainly learned to use language as a powerful tool of manipulation; but in such a way that sometimes its perversity is laid bare, while on other occasions, it shows itself to be simply ridiculous.

The destruction of the family has taken its toll also on marriage as a Sacrament. The so–called *free unions*, and sometimes *sentimental companionships*, have become the norm. Including unions (marriage) between homosexuals, recognized as having all the rights and duties as (other) legitimate unions; however, I must confess to you, concerning this last bit, that even though on my part I might be able to understand here what is meant by *duties*, I admit myself incapable of comprehending what is meant by *rights*. There is no need to tell you that many are the Shepherds who support the theory that consummate realities must be accepted, which leads them to allow such things with resignation. And it should be noted that I do not think that what is *consummated* is referring here to the *marriage* between homosexuals.

Modern ecumenism has indeed taken steps forward. As for our *separated brethren* we must highlight that, if it be true that Catholics have insisted more on the *brethren* aspect, the Protestant churches seem to have underlined more the *separated* aspect. Everything indicates that the most notable result, obtained up till now, has been that of disseminating among Catholics the idea that all Churches are the same. We can also count, as considerable progress, how Catholics in our time consider the *Koran* to be a sacred book, no doubt with the good intention in mind of drawing closer to the Muslims; though, someone might say in this case that the *Ramayana* and the *Mahabharata* are considered as sacred by the brahmans of India, and that something should be done about it.

The clergy in general has seen its field of competence flooded by a multitude of *promoted* laymen and experts capable of doing anything, namely, anything human or divine; but especially divine. Which has led to the fostering of an inferiority and inutility complex, known otherwise as a *crisis of identity*, among the simple clergy. It is funny that twenty centuries of the History of the Church had to pass before the priest discovered that he does not know who he is: *I know only that I know nothing,* said the Ancient Wise Man, *and that only because someone else told me...* a friend of mine would add.

And as a direct result of what we have just mentioned, vocations to the consecrated life, to the priesthood or to religious life, have plummeted to a level one can only describe as zero level. The Church in our time has no priests, although that is not yet the worst of it.

The worst of it all is the remedy that many have found for such a scarcity. For now, homosexuals are admitted into the seminaries, no questions asked. In the Anglican Church there is even talk of the possibly consecrating as Bishops certain characters who recognize themselves, publicly and solemnly, as homosexuals. As a matter of fact, the official acceptance of homosexuality among the (high and low) clergy has already been established.

The Bishop's Conferences choose their new candidates according to their views on ecclesiastical and administrative politics, without paying much attention to pastoral criteria. Of course, all of this is part of a specific movement of ideas, according to which it is absolutely necessary to do away with men who have firm and steady principles. Those chosen for places of such responsibility must be from among the *moderates*; though some might say that now we name as such those whose faith is ambiguous (if not doubtful) and who are convinced, moreover, that the only certainty is to have no certainties.

These last ones are those who have wholeheartedly embraced the theory of *legitimate discrepancy* with respect to the Magisterium of the Church, a theory invented by avant-garde theologians and which seems to be spreading above all in the United States. Needless to say, if we admit the possibility of discrepancy, and if the legitimacy of the Magisterium depends on each one of us, the inevitable conclusion can be nothing but the futility of the Magisterium.

Currently one might stumble upon a high-ranking Shepherd proclaiming to the four winds, after calling the *media*, that the Church would do well to revise her criteria and her laws concerning contraception and abortion; concerning the need for the ordination of women; concerning the acceptance of homosexuality as something legitimate; concerning the *legitimate dissent* with respect to the teachings of the Magisterium..., and anything else, really. Unfortunately, all these anomalies do not become an obstacle for this Shepherd to receive the Cardinal's hat shortly after his declarations.

The President Cardinal of a certain Pontifical Council does not believe in the historical reality of the resurrection of Jesus Christ.

And I am going to stop here, though I could go on for a long time and extensively, because I would rather not fill your hearts with even more sadness. If I have presented this list to you, by no means exhaustive but disagreeable and disheartening in excess, it is simply because I want you to realize that all this seems to be happening *because Jesus was not there*. In fact, countless are the Christians who now cry and feel crushed by the absence —*kenosis?*— of Jesus. It does indeed seem as if He has abandoned us; or as if someone has taken Him from our midst, depriving us of His presence:

—*Woman, why do you weep?*— Jesus asked Mary Magdalen.

—*For they have taken my Lord and I know not where they have placed him...*— she answered.

Jesus Himself had already stated very clearly His absence:

—*But the days will come, when the bridegroom shall be taken away from them, and then they shall fast.*[24]

That is why Saint Paul, grief stricken and in all sincerity, once spoke about how *while we are in the body, we are absent from the Lord.*[25]

And quite absent, of course, for now it seems we are farther away than ever. He has either gone or has disappeared from our midst. Or perhaps we are the ones who have asked Him to leave, as the Gerasenes did after having lost their entire herd of pigs. In any case, how is the wife in love not to feel anxious and full of yearning on account of the absence of her Spouse? She knows He is not there, and moreover she is unable to find Him and is completely lost without the Beloved of her soul. We place in Him our trust because we are convinced that He alone can take care of His Church and save all of us who feel helpless.

> *Where have You hidden Yourself,*
> *And abandoned me in my groaning, O my Beloved?...*

---

[24] Mt 9:15.
[25] 2 Cor 5:6.

Thus wept Saint John of the Cross. Or in the same way the wife of the *Song* also lamented:

> *I sought him whom my soul loveth:*
> *I sought him, and found him not.*[26]

So also spoke the poet, hinting at the grief the weeping willow felt when it heard the pitiful and nostalgic song of the sweet nightingale:

> *Sweet Philomena again*
> *Calls to her love from among the highest leaves*
> *Of a green willow tree in the shaded ford.*
> *And the tree shares the great pain*
> *Of the bird who seeks her love with no reward;*
> *Who in lonely sorrow grieves,*
> *Feeling herself die in sweet flames of love's blaze.*
> *And, from that hour, whenever*
> *He hears her grieving, the willow weeps for her.*

A lover cannot feel happy if the beloved person flees from her side or hides Himself. If their love is deep, the lover will feel insipid, lost, and even fearful when the Beloved One disappears. Perhaps He has gone far away, or maybe He is hiding. But the feeling of abandonment, of insecurity and confusion, is inevitable for the lover. What to do? And will the Beloved return? Will He come to put an end to the miseries and sufferings that His absence has caused? He will return, beyond any doubt. And His voice will be heard again, and *the fig tree will put forth her green figs, the vines in flower will yield their sweet smell, while the voice of the turtle dove is heard in*

---

[26] Song 3:1.

our land...[27] Then the bride will once again hear the voice of the Bridegroom *and He will give her His love again.* And both shall then be together forever, when all the rest has past, and relegating all else to complete oblivion:

> *I will rise with haste and go*
> *To wherever my Beloved wishes me;*
> *To where eagles nest below*
> *Soaring heights majestically;*
> *To mountain tops all forgotten already.*

When Jesus arrived in Bethany, Lazarus had already been in the tomb for four days. Martha rushed out to meet Him and spoke to Him the words we have already heard: *If you had been here, my brother would not have died.* Do these words express a complaint or rather an explosion of love, hope, and faith in the Master? Probably both. Perhaps this is a loving and sincere complaint, although with a certain hint of fearful hesitancy, based on the full assurance that the Master can handle everything and that He never abandons us. It is exactly the same thing that happens to us, no more and no less. Human nature is always the same, and that is why its reactions and its psychology are repeated over and over again. Human beings are human beings after all. Thus the Apostles, frightened in the midst of a stormy and fierce sea, saw however that Jesus was with them in the boat; but He was asleep, and the boat was filling with water and sinking!

Jesus tries to calm Martha, reassuring her that her brother will rise again. This affirmation, as we have been saying, is understood by her in a lesser tone: *I know that he will rise again on the last*

---

[27]Song 2: 12–13.

day. Making it true again that the thoughts of men always walk on different paths, and at a much lower altitude, than the thoughts of God. Always our human nature, with hesitations and doubts that should no longer have any place. That is why Jesus demands at this moment from Martha a profound act of faith, to which she does not hesitate to respond generously and courageously. It is only then that the paths along which the prodigies and wonders parade themselves can be opened...

Martha then went to tell her sister and said in her ear: *The Master is here and is calling you.*

Many years have passed and I still have a vivid memory of something that happened to me during my first year of college. When I first entered the *Colegio Mayor Cardenal Belluga* (now long gone), I was struck by those words in a way that had never happened before in my life. They were written in Latin on the door of the almost hidden chapel of the College: *Magister adest et vocat te.* So, the Master is here, I said to myself, thinking of the Eucharistic Sacrament. Perfect, then. But He is also *calling me.* And it was then that something strange touched my heart. He was calling me! But, for what? I had never imagined that a *call* could so strongly alter the beating of a heart. Surely because in this case the call came from Him, which gave it an unsettling character because, as if that were not enough, it was addressed precisely to me. And could He think of me and ask me to come to His side... for something about which I could know nothing?

I admit that up to that moment in my life, God had been for me, as for so many others, nothing more than a good God, albeit distant and hidden. Our personal relationships had never existed; or at least as I understood personal relationships to be. And although until that moment the idea of a *vocation* had never crossed my mind, let alone my heart, something in my subconscious told me that this call could only be a loving call. And a loving call, as everyone understands, is a call to follow, to be close to the one who calls, to share his life..., and even to live it to the point of identification. And while all this, as I have told you, remained for me at the subconscious level, I could not help sensing something incredibly marvelous in it.

> *The voice of my beloved, behold he cometh;*
> *behold my beloved speaketh to me:*
> *Arise, make haste, my love,*
> *my beautiful one, and come.*[28]

To be like Him! To live His own life and without the need to introduce any change! It had never occurred to me that such a challenging and yet astonishingly beautiful adventure could be proposed to me, with a view to living it out. I had always wondered, without ever finding an answer, about the meaning of my life!

With the passing of the years, and in view of what I now see in the world in which we live, I wonder with admiration how it is possible to speak of a *priestly identity crisis*. When the priest is the only man in the world *who knows exactly who he is and what he is, and that no one, absolutely no one on this Earth of ours, will ever be able to live up to his ineffable and divine identity...*

However, I have not yet told you about something that is contained in the text, and which is perhaps the most endearing thing about it. For, as you have already noticed, the words that Martha addressed to her sister to inform her of the Master's arrival, were spoken *in her ear.*

---

[28] Song 2: 8.10.

It could not be otherwise, since it was something that surpassed the limits of the marvelous. In those moments of greatest pain, someone gives the news that the Master has arrived and is already there. But that which is most dear and which, because it concerns the most beloved person, absent until now but most awaited, touches the deepest part of the heart in love, must be communicated in intimacy. For, listen carefully: the most tender and intimate communications of love that take place between lovers, *are always made in silence* and fleeing from all other things. And it is not that other things are despised, but that, in the presence of *the only thing necessary*, they lose their relevance in order to take their rightful place. Since the dialogue of love has always taken place between a *thou* and an *I*, everything that could interrupt or hinder it remains in second place:

> *At my Love's side I lingered,*
> *In the silence of Love's mutual sweet word,*
> *While still at his side I heard*
> *Soft in my ear he whispered*
> *That he too, wounded by my love, has suffered.*
>
> *Come to me; be with me; stay.*
> *While brisk North winds gust over the high meadow;*
> *Leave the flock to find its way,*
> *Whisper to me, faint and low,*
> *That you feel wounded by my love's tender blow.*

Which is exactly what the beloved bride in the *Song of Songs* said to her Bridegroom. It has always been so and will always be so. The search for solitude and the forgetfulness of other things that, although they keep the traces of the Beloved, are not yet the Beloved:

> *Come, my beloved, let us go forth into the field,*
> *let us abide in the villages.*[29]

That is why the whole of Creation keeps silence so that the intimate dialogue between the bride and the Bridegroom can take place:

> *As I was told by the deer*
> *He lives in the forest of the cedar tree.*
> *I ran to Him to be near,*
> *And as He spoke, just to me,*
> *No sound was heard, though the wind whispered softly.*

It would be interesting to note here that, precisely because of what we have been saying, the call to discipleship always takes place in the silence of loving intimacy; as if God did not like to communicate with people amidst the sound of fanfare. This explains why a young man or woman will not be able to understand what a vocation to total dedication in the following of the Lord is *if they themselves do not listen directly, person to person,* to the voice or whistle of the beloved Shepherd. And there is no room here for intermediaries. If they exist at all, their function is none other than to bring the two persons concerned into immediate contact with each other. But, in the final analysis, it is always the Good Shepherd who knows His sheep *and calls each of them by name.*

In the relationship of divine–human love —and the call of a vocation is its finest form of expression, or at least its beginning—, there is no room for declarations by correspondence, nor for mediations of any kind, which in this case would serve no purpose.

---

[29] Song 7:12.

Now and at this time, only person–to–person treatment is possible. Given that, in this concrete circumstance, the only possibility for the desired person to respond affirmatively, seduced by a voice that enamors her, is none other than for her to hear for herself the enamored request that solicits her. For only that voice is the one that can captivate:

> *The voice of my Beloved...! Hear what He speaketh to me: Arise, my beloved one, and come...*

I have often been surprised, negatively and, unfortunately, painfully, by the campaigns that dioceses usually organize to recruit vocations. First of all, it should be said that vocations are not *recruited*. But they also use methods of which the least that can be said, in an enormous excess of benevolence, is that they are wrong. To give an example, it does not seem to have produced spectacular results (nobody has seen them) the sending of small seeds to the schools to be distributed to the children; something that has been done with the purpose of exhorting them so that, once sown in their respective gardens, the little ones would raise to God their prayers so that the priestly or religious vocations would *flourish* among them. No, no, and no, of course, and we must admit it: taking the help of Botany has not been a success. Nor does the idea of sending the boys photographs of priests, each accompanied by a short summary of the biographies of the priests themselves, seem to have been a good idea; the mustached image of a former army sergeant, for example, ordained as a priest in his forties, has so far failed to drive any youngster crazy with enthusiasm (at least as far as I know). Diocesan experts in youth ministry have not yet been able to explain the failure of this wonderful idea, despite its obvious brilliance. As for the propaganda leaflets of some seminaries, perhaps it would be better not to speak about it and keep silent: the pictures of boys —and girls— playing the guitar on the seminary premises, with forced smiles and eyes gazing dreamily into a strange infinity, have not worked either; etc. Astonishing beyond belief, and even more than astonishing.

A friend of mine commented to me not long ago that the youth ministry that is practiced in the dioceses usually suffers from a serious defect of myopia, or perhaps something worse. The diocesan experts on duty, instead of looking at the children with suitable optical lenses, seem to be looking at them as if through a mirror. And perhaps, my friend said, this is why they think that children are idiots.

The fact is that the voice of God is not usually heard in the midst of the roar of the drums and cymbals, as it was said by the prophet Elijah so long ago that we have forgotten it: *Yahweh said to him, "Go out and stand on the mountain before Yahweh," for behold, Yahweh is about to pass by. And there passed before him a mighty and strong wind, which rent the mountains, and broke in pieces the rocks: but Yahweh was not in the wind. And after the wind came an earthquake; but Yahweh was not in the earthquake. And after the earthquake came a fire; but Yahweh was not in the fire. After the fire came a light, soft whisper. And when Elijah heard it, he covered his face with his mantle, and went out, and stood at the entrance of the cave, and heard the voice...*

Many modern specialists, experts in children's pedagogy, have not yet learned that the child only allows himself to be seduced at this point, to the point of feeling capable of joyfully immolating his life for love, *when he hears the voice of Jesus Christ Himself*. Which is impossible to be heard, as a silent and soft whisper, if it is not within an environment where Jesus Christ is loved, and where the child —the young person— can *perceive* Jesus Christ. The child (or the young man or woman) will never know Jesus Christ except through *another Christ* —who in turn will disappear to make way for the authentic one— and never through a mere expert. Hence the need for priests in love with the Lord. Only they, and since love always transmits love (if they are ardently in love with Jesus Christ), will be able to lead young people to the place where, in the silence that makes whispering possible, the Lord will show Himself to them to tell them that He loves them and invite them to follow Him. The serious imitation of Jesus Christ, lived especially by a priest who is in love enough to practice it, is the only thing that can encourage young people to follow Jesus Christ. This also includes keeping prayer in mind, since it is the great solution offered to us by the Lord himself: *Pray to the Lord of the harvest to send out laborers into his harvest.*[30]

In a spirit of jest —because it is always better to laugh than to cry— we have alluded, as if in passing, to one of the most serious problems facing the Church today. There is a choice: either the orientations of the Youth Pastoral activity are completely changed, or the Church at the beginning of the twenty–first century will be left without youth. And then it will happen that the Youth Meetings and Youth Councils, for example, will have served only to fill the pockets of hoteliers, travel agents, unscrupulous organizers... and even worse, namely: to keep all the faithful under the delusion that there is still a Christian youth.

The sweet news that the Master *is here and calling you* is always transmitted *to the ear*. Rumblings and fanfares are not the most appropriate thing in this matter, and hence the Meetings and Concentrations do not produce the results that might be expected. And although it is even possible, or rather certain, that some achieve-

---

[30] Lk 10:2.

ments are derived from them that for many are successful, these are always results that correspond to another level of things but do not belong to the supernatural world. Excessive noise and trumpet blasts sometimes serve to conceal either the lack of content and solidity of a Christianity that has ceased to be Christian, or the spiritual emptiness that currently suffocates so many souls who suffer from the absence of Jesus Christ.

Everything would seem to indicate that the Lord has gone and is no longer with us. Or perhaps it is we ourselves who have asked Him to leave? Be that as it may, or for whatever reason, it is as if He is not here. And hence we are overwhelmed by the pain of an illness whose possible consequences we fear.

But we know that He will soon return and be with us again. None of us will ask the reason for His delay, for we will be overwhelmed by the joy of His presence. And maybe one day, in the morning, in the late afternoon, or in the dead of night —who knows—, when we are most in pain, someone will announce to us that He is already here and is calling us. With words that will surely be spoken in our ear, and that we will therefore only be able to hear in the silence that gives way to true love: when we have put aside so many things that hinder us, in order to concentrate better on listening to the loving whistle of the Good Shepherd Who is already arriving. Then we will remember the times and sighs of ages past:

> *My Love asked me, soft and low,*
> *To forget all things and not let worries rise,*
> *And in the lush green meadow,*
> *Contemplate only his eyes*
> *And listen to the words of love in his sighs.*

And here we leave it, as we have far exceeded the time available.

OUR FIRST MEETING WITH THE LORD, OR ABOUT VOCATION

(REGARDING SAINT ANDREW'S VOCATION)

MEDITATION

(December 1st, 1976. Jn 1:35 ff.)

Yesterday, November 30, we had the opportunity to celebrate the feast of Saint Andrew the Apostle. I have always felt a tender devotion to this apostle, especially since I was sent, as a recently ordained priest, to my first assignment in a parish under the advocation of this Saint. I had the opportunity, therefore, to exercise the first years of my priesthood in the shadow of his protection.

The Gospel gives us some details about his life, although we are more interested at this time in those that refer to the early days in which he accompanied the Lord. It tells us about his vocation, or his first encounter with Jesus, and later about the definitive confirmation of his vocation. The Gospel gives us little more about his activities during the years in which he accompanied the Lord; and after the Ascension, nothing is said about him, so we have to rely on Tradition and what is told in some other documents, such as the *Book of the Acts and Martyrdom of St. Andrew*, written in the second century.

Let us speak then of his first encounter with the Lord and of his definitive vocation to the apostolate.

The event is narrated by Saint John, since it was the two together (John and Andrew) who met the Lord for the first time and then spoke with Him on a certain evening. The author of the fourth Gospel tells it thus:

The next day again John [the Baptist] *stood, and two of his disciples* [Andrew and John the Evangelist]. *And beholding Jesus walking, he saith: Behold the Lamb of God. And the two disciples heard him speak, and they followed Jesus. And Jesus turning, and seeing them following him, saith to them: What seek you? Who said to him: Rabbi, (which is to say, being interpreted, Master,) where dwellest thou? He saith to them: Come and see. They came, and saw where he abode, and they stayed with him that day: now it was about the tenth hour. And Andrew, the brother of Simon Peter, was one of the two who had heard of John, and followed him. He findeth first his brother Simon and saith to him: We have found the Messiah, which is, being interpreted, the Christ. And he brought him to Jesus. And Jesus looking upon him said: Thou art Simon...*[1]

After this first encounter, they returned to their work: their boat, their nets, and their fishing. Until one day the Lord called them to go with Him, definitively. This is how Saint Mark tells us about it: *And passing by the sea of Galilee, he saw Simon and Andrew his brother, casting nets into the sea (for they were fishermen). And Jesus said to them: Come after me, and I will make you to*

---

[1] Jn 1: 35–42.

become fishers of men. And immediately leaving their nets, they followed him.[2]

We have read earlier that the Baptist was with two of his disciples —John and Andrew— when the first meeting of the two young men with the Master took place. It should be noted, as if in passing, that the school of John the Baptist provided the Lord with very good followers. For the Forerunner knew how to train his men well, and then detach himself from them and lead them to the Lord; limiting himself to show them the way at the same time that he hid and disappeared: *He must increase, but I must decrease,*[3] as he used to say. Then, looking at Jesus as He passed by, he said to his two disciples: *Behold the Lamb of God.*

Looking at Jesus... And indeed, if we want people to look at the Lord and fix their attention on Him, we must first have done so ourselves (the text of the Latin version uses here the verb *respicere*, which means to look deeply, to observe carefully or attentively). To the extent that, if we are not accustomed to doing that, we will not be able to get people to turn their attention to the Lord and fix their gaze on Him. The inanity and sterility of many apostolic lives lie in a superficial attention to the Lord and in the consequent lack of intimacy and contact with Him.

So, when the two disciples heard the Baptist's statement, they followed Jesus. And if you remember the way in which our own vocation took place, you will realize that everything happened in the exact same manner. Someone told us about the Lord and pointed Him out to us in some way. And we, for our part, even though we did not yet understand very much, also began to follow the Master. In reality, we still did not know very well what it was about or Who

---

[2] Mk 1: 16–18.
[3] Jn 3:30.

it was about, although this was not an obstacle for us to continue forward. The truth is that we heard about a marvelous and seductive man, who was also God —God and Man at the same time—, and Whose name was Jesus.

In any case, notice that the definitive and authentic vocation had not yet taken place for the two disciples. This, as we have read in Saint Mark, happened later; for until then it was merely a matter of a first contact with the Lord. We must be aware how important are those who do the preliminary work that the Baptist did. For it is certain that at some time or other we have come across someone who caught our attention about a wonderful character, for us until then virtually unknown, who was called Jesus, the Man-God. It is, therefore, evident that such people, who know how to point out properly so that men may take notice of Jesus, have an extraordinary importance in Christian life; as Saint Paul indicated in his *Letter to the Romans*: *How then shall they call on him, in whom they have not believed? Or how shall they believe him, of whom they have not heard? And how shall they hear, without a preacher?*[4]

So, if we want men to call upon the Lord, or turn to Him, we must speak to them and preach to them about Him... *Master, where do you live?* Accordingly, any attempt to make Jesus invoked and known, by approaching Him, must use this procedure if it is to succeed.

And hence the failure of so many *vocation campaigns*, which emphasize anything but the *true Jesus*, by making truly ridiculous allusions to Jesus orally, in writing, or graphically; as through *posters*, for example, which rather present an effeminate, or at least decaffeinated, Jesus; or by insisting on sociological, psychological, or merely human procedures, which are incapable of attracting any

---

[4]Rom 10:14.

young person with a normal mind and heart. And often it does not even come to this, since the vocation problem does not revolve around the Person of Jesus, but rather insists on purely human issues without supernatural value: commitment to the marginalized, work for social peace..., and a long litany of like issues known to everyone. This is undoubtedly because the promoters of such campaigns *have never fixed their attention* on the Person of the Master; in other words, they lack interior life.

Any attempt to promote vocations is doomed to fail if it does not take into account something fundamental here: What we are accustomed to call vocation —the call to follow Jesus Christ— is in reality *an act of love*, or *a declaration of love*; even more: a *courtship asking for one's hand in marriage*, which is nothing more than the impulse towards a betrothal that will later be consummated in an authentic spiritual marriage. These statements may seem exaggerated to those who are not familiar with the essence of Christian existence (being an ecclesiastic, or a consecrated person, does not mean *per se* that one possesses intimacy with the Lord, or a deep knowledge of His Message).

First of all, it should be taken into consideration that a vocation is something like the grace of all graces. This could seem a hyperbolic statement, but the fact remains that a vocation is at least one of the most sublime, delicate, and ineffable graces that Jesus can bestow on someone (ordinarily a young man). While every Christian is called to union with the Lord to the point of a certain identification of lives (Jn 6:57; Gal 4:19; Eph 4:15), here it is something different, in that the vocation or call pursues something much more tender and elevated (although the starting point is the same, in this case it is a matter of deepening and reaching the most intimate and tender consequences: love brought to its fullness). Something like perfection within perfection, or perfection taken to the highest degree that can be reached in the earthly stage of life. To say that a vocation is an invitation to friendship —a friendship such as God understands it, entering already the paths of true love— would not yet be the whole truth. For the call means that the one chosen (for love) consents to everything which love expects, namely, the affirmative response to a true and more complete exchange or transfusion of lives: *I live, though it is no longer I, but Christ who lives in me,*[5], said the Apostle; and hence it can be said in all truth that *sacerdos est alter Christus.* Here we are no longer faced with something that, superficially seen, could be described as an exchange of hearts. There is no longer here a mere exchange, but the surrender to the beloved, on the part of the Lover, even of the functions and privileges most properly His own (Jn 20:21; Lk 10:16; Jn 20:23, etc.). What the Lover most desires is to identify His life with the life of the beloved. Or, to put it another way and as far as vocation is concerned: that the love between Jesus and the person called by Him to the intimacy of His heart may reach its most intimate fullness.

Because of its spousal or matrimonial character, the initiative in this case normally seems to correspond to the future Bridegroom Who calls and invokes His future bride, for whom He dies out of love: *Neither doth any man take the honour to himself, but he that is called by God, as Aaron was,* as is said in the Letter to the Hebrews.[6]

Since Love is a devouring fire (Heb 12:29), not surprising is the impatience or anxiety shown by the Bridegroom in the search for His chosen bride. The vocation or call to total discipleship is but this very thing, but carried to its deepest and most intimate consequences:

---

[5] Gal 2:20.
[6] Heb 5:4.

> *Arise, make haste, my love,*
> *my dove, my beautiful one, and come.*[7]
>
> ....
>
> *Open to me, my sister,*
> *my love, my dove, my undefiled...*[8]

So it is said in the *Song of Songs*, although modern poetry expresses it in the same way. To which we should add here, as if in passing, that authentic poetry always refers to love or is a song of love:

> *Beloved, I searched to see,*
> *In my orchard, the path where lemon blooms burst,*
> *There I stayed in wait for thee,*
> *Out behind my lemon tree,*
> *To see if, My Beloved, I found you first.*

Someone might remark here that it is not normal to reach betrothal, let alone marriage, without first falling in love. And so it is, in fact. The young person (the Christian) will not respond to the call he receives to a total following if he is not in love with the Lord. And this is how it always happens (we do not speak here of the aberrations meant by the modern term and concept of love), for one does not fall in love if the two lovers have not previously contemplated each other and have not realized their mutual beauty. In other words, it is true that love requires a certain previous period (moment) in which goodness and beauty are already perceived:

---

[7] Song 2:10.
[8] Song 5:2.

> *My beloved is white and ruddy,*
> *chosen out of thousands.*[9]

And now we could allude again to the previous work of preparation that the Baptist carried out; which, in this particular case, would be with respect to his two disciples Andrew and John. Prior work of training without which the two men in question would not have been determined to follow Jesus in order to know Him more closely and more intimately.

This is another reason why vocational campaigns often end in failure. Since the modern Church has given up any work of authentic catechesis (in the broad sense of the word), the Christian people (and even more so the youth) find themselves in a situation of extreme ignorance regarding the content of the Christian Faith: *How can they believe if there is no one to preach to them?* as the Apostle said in his Letter to the Romans.

And there will also be those who will point out here a new observation or objection in this regard:

Perhaps it seems exaggerated to try to relate the mystical life to something as simple as a vocation to follow (and specifically the priesthood). To which we could respond by saying, in the first place, that a vocation is not something so simple, if by simple we mean here something unassuming and of minor importance. Secondly, it also happens that such a presumption of exaggeration is precisely another of the causes —surely the main one— of the failure to which we are alluding. If one does not fall in love with Our Lord (call it mystical life or whatever you want), he will not feel determined to follow Him faithfully and completely. Especially not the young man.

---

[9]Song 5:10.

After all, it was the Lord Himself who made prayer the basis of any vocational campaign (Mt 9:38).

Unfortunately, in this field of Christian Pastoral Ministry that relates to the recruitment of vocations (and in any other field of Christian life), a third party has nothing to do with it. It is useless to play the role of go–between if one wants to lead someone to the love of Jesus Christ, since whoever wants to do so must also be in love; or if you wish, as they say nowadays, committed (with the Lord, of course). For only love produces love. But no one can doubt that the Baptist was a truly *committed* man; hence his success.

The mediocrity of priestly lives, which so many apostles of pastoral work present to young people today, does not seem to be the most suitable way to seduce them. And even less so when they are offered a program of education with merely human welfare content (Human Rights, social peace, commitment to the marginalized ... etc.; you already know the litany). It is a total ignorance of youth to believe that young people fall in love with *programs* —and what programs, Lord!— When the reality —the beautiful reality indeed— is that people fall in love with *people*; and, in this particular case, with the Person of Jesus Christ.

The Gospel text goes on to say that Jesus, *turning to them, and seeing that they were following Him, said to them, "What do you seek?"*

After having been led to Him, the personal encounter takes place. The same thing happened to us, and that is why we can recall, with real emotion, the moment of that first meeting that moved us to begin to follow Him. Although we did not really know exactly Who He was, something knocked at the door of our hearts to tell us that that moment was wonderful and great. And then He turned to us...

Saint Augustine once said that *we would follow Him in vain if He had not turned toward us.*

And He asked the two disciples with those words, as brief as they were filled with meaning: *What do you seek?*

And in questioning them He was also questioning us. Each one of us. With this type of questions, charged with such a personal and intimate character that have so much to do with love.

Of course, the Lord knew well what those two men were looking for. Exactly the same thing that all human beings seek, consciously or unconsciously, openly or without wanting to recognize it: happiness. Soon Andrew would realize that what he was anxiously seeking was not some *thing* but some *One*. In short, Jesus Himself.

Men search anxiously for happiness and often never really find it when they are looking for it in things. On the other hand, we know well that happiness is only found by those who do not seek it or are not concerned about it; precisely because the only thing that matters to them is the Lord. When you began to follow the Lord, with such little knowledge of His Person, you had not thought of attaining happiness, but only the Lord... Until He turned and... A wonderful thing, since it was He who reached out to you (Phil 3:12). It was thus that the first love for the Lord knocked at the door of your heart. And it was thus that the first great love was born in you; it was not for some *thing*, but for some *One* who alone could fulfill your insatiable desires for happiness: Jesus, the good Master, the Lord.

From which it seems to be deduced that the ultimate end (no doubt this is a redundancy) of man is not so much *Beatitudo* as *Love*; as if Love demanded a first place in a correct hierarchy of values. And rightly so, for happiness is the first —and last— consequence of the reality of *being in love*. Someone is happy when he possesses the loved one. And this is how everything seems to indicate that happiness is the consequence of love, and not the other way around. Therefore, it is when we have reached infinite Love that we have arrived at the possession of infinite Happiness (insofar as it can be shared by the creature), and which many call *Beatitudo*:

> *I am not moved to love Thee, O my Lord,*
> *By any longing for Thy Promised Land;*
> *Nor by the fear of hell am I unmanned*
> *To cease from my transgressing deed or word.*
>
> ....
>
> *Yea, to Thy heart am I so deeply stirred*
> *That I would love Thee were no heaven on high,*
> *That I would fear, were hell a tale absurd!*

As the old and anonymous poem said. And it was Jesus Himself Who related the Complete Joy (Jn 15:11) that He intended to bestow on His disciples in His own Person (Jn 16:22), which is precisely what identifies Him with Perfect Joy.

In this regard, with respect to the well–known passage narrated in the book of *The Little Flowers*, in which Saint Francis dialogues with his companion Friar Leo about Perfect Joy, I would dare to qualify here some aspect of the question.

Of course, the episode is one of the most beautiful of those contained in the book. Saint Francis demonstrates in it once again his holiness, in no way inferior to his genius in terms of understanding the spirit of the Gospel. However, everything seems to indicate that Perfect Joy cannot consist, in the last analysis, in sufferings borne with patience and out of love. Since suffering is pain, it is impossible to combine it with joy, no matter how much it is borne out of love for Christ. What is really happening, in my opinion, is simply that the Saint's immense perspicacity accurately understood something fundamental: that sharing the sufferings, and even the death, of the Beloved (Christ, in this case) is the only, quickest, and most direct way to be close to Him; *which is precisely what leads to Perfect Joy.* Hence, according to this, suffering for the Beloved —through the certainty of being close to Him— would be the penultimate thing; or, to put it more clearly, the thing immediately preceding the end of the journey, which is Perfect Joy. It is impossible to suffer while being with the Bridegroom (Mt 9:15). And this is how the Baptist also felt when he said: *The friend of the Bridegroom, who "accompanies him and hears him, rejoices greatly" when he hears the voice of the Bridegroom. Therefore my joy is complete.*[10]

What do you seek? the Lord asks John and Andrew, when He sees that they are following Him.

The question addressed to Mary Magdalene, when she was tearfully looking for her Master, although it seems to be the same, contains however a different nuance: *Woman, why are you weeping? Whom do you seek?* It is no longer a question, therefore, as to the object of the search, of a *what,* but of a *who.* Mary Magdalene was no longer seeking any particular thing, not even happiness (which no longer mattered to her), but only the Lord. Hence the question of Jesus, Who knew very well that Mary Magdalene was not looking for any particular thing, but only for Him.

Ultimately, one does not love things, but people. Love is interpersonal and always flows from heart to heart. If things are loved, they are always loved through and because of the love professed for persons. The saints loved created things as the work and vestiges of the Creator and, therefore, through their love for God. The Saint

---

[10] Jn 3:29.

of Assisi, for example, loved things with the same simplicity and ingenuity with which man loved them in the first days of Creation; so that, being God's work as well as his own, he considered them as his sisters: Brother Sun, Brother Fire, Sister Moon, or Sister Stars...

Scattering a thousand graces,
He passed through the groves in haste,
And looking upon them as he went,
Left them, by his glance alone,
Clothed with His Beauty.

....

My Beloved, the mountains,
The solitary, wooded valleys,
The strange islands,
The roaring rivers,
The whisper of the amorous breezes.

As Saint John of the Cross also says in his beautiful verses, so sublime that they have become immortal.

But let us continue with our story. It was then that *He said to them: Come and see. So, they went and saw where He dwelt, and abode with Him that day. It was about the tenth hour.* They always remembered with emotion the moment of their first meeting with the Lord, as is shown by the fact that Saint John even notes the hour at which it took place.

So deep was the impression and so profound the impact those two men received that Andrew, full of enthusiasm, ran at once to convince his brother: *Then he found his brother Simon and said to him, "We have found the Messiah" —which means Christ—. And he led him to Jesus.*

Then they went back to the work of their trade: their boat, their nets, their fishing... Until one day, as we have read before, *while walking along the Sea of Galilee, the Lord saw Simon and his brother Andrew casting their nets into the sea, for they were fishermen, and he said to them, "Follow me, and I will make you fishers of men."*

Now they knew what the Master wanted. And, at last, they understood what their hearts were longing for and the true meaning of their lives. They had clearly heard the Lord's call and knew that they were destined to undertake the greatest of all adventures. The previous stage of preparation was necessary to better understand Jesus and to not be afraid of what He was going to propose to them.

The Gospel tells us of a few episodes in which the apostle Andrew appears, more or less accidentally: At the first multiplication of the loaves when, together with Philip, he tells the Lord about a young man who was carrying a few loaves of bread and a few fish —although his consternation was great, for what could such a little thing mean to feed so many people?— Or when, also together with Philip, he tells the Lord that some strangers have arrived and wanted to speak to Him and know Him... After that, we know hardly anything certain about the way in which his life passed. It seems that he evangelized certain parts of Asia, together with his brother Peter according to some, although it is practically certain that he died a martyr's death, crucified on an X–shaped cross, as many claim.

In the *Book of the Acts and Martyrdom of St. Andrew* —whose absolute historicity I cannot guarantee, in spite of its extreme antiquity, although there is nothing to prevent us from believing it— we read of the words spoken by the Apostle when he was being led to his death. As you know, the last words of men who have passed into history often summarize, in the form of a compendium, what their lives have been; and sometimes they even tell us more about them than many of the marvelous episodes that punctuate their lives:

> *O good Cross,*
> *Made beautiful by the body of the Lord:*
> *Long have I desired you,*
> *Ardently have I loved you,*
> *Unceasingly have I sought you out;*
> *And now you are ready for my eager soul.*
> *Receive me from among men*
> *And restore me to my Master,*
> *So that he, who, by means of you,*
> *In dying redeemed me, may receive me.*
> *Receive me from among men*
> *And restore me to my Master...*

Indeed, for when we contemplate this world of ours in which God has willed that we should live, and in which Evil reigns everywhere (Jn 14:30), even if we do not want to admit it... When the crisis that the Church is suffering has allowed the ideas of the world, or the smoke of Satan in the words of Paul VI, to penetrate even into her bosom. When paganism is displacing Christianity throughout the whole wide world, and everything seems to indicate that the end of History is near (Mt 24:15; 1 Pet 4:7; Rev 22:12). When Christians are being persecuted everywhere in a thousand ways and means. When all this happens, how can we not feel the desire to go to the Father's House, to our true City, which is the Homeland of Heaven (Heb 13:14)?

This Earth, on which we still live, is good and beautiful because it has been created by God, after all Of course, it is. But it is so insofar as everything it contains is a vestige and imprint of God. And also, and above all, because it has been for us the means and the platform that have allowed us to share the life and the cross of Our Lord. And just as it is true that Christian hope is absolutely contrary to pessimism, do not forget that it is this virtue of hope which makes us look towards the City of Heaven and which induces us to feel the nostalgia of soon being full citizens there:

I die because I am not dying...

As our Saint Teresa of Avila used to say. Or as Saint Paul also declared in his *Letter to the Philippians*: *But I am straightened between two: having a desire to be dissolved and to be with Christ, a thing by far the better...*[11] Now more than ever, and thanks to Jesus Christ, we Christians have the right to contemplate death as a liberation rather than a punishment. The child–angel Tiberius, or the angelic child Tiberius (in *Las Campanas Tocan Solas*, by José María Pérez Lozano), when asked about what he would like to be in the future, answered —or perhaps he could have answered:

> *A gardener of the air,*
> *So as to live among the birds and the clouds.*
> *To be farther away from men*
> *And closer to God.*

Our vocation was the first call that the Lord made to us, urged by the goodness of His heart, for He loved us more than He loved others. Now we groan as we await the second, which will sound louder and

---

[11] Phil 1:23.

clearer than the first. It will happen when the impatience of His love can no longer bear the waiting, which will coincide with the moment when our heart no longer wishes to live in nostalgia and absence. It will be then when we will forget forever the icy cold of this Earth of ours to go away with Him:

> *Open to me, my sister,*
> *my love, my dove, my undefiled...*

So spoke the impatient Bridegroom from *The Song of Songs*. And Saint John of the Cross, on his part:

> *But how, O life, dost thou persevere,*
> *Since thou livest not where thou livest,*
> *And since the arrows make thee to die which thou receivest*
> *From the conceptions of the Beloved*
> *Which thou formest within thee?*

And so it is, to our joy. *The Cross desired for so long, loved with so much care, searched for so tirelessly, and prepared with so much encouragement...* Sartre was right, without knowing what he was saying, when he declared that man is a being meant for death. Of course, the reality is of a very different meaning from the one that his disturbed mind intended. For Saint Paul himself seems to agree with the French writer, although *a sensu contrario*, if one takes a closer look: *Do you not know that as many of us as have been baptized into Christ Jesus have been baptized into his death?*[12] Evidently, once again it is clear that the ideas of the world are a

---

[12] Rom 6:3.

sad imitation that leads to a desperate, ridiculous caricature and inverted image of the ideas of God.

The day and the moment when we felt the first call of the Beloved —His loving whistle, addressed to us— we will never forget. *It was about the tenth hour.* Now it is our turn to await, with all the impatience that a heart in love can bear, that other call which will lead us to be reunited with Him forever.

THE HEALING OF THE BLIND MAN BARTIMEUS

MEDITATION

(October, 26th, 2003. Mk 10: 46–52)

And they came to Jericho: and as he went out of Jericho, with his disciples, and a very great multitude, Bartimaeus the blind man, the son of Timaeus, sat by the way side begging. Who when he had heard, that it was Jesus of Nazareth, began to cry out, and to say: Jesus son of David, have mercy on me. And many rebuked him, that he might hold his peace; but he cried a great deal the more: Son of David, have mercy on me. And Jesus, standing still, commanded him to be called. And they called the blind man, saying to him: Be of better comfort: arise, he calleth thee. Who casting off his garment leaped up, and came to him. And Jesus answering, said to him: What wilt thou that I should do to thee? And the blind man said to him: Rabboni, that I may see. And Jesus saith to him: Go thy way, they faith hath made thee whole. And immediately he saw, and followed him in the way.

The first thing that calls one's attention when reading this text is the state of misery in which blind Bartimaeus found himself. Sitting by the side of the road, at the entrance (or exit, if you prefer) of Jericho begging for alms. And I am not referring so much to his material misery as to that which refers to his predicament in general.

We may imagine, with the certainty of being right, that the comforts that surrounded him would not be abundant, and that the satisfaction of his hunger would not be a pleasure he would often enjoy. These poor wretches lived on the few scanty alms thrown to them, out of compassion, by other people almost as poor as Bartimaeus.

And yet, all things considered, it was by no means this that made the situation of blind Bartimaeus tremendously unhappy.

The unhappy man was sitting by the roadside, listening to the people coming and going, but unable to move from the place where he was. But roads have been made to be traveled and walked upon, not for one to be seated at their side while people come and go along them. Think of someone who remains indefinitely immobile and sedentary in the place where everyone is on his way in search of a goal which always lies beyond... and we will be overwhelmed by confusion and sadness. For it is true that roads can only be imagined as destined to lead to a certain end —or perhaps to an uncertain one, but an end all the same?

What is important here is that the Christian is fundamentally *a being who walks* —like the Church of this Earth which is always itinerant and of which he is a part— inasmuch as he has been called to make Jesus' life and existence his own. He said of Himself that He is the Way, and that one cannot even reach the Father unless one goes all the way to the end (Jn 14:6). Hence, the Christian cannot claim any other destiny than that of walking beside Him, in Him, and with Him.

But the blind beggar stood still and unable to move in a place where everyone was walking. Sitting on the side of what had been made to move forward and with no hope of getting anywhere. Forced to earn a meager livelihood by living the paradox of stillness and obscurity where only movement and light made sense.

It is evident that to stop in perpetuity at the edge of a road seems the greatest of incongruities.

A Road always possesses a certain air of restlessness and excitement, like a path in which the unexpected could appear at any moment, perhaps at the turn of one of its many zigzags, where the strange or the inexplicable may await; and more surely something hitherto unknown that may be able to gladden —or perhaps sadden— our hearts. Destined to be lost in the distance, the road does its job even better when we do not know where or when it will end. Sometimes it bifurcates, or even seems to get lost or hide, perhaps to make us doubt the direction that suits us; as if it were a kind of strange joke that seems to smile to itself contemplating our incapacity. It was opened so that, by following its path, mortals could know of weariness and fatigue (Jn 4:6), the only and exclusive way to reach an intended end (for someone already said *that battles have always been won by weary soldiers*).

> *As you walk towards hills above*
> *Allow me to walk with you, Pilgrim, my friend*
> *And see if he whom I love*
> *Gives us his wine to drink of*
> *In reaching together our long journey's end.*

The horrendous misfortune of our blind beggar is that he found himself in a situation all the more distressing because he had no way out. Double misfortune, to be more precise. For in reality the proper end of the Christian is to walk: *Go and teach all nations...*[1] *Men of Galilee, what are you doing there, looking up to heaven?*[2] As well as to be able to see and contemplate Him of Whom it was said that *He was the light of men.*[3] It is precisely to this last point that his path leads.

> *The Road goes ever on and on,*
> *down from the door where it began.*
> *Now far ahead the Road has gone,*
> *and I must follow, if I can,*
> *pursuing it with weary feet,*
> *until it joins some larger way,*
> *where many paths and errands meet.* [4]

The Road goes ever forward, continually onward and onward (Phil 3:13), and no one is allowed to look back (Lk 9:62). For the heavenly Jerusalem was not made for cowards (Rev 21:8), nor for those who, after having tried to flee from the filth of the world, return like a dog to its vomit; or like a sow, which, having been washed, returns to wallow again in the mire (2 Pet 2: 20–22).

The end of the Road can be guessed at or felt, better than seen in the distance; although it is still too far away to have to walk it with tired feet. But with the certainty, of course, that there is no danger of getting lost, since it has been duly marked and prepared by the One who has already traveled it first (Jn 14:34).

---

[1] Mt 28:19.
[2] Acts 1:11.
[3] Jn 1:4.
[4] From the poetic work of J.R.R.Tolkien.

A good connoisseur of human nature that Saint Augustine was nevertheless contemplated this sad possibility: *Bene curris, sed extra viam*, the Saint once said.[5] In any case, it is never licit for the Christian to abandon the Road (Mt 10:22), rather he must follow it, whatever happens: *But I must follow it, if I can.* And although it is evident that he would never be able to do it on his own (Jn 15:5), he can always resort to exclaim with the Apostle: *I can do all things in Him who gives me strength*[6] and Who will never forsake me.

> *If ere from thy side I flew,*
> *Search for me again, my friend, come look for me,*
> *And when you find me anew,*
> *Take me to the path, I plea,*
> *There where you first met with me and I with thee.*

The destiny of the disciple of Jesus consists in walking the Way always with feet exhausted by fatigue, because, as we have mentioned before, *battles are always won by tired soldiers*. And it cannot be otherwise, since, as the Master warned His followers, *the gate is narrow and straight the path that leads to Life, and few are those who find it.*[7] His goal, therefore, is to advance weary and burdened; until the Path finally converges upon another wider and happier one, where so many destinies that remained faithful will ultimately coincide. Otherwise, he would not be sharing the life, the cross, and the death of his Lord.

To try to go elsewhere is to run *extra viam*, as Saint Augustine said. It would mean having chosen the broad and spacious path,

---

[5] *You run well, but off the road.*
[6] Phil 4:13.
[7] Mt 7:14.

which would be tantamount to running towards perdition (Mt 7:13), depriving life of its meaning and of the possibility of ever knowing Perfect Joy.[8]

A life is not a life as such, much less an abundant one (Jn 10:10), if it has been devoid of all difficult and adventurous content. Life that is not a risky *quest* is not true life. Just as an easy Christianity or a Christianity to be accepted by the modern post–Christian world has nothing to do with the Person and the Message of Jesus.

Hence the perplexity of many Christians in light of the attitude that part of the Hierarchy of the Church seems to have adopted.

It is not clear, for example, that *forgetting what separates us in order to insist on what unites us* will solve any problem, since the results seem to point in the opposite direction. According to classical logic, the purpose of definition is to set limits and differences, which is the only way to distinguish one thing from another. When such differences are set aside, the definition is blurred, and with it the identity of the thing defined. It is not surprising, therefore, that the Church today is facing a crisis of identity with herself. This does not affect the Church as such —which has never had any doubts about her nature or the purpose for which she was founded—, but rather many of the Christians who are part of her and who seem to have lost their faith.

For twenty centuries, the One True Church was known as the *Catholic Church*. Nowadays, however, the official ecclesiastical jargon (documents and speeches) refers to her as the *Church of Christ*,

---

[8]Must we repeat here, once again, that Perfect Joy, far from being purely eschatological, already begins on this Earth, also called the *valley of tears*, even though it is destined to unfold in total fullness in the Homeland? Far from there being any hint of contradiction here, the fact that our world is *a valley of tears* is precisely the indispensable condition for attaining Perfect Joy.

with the intention, no doubt, of favoring ecumenism.[9] An honest consideration, however, of the statistics would show bleak conclusions. Not only have there been no signs of rapprochement to the One True Church on the part of the *separated brethren*, but the concessions and weaknesses indulged in by the Catholics have further confirmed them in their beliefs. While the defections, on the other hand, in the Catholic Church can be counted by thousands and thousands.

Religious syncretism has never produced beneficial results. At least in favor of the good cause. Although practicing worship in conjunction with *religions* which are not really such (including heretical, occult, pagan, and even suspiciously perverse cults) may be a sign of good will, it undoubtedly succumbs to the blunt dictates of Logic. And those who apply it in this case are the simple people. For whom, however one may put it, if all religions are more or less equal, it is not worth getting on the wrong side of life for any of them. Evidently the official jargon used by many ecclesiastics tries to disguise this statement. And modern philosophies [of manipulation] of language have also gained a foothold within the Church, so that political and diplomatic jargon is now in common use in the Chancelleries and ecclesiastical Curias.[10] If anyone still has doubts, he can always free himself from prejudice and hesitation and honestly and objectively check the results.

---

[9]But just as the study of any doctrine or concept presupposes beginning, as Epictetus said, with a certain *consideratio nominis*, it is evident that, once the name is eviscerated, the thing referred to will also evaporate, or at least suffer serious detriment.

[10]The examples would be innumerable; to cite but a few: A resounding failure at a *dialogue* conference held between separated Christian denominations is presented to the *media* with the pretense that, *although no definitive positive agreements have been reached, the doors have not been closed*. Let us also recall the pitiful *post hoc, non propter hoc*, in reference to the Second Vatican Council.

Even more dangerous is to play with the sacred Magisterium. I am referring to problematizing, forgetting, or falsifying its authentic scope and content, its legitimate boundaries and limitations, its interpretation... etc. To consider as obsolete or outdated Documents or Declarations of the Magisterium (even solemn ones), which are part of the sacred Deposit of Teachings of the Church considered as unbreakable, can lead to disastrous results. If it is established, for example, that the condemnations contained in the *Syllabus* no longer have any relevance (the religious, social, or political conceptions that dictated them have changed), or that even solemn definitions of the Council of Trent now require a different interpretation (the meaning of the language has changed, while the philosophical concepts proper to the time, and which served as their basis, are no longer accepted by modern thought), it would not be strange if many people were to doubt the validity of the Magisterium. Both ancient and modern. For if the Magisterium of past times is susceptible to reinterpretation, why shouldn't the present one be so in a certain number of years? It is impossible to prevent people from drawing conclusions and thinking logically on their own. It is well known that the laws of rational thought (Logic) are immutable and unbreakable, inasmuch as they respond to the very constitution of human nature and, when it comes down to it, to the very reality of being; so that not even the Devil could change them, so that he has only the recourse of lying to conceal and disguise the truth. Therefore, it is impossible to avoid that so many normal people draw their own conclusions, even if they are wrong; in fact, they have been induced to error by nefarious, or at least notoriously mistaken, approaches.

There is no point in hiding or misrepresenting the content of the Gospel. If the Road offered in it is narrow and difficult, and therefore hard to sell, there is no point in changing it for another more comfortable and spacious which, moreover, we know leads only to perdition. The complicated problem of modern Catholic Pastoral activity revolves around the fact that, facing the social phenomenon of the desertion of the masses,[11] it has found no other solution than to lower the bar: *If the mountain does not come to Mohammed, Mohammed must go to the mountain.*

The modern ecclesiastical policy of rapprochement (to separated brethren, to atheists and agnostics, to the youth, to the working class, and even to strange forms of thought such as Communism —the Chinese State Church, for example—, Feminism, or the Pro–Gay Movements) is not due to ill will. What does seem significant, however, is that a certain wave of fear or dread swept through the High Ecclesiastical Spheres, and even through the halls of Vatican II, from the beginning, at least, of the second half of the twentieth century. Does the current approach still respond to that fear, or is it perhaps due —as some claim— to a certain feeling of affinity with neo–modernist ways of thinking on the part of certain theologians and some Church Officials? Here is a question for history.

While respecting the ways of thinking of certain modern experts in pastoral approach, and assuming their good will, it is difficult to admit as an adequate policy the implementation of a certain mass pastoral as a means of attracting young people. If one honestly admits the facts, it is necessary to recognize that the great religious gatherings of young people, for example, have not only not resulted

---

[11] *The Rebellion of the Masses*, by Ortega y Gasset, was only a beautiful literary pirouette. What we have now is not a rebellion, but a desertion, which in some respects is perhaps worse in that anti–religious warmongering implies at least a *concern* for religion (one can compare the indifferentism of modern post–Christian society with the anti–theism that, starting with the French Revolution and passing through the Enlightenment, reaches to the present day). Of course, the modern Catholic Pastoral action will hardly admit the fact, although the mere implementation of the policies adopted is the most obvious demonstration that it recognizes it.

in an increase in their Christian life and a greater closeness to the Church, but rather the opposite has occurred.[12] This is not strange if one considers that the Gospel Message cannot be preached through the merely human means of modern Sociology (1 Cor 2: 4–5). The techniques of today's powerful advertising systems have nothing to do with the Gospel and are even counterproductive when they are used as an almost exclusive working tool.

No matter how little one knows about the youthful world of our times, anyone can see that they live immersed in a playful and fun environment in which, through noise and din, together with sex and often with drugs, they try to fill an anguished inner emptiness. They try to cloak their hollow and meaningless life with the *show*, the din, and anything that allows them to escape from the abyss of their inner nothingness. The *show* and the appearance create a world of dreams —no matter how false and ephemeral— entirely opposed to the possibility of an inner reflection that would lead to reality. It goes without saying that, when these conditions are considered and practiced as normal, the world of the supernatural, of the sacred, and of the metaphysical realities of being and truth, cannot find its place here. [13]

---

[12] It is a well–known fact that the Protestant denominations, taking advantage of the most prominent moments of these youth rallies, have carried out abundant and apparently successful proselytizing. It would be urgent to recognize with sincerity that the young people go to these massive events, more driven by a desire for tourism and amusement than by religious concerns.

[13] It is frequent in these massive ceremonies that, at the same time that the bishops and priests remain seated, adolescents of both sexes distribute the Eucharist in bulk by means of hand baskets, in the midst of a general tumult and even in the presence of the Pope. In the face of such events, and many others like them, it is very difficult not to realize that, in such circumstances, the meaning of the *sacrum* has completely vanished.

Of course, it is obvious that *one should not provide young people with the same old thing —or what sounds like the same old thing— to get them out of the same old thing.* Young people need *to feel something different* —someone would rightly say revolutionary— in order to make them feel strongly shocked and thus ready to give up their reverie of death. It is necessary to take them out of the noise and crowd of a fallacious and criminal world, in which they live deceived, so that they can recover again the vision of reality (Mk 8:23). The proclamation of the Christian Message must contain for them, and for all men, something not only different, but in every way contrary to what the world offers (1 Cor 1: 21–23). According to the Apostle, the preacher of the Gospel can in no way seek the pleasure or applause of those who listen to him; inasmuch as the fruit of his sowing is inversely proportional to such intentions: *For do I now persuade men, or God? Or do I seek to please men? If I yet pleased men, I should not be the servant of Christ.*[14]

The modern experts in pastoral work with youth need to discover something that, although it may come as a surprise to many, is nevertheless as (apparently) incredible and paradoxical as it is true: *It is not the broad and easy path that attracts young people; rather on the contrary, only the arduous and steep path can seduce them.* Who would have thought that the spirit of adventure, of heroism and generosity, is more characteristic of the old? And I am not referring so much to the old in years as to the old in spirit.

Of course, the same thing can happen to us, in a more or less conscious way, as happened to blind Bartimaeus: we may find ourselves at the side of a road, motionless and without moving forward; he compelled by his disability, we due to our lack of heart.

---

[14] Gal 1:10.

The great danger that lurks in the spiritual life is lukewarmness or mediocrity: *I know your works and that you are neither cold nor hot. Would that you were cold or hot! But because you are lukewarm, and are neither cold or hot, I will vomit you out of my mouth.*[15] Bartimaeus stood by a road along which everyone was moving except him; whereas we stand by the One who said of Himself that He is the Way..., but without excluding the horrendous possibility that we remain anchored and fixed in the same place and without advancing. And to make matters worse, we are also blind, since we do not realize what our situation entails.

It is not possible to march with Christ and stop. The good athletes who are His followers must carefully enter the race without giving in to fatigue, conscious of the competition and of the goal that awaits the winner.

I therefore so run, not as at an uncertainty: I so fight, not as one beating the air...[16] *Know you not that they that run in the race, all run indeed, but one receives the prize? So run that you may obtain.*[17]

Love always necessarily involves a race between lovers, even if it takes many forms and meanings, to reach the finish line and thus meet each other as soon as possible; to give more than the other and defeat him in the love contest...

> *He has taken me to his cellar,*
> *And his banner over me is love.*[18]

---

[15] Rev 3: 15–16.
[16] 1 Cor 9:26.
[17] 1 Cor 9:24.
[18] Song 2:4.

> *Come, my beloved, let us go forth into the field,*
> *Let us abide in the villages.*
> *Let us get up early to the vineyards,*
> *Let us see if the vineyards flourish,*
> *If the flowers be ready to bring forth fruits...*
>
> ....
>
> *Flee away, O my beloved,*
> *And be like the roe, and to the young hart*
> *Upon the mountains of aromatic spices.*[19]
>
> ....
>
> *Draw me: we will run after thee.*[20]

And so it was that blind Bartimaeus, in fact, ran with all his might after the Lord: *When he heard that Jesus the Nazarene was passing by, he began to cry out and say: Jesus, Son of David, have mercy on me!*

The poor blind man heard the tumult —blind people are not deaf—, and when he learned who it was that was passing by, he understood that he could not miss that unique opportunity of his life. Saint Augustine would later say: *Timeo Deum transeuntem et non revertentem,*[21] since we do not know how many times He will pass by us or the opportunities we will receive.

Many rebuked him to be quiet; but he shouted all the louder...

Throughout our lives, there will be many who, in addition to trying to drown out the voice of our anxious calls to the Lord, will try

---

[19] Song 7: 12–13; 8:14.

[20] Song 1:4.

[21] *I fear that God may pass by me and never come back.*

to impede, by whatever means, our efforts to reach Him. The post-Christian world in which we live is not willing to tolerate anything other than either total indifference to Jesus Christ or mediocrity at best. And our own brethren will also take part, even more fiercely than outsiders, in the coercive campaign of silence (Mt 10:36; 2 Cor 11:26).

This should not surprise us in any way, since the Master has already announced that *if they persecuted me, they will also persecute you.*[22]

The serious and determined will to love and follow Jesus Christ usually arouses the hatred of many, both near and far. This is one of the most obscure mysteries of human existence, by no means completely clarified even by the Lord's words: *If the world hate you, know ye, that it hated me before you. If you had been of the world, the world would love its own: but because you are not of the world, but I have chosen you out of the world, therefore the world hateth you.*[23]

In the face of the crisis currently affecting the Church, perhaps the deepest crisis in its history, there are three different positions to be adopted by its members. Two of them are extremely easy to follow, while the third one involves a host of difficulties and problems for its supporters. We will call them here, simply for the sake of simplicity and ease, Positions A, B, and C.

Position A is simple to understand and relatively easy to adopt. Some convinced Catholics subscribe to it who think that a certain number of principles, to which must be added the teachings of the

---

[22] Jn 15:20.

[23] Jn 15: 18–19. An explanation that refers to first causes: *Because I chose you out of the world.* But it is evident that one could still ask about other second and deeper causes, the answers to which, however, remain for the moment among the secrets of God's heart.

Magisterium, besides being immutable are also intangible; while to forget them, to conceal them, or to falsify them, is an attack against the Faith. Which is precisely what the current Hierarchy of the Church has done, according to the supporters of this position. Things being so, and in the face of the impossibility of reaching any understanding, the followers of attitude A have opted to cut the link that united them to the Hierarchy. All this in order to maintain the principles, and in spite of the fact that the Canon Law typifies such a behavior as schismatic.

It is necessary to honestly recognize the verisimilitude of what this Position defends, inasmuch as it seems true in at least almost everything it proposes. The honesty and integrity of its followers is also to be commended, in whom the best of intentions can be assumed.

It suffers, however, this Position —at least that is how I understand it— from a major flaw that affects precisely one of the principles it claims to uphold: fidelity and submission to the legitimate Hierarchy, however inoperative and mundane it may seem in the best of cases, or even corrupt in the worst of them. What is certain is that a Catholic can never dispense with the fundamental principle, *nihil sine Episcopo, nihil sine Ecclesia*. On the other hand, it is well–known that cases of corruption of the Hierarchy, even among the Highest Officials, are not entirely foreign to the long–suffering history of the Church. And yet the true faithful have never felt justified in breaking with her: *Ubi Petrus, ibi Ecclesia*.

The problem is certainly as serious as it is delicate, as befits the difficult times in which we live. As for the possible submission to a worldly Hierarchy, and even one that is dubiously faithful to the principles of the true Faith and sound Tradition, it seems that it will be one of the tests that the Lord will allow His disciples to undergo;

especially when the end times draw near (Mt 24:15). If participation in the sufferings of his Lord has always been the condition of the true faithful, it is evident that, as the time of the final confrontation approaches, that participation will have reached its climax. And there is also something that true disciples do not forget, which is that participation in the Lord's cross, although it cannot be borne except upon pained shoulders, nor contemplated except with eyes filled with tears, is in reality, something glorious and a foretaste of the final Crown.

Position B is easy to understand and even easier to follow. Its adherents steadfastly maintain fidelity to the Hierarchy, even though such determination may at times seem somewhat excessive. Ignorance about the true scope of the due submission to the Magisterium and to the Hierarchy, on the part of so many of the faithful, allows certain ideologues and pressure groups to take advantage of the circumstance. Putting in parenthesis, even for the moment or indefinitely, fidelity to the intangible principles —dogmas included—,[24] the followers of this Posture decisively support what the Pope says, speaks, thinks, or does; although without putting too much emphasis on the true content, meaning, and limits of the Magisterium.[25] Still less do they think it necessary to distinguish between the Ordinary Magisterium, the Solemn Magisterium, or simple discourses or opinions poured out here or there; nor even that it is necessary

---

[24]Note that here we speak of bracketing, not of denying them. To deny the intangible principles would be absolutely improper of a Posture that defends for itself the monopoly of maintaining them.

[25]It must not be forgotten that the guarantee of supernatural infallibility enjoyed by the Magisterium of the Church, when exercised within the necessary limits and conditions, absolutely precludes the Magisterium from ever being able to contradict the Magisterium. If this were not so, it would be necessary to recognize that the Magisterium does not exist at all.

to integrate what the present Pope says with what has already been said by previous Popes, which can also form part of the one and only sacred Magisterium. In short, and to sum up: as strange as it may seem, for the supporters of position B everything the Pope says or does, including what is most frivolous, is dogma of faith; to the point that the slightest discrepancy in this respect supposes, according to them, to cease to be faithful to the Church.[26]

Of course, it must be recognized that Position B is the safest position. It involves leaving the principles and their interpretation in the exclusive hands of the Hierarchy —but is it certain that it is always the Hierarchy?— and to follow it faithfully and blindly. Thus, fidelity is assured and problems are solved. On the other hand, adherence to this Posture is also absolutely necessary, if one aspires to possessing a certain position within the Church that otherwise one would never attain: *Si quis episcopatum appetit, bonum opus desiderat*;[27] moreover, he will probably achieve it, which would not be possible at all without subscribing to this Posture.[28]

Position C, however, is the most difficult to understand and the hardest to practice. Since it is the Cinderella in this kind of singular contest (although without an enamored Prince or happy ending),

---

[26]We have already said before that the leaders of this Position, and their most allied and erudite supporters, have induced the vast majority of the Christian People, otherwise uneducated, to join it. And who would dare to reproach a multitude of simple faithful who lack the means to verify their own criteria?

[27]1 Tim 3:1.

[28]Position B, whose good will in the search for legitimate security we will not doubt here, also forgets something important. Admitting the principle of fidelity to the legitimate Hierarchy —without which there is no Catholicism worthy of the name—, a healthy theology cannot fail to consider that the Hierarchy also needs the faithful, inasmuch as the Church is a composite and complete organism. It is to be noted, therefore, that the legitimate authority, exercised by the Hierarchy, cannot dispense at all with the *sensus fidei* given in Baptism to all the faithful.

perhaps someone might think that it is not worth talking about it, and perhaps he would not be wrong. We can assure in advance that it is doomed to be an approach despised, and even abhorred, by one or the other. Positions A and B agree in this to condemn it (like Herod and Pilate), and hence its followers are always few and deserving (even if they are not recognized as such) the label of heroes.

The followers of this Position are convinced that they cannot desert the intangible principles of the Gospel, nor can they abandon their unwavering submission to the legitimate Hierarchy of the Church. This places them, at the present juncture of the Church, in an extremely unstable and difficult position of equilibrium. The supporters of Position A will always point to these faithful as having miserably sold themselves out to the System. While the followers of Position B will never recognize the struggle of these people to maintain fidelity to the true Faith; and they will never cease to accuse them at all times of being insubordinate and fundamentalists, no matter how much they have always obeyed, to the point of heroism.

Those who subscribe to this Posture know that they are condemned beforehand to not be taken into account in the Church, to never be conferred responsibilities or prebends of any kind. Neither do they desire them under any concept, perhaps thinking that the authentically deserved attribution of ranks, as well as the distribution of rewards, will not take place until He comes again Who will give to each one according to his works (Rev 22:12).

Thus, despised and abandoned by all, their own folly —which they think is divine— leads them to consider their condition as a mark of glory, and even as a guarantee of their participation in the existence of the Lord. Since they know that they are destined, as I have already told you, to anonymity and to be despised, it is for this reason that they expect with certainty to enjoy beforehand a foretaste of the happiness of Heaven. Convinced as they are that, after all, *blessed are those, individuals as well as nations, who have no history.*[29]

Upon noticing the cries of the blind man and the scandal produced around him, *Jesus stopped and said: "Call him!"*

This attitude of Jesus is in line with practical pastoral care as it often emerges from the Gospel. Which consists in using others —those who are closest to Him— to call those He wishes to bring closer: *And the Lord said to the servant: "Go out into the highways and hedges, and compel them to come in, that my house may be filled"...*[30] *The kingdom of heaven is likened to a king, who made a marriage for his son. And he sent his servants, to call them that were invited to the marriage; and they would not come... "but they that were invited were not worthy. Go ye therefore into the highways; and as many as you shall find, call to the marriage"...*[31] *"Go you also into my vineyard, and I will give you what shall be just."*[32]

---

[29]Curiously, there is a fourth Position, quite peculiar and unique: that of the Chinese State Catholic (?) Church, entirely subjected to the Chinese Communist State and completely separated from communion with Rome. Thus, as can be seen, it participates, together and at the same time, in Positions A and B. Strangely, however, this Church enjoys the sympathies and understanding of High Vatican Officials; contrary to what happens with the *underground* Chinese Catholic Church, which has remained faithful to Rome in spite of the persecutions it has suffered on the part of the Communist Authorities, but which does not usually receive such gestures of affection and encouragement on the part of the Vatican. Just as the unfortunate followers of Archbishop Lefebvre have exhausted the anathema jar against them, this has not been the case, far from it, with the *Chinese State Catholic Church*. The reasons that may justify these differences in treatment are as yet unknown.

[30]Lk 14:23.

[31]Mt 22: 2–3.8.

[32]Mt 20:4; Cf. Mt 28:19; etc.

The call is always personal and direct... unless circumstances[33] make it more feasible to do otherwise for the time being. In this case, the meaning of the word *apostle* as *one who is sent* makes full sense. And since the Lord has decided to work in collaboration with His creatures,[34] we can thus understand the role that His Heart has entrusted to His priests or ministers: He has made them envoys, messengers, and angels from on High, charged with summoning and drawing all men to Himself. And for this reason Scripture says that *he has as his messengers the winds, and for ministers flames of fire.*[35]

According to which the priest —the apostle, or the one sent— is a hurricane wind and a flame of fire. A wind that blows where it wills and one does not know where it comes from or where it goes (Jn 3:8), or fire that scorches the forest and burns the mountains (Ps 83:15). Who has spoken of the identity crisis of the priest...? Who has dared to attribute to the simple layman (in spite of all the greatness he possesses as a Christian and a child of God) the same dignity as to a minister who is wind and flame of fire at the same time...?[36]

---

[33]Or love, which usually impels the lover to have the loved one take part in his own tasks, as a way for both to participate in the same existence.

[34]Hand in hand with His beloved creatures, whom He no longer wishes to call servants, but friends (Jn 15:15).

[35]Ps 104:4.

[36]The attribution to the priest of the office of apostle or envoy is rather a tranquilizer terminology; so as not to disturb the weak or easily scandalized spirits. The priest is an envoy and at the same time he is much more than that, insofar as he identifies himself with the One Who sends him: the priest is another Christ. In fact, he does not come simply *on behalf of* Christ, because, if we think about it, acting as he does *in persona Christi,* Jesus' words are fulfilled: *whoever listens to you listens to me; and whoever rejects you rejects me* (Lk 10:16).

In recent times, however, the profound crisis that the Church is undergoing has affected the priesthood with particular intensity. It could not be otherwise. In a post–Christian world, in which many of the faithful, including members of the hierarchy, have seen their faith in Jesus Christ fade away, this could not but have negative repercussions on those who have been called to be other Christs. The much–touted promotion of the laity has caused a multitude of priests to be displaced from their functions by the laity. The questioning of their identity by theologians in the limelight and irresponsible hierarchs, together with the dedication of Bishops to so many tasks so often alien to a true Pastoral activity, have left thousands of priests in a lamentable state of abandonment and oblivion; or in a situation that some would qualify as spiritual and even material misery. For though it is true, as we have been saying, that the priest is another Christ, it is also true that he is first and foremost a human being, and, therefore, in need of a Father, who can be none other than his own Bishop. For a human being without a father, whether according to the blood or according to Christ, is nothing more than an orphan whose situation is aggravated when it comes to the supernatural plane. Unfortunately, however, there has often been a lack of true Shepherds who should have taken care of the spiritual, moral, doctrinal, and personal care of so many priests. If in these circumstances some have sullied the high dignity with which they were invested, it would not be right to forget, in attributing responsibilities, the ultimate and most culpable causes that have led to such situations.

But the Christian priesthood is too great and sublime a thing to be tainted, much less destroyed, by the insidiousness of the Evil One. The promises made at the Last Supper, and what happened there, are things too lofty and beautiful to be overtaken by ugliness or creeping malignity. The waters will return to their course, the

Mother and Teacher Church will set things right again, the threatening clouds that now darken the sky will be torn away to make way for the fiery and life–giving rays of the sun. The army of holy priests will have made its appearance once again, and they will then be, as they always were in the past, the only ones who can save the Church in the future.

As for some of us, who are now in the twilight of our lives, we look back and see once again that we have never been accepted by men. And yet we have never pretended to do anything other than strive to spread the love of Jesus Christ. Perhaps that is why all doors have been closed to us and barriers have been placed in our way? We do not know, although we have never been concerned about the answer to that question. In the plunder to which the nothingness of our existence has been subjected, we have not even dared to console ourselves with the memory that *He also came to His own, but His own did not receive Him.*[37] Like Saint Peter, we too are not worthy to die in the same way as our Master.

All that is gold does not glitter,
Not all those who wander are lost;
The old that is strong does not wither,
Deep roots are not reached by the frost.

From the ashes a fire shall be woken,
A light from the shadows shall spring;
Renewed shall be blade that was broken;
The crownless again shall be king.[38]

What Tolkien says of his mythical Aragorn could properly apply to today's priest. Although without a horse, without a sword, and

---

[37] Jn 1:11.
[38] From the poetic work of Tolkien.

without spectacular victories, of course. Of course, Tolkien writes an epic novel in which, through beautiful language, he draws a passionate metaphor intended both to construct literary language with the beauty of poetry and to convey the profound message of human existence and, ultimately, of human–divine love relationships. The victories of the Lord's disciple are never spectacular, and even take on the appearance of defeats; or at least that is how they appear to the world. Like the Lord in His Passion and in His Death. Satan takes good care that his own defeats are not trumpeted before the public of the world. Hence the struggle that the Lord's minister wages against the Evil One always takes place in the abysses of the depths: in the innermost depths of the human heart, in the dark and even tenebrous immolation of himself —as real as it is unknown to the world—, in the mysterious abandonment and emptiness of those moments of prayer in which he shares the Hour of Gethsemane..., and always in such a way that it goes unnoticed even by the Dark Powers. They will never be able to understand the humility of the silent and hidden surrender of one's life for love. But, at the end of the day, and in any case, the comparison of the priest with Gandalf is legitimate, even if the reality goes beyond all that this character means.[39]

---

[39]Tolkien's Gandalf the Wizard–warrior is much more than a hero of battles and legends. His fight against the Dark Lord has nothing to do with a mere epic narrative in which fabulous armies, whose composition and number surpass what is conceived by the most exalted imagination, would face each other. What happens is that Tolkien writes a grandiose epic novel of pure literary language... for those who read at a stretch; with an arcane language, but of high meaning and content, for those who know how to read underneath and deeper. In the struggle of Good against Evil, only one character can decide it in favor of Good. Not precisely in the form of a Victorious Rider with his sword, but at the price of his disappearance, which is tantamount to his immolation.

The Christian priesthood may seem buried today amidst the discredit of many people, the oblivion of many Hierarchs, its omissions in Documents and Declarations, and the appropriation, by the laity, of tasks that in times past denoted their sacred character inasmuch as they were carried out by the priest. *But all that is gold does not glitter.* Because the precious metal can still be hidden, perhaps in the depths or in the crevices of the stones, waiting for someone with a determined spirit to extract it again to be, once more, light and brightness that attracts men. Now it lies unknown and unseen; but gold, like light, has no other destiny but to dazzle men. *The old that is strong never withers, nor do the frosts reach the deep roots.* And hence Christian Hope forbids doubting that soon the age of the saints will rise again: *Out of the ashes a fire will rise, a light will spring up again among the shadows, the sword that was broken will be mended, and he who had been stripped of his crown shall be king again.*

At last they took pity on the blind man *and said to him, "Courage, get up for he is calling you!"*

The expression is a true slogan and a good apostolic program. To encourage those who are downcast and dejected, to exhort them to get up... and even more than all that, to give him the main reason to do so: *For He is calling you.*

The latter is perhaps the only determining motive that can propel those who are down to rise to their feet. The infusion of encouragement and understanding dispensed to the unfortunate, together with the exhortation that they put down their marasmus and abandon their state of misery, may not be sufficient; even if we were honest, we would have to say that quite often they are not. But that *He calls you,* uttered in the ears of the sufferer in the midst of his misfortune and misery; and even the simple knowledge that

He has fixed His attention on the despondent, called him by name (Jn 10:3), and requested him to come to His side, seem to possess a magical power of evocation. *He calls me...!*

I remember the impression I received when, at the beginning of my university studies, I entered the Campus Residence of the University of Murcia, and read for the first time the inscription on the chapel doors: *Magister Adest et Vocat te.*[40] I could not explain why or how I immediately felt emotionally alluded to.

I have often thought that the reason for the ineffectiveness of so many pastoral impulses lies in their lack of reference. Or to put it more clearly, in the lack of due reference to Jesus Christ. *He calls you and waits for you.* As Saint Peter did, although in the opposite direction, when he exhorted the paralytic lying at the door of the Temple to get up in the name of Jesus Christ (Acts 3:6). Many are the pastoral programs —often so bulky and erudite— that emerge from the laboratories of the Curiae and are so elaborated by highly specialized experts, that they seem more like treatises on sociology than anything else. It is therefore possible that, when the Church decides to free herself of some of the dead weight that impedes her impact on the modern world, she will include experts in pastoral alchemy on the list of things to get rid of.

Who casting off his garment leaped up, and came to him. And Jesus answering, said to him: What wilt thou that I should do to thee? And the blind man said to him: Rabboni, that I may see. And Jesus saith to him: Go thy way, they faith hath made thee whole. And immediately he saw, and followed him in the way.

We began this reflection by alluding to the fact that blind Bartimaeus, sitting by the side of a road, was nevertheless immobilized and prevented from walking along it. Now, on the contrary, at the

---

[40] *The Master is here, and He is calling you* (Jn 11:28).

end of the episode and after what happened there, the Evangelist tells us, as in a cry of triumphant enthusiasm that culminates and brings the narrative to a close: *And he followed him in the way...*

Before reaching this moment, some beautiful episodes that would have required our attention have been left behind... if we still felt we had the strength to do so. Hence, we can well say that it has been tiredness and impatience both at the same time that have driven us to arrive as soon as possible to this last and exciting moment of the narration.

Ever since I began to read the Gospel, while I was still an adolescent, I have always been affected by those words: And the blind man, when he had recovered his sight, *followed him in the way.* And this is how, strangely and without knowing the ultimate reason that would allow us to explain it, the Way has come to be, in some way, the main thread that has been weaving this beautiful Gospel story.

Upon the hearth the fire is red,
Beneath the roof there is a bed;
But not yet weary are his feet,
Still round the corner may wait
A new Road or a secret gate,
And though he passed them by today,
Tomorrow he may come this way
And take the hidden paths that run
Towards the Moon or to the Sun.
Home is behind, the world ahead,
And there are many paths to tread
Through shadows to the edge of night,
Until the stars are all alight.
The world behind and home ahead,
He wanders back to home and rest.[41]

---

[41] A poem written by Tolkien.

It is true, as the poet says, that *upon the hearth, the fire is red and that under the roof there is a bed.*

That is why, in the face of the madness of the world, the disciple could have turned his eyes elsewhere, and then taken refuge in the comfortable security of a home under a roof. And even more so when, after having tried something else, he would have received only the rejection of all.

But then, where would have been the great adventure of the search for true love? And has Love ever been found on the quiet paths? And how can the madness of men be saved except by means of another madness?

> *In search of my Love*
> *I will go over mountains and strands;*
> *I will gather no flowers,*
> *I will fear no wild beasts;*
> *And pass by the mighty and the frontiers.*

Saint John of the Cross said. That is why the disciple wants to believe that his feet are not yet tired, and that, in any case, around a bend, a new Path or a secret door may still await him. He remembers having heard the Master say that, if you are expelled from one city, go immediately to another; for the cities of Israel will not end until He comes (Mt 10:23). And because all the gates can never be closed to us, for there will always be another of whose existence we would not have known; and because at any moment a new Way awaits us, there is no room left to think of weariness.

And even if we have often passed by them, *tomorrow we can still retrace our steps, in order to take the hidden paths that run... towards the Moon or to the Sun.* Towards the paths whose final horizon we can only sense, and never see. Towards the unknown paths that run, above the stars, towards the Moon or the Sun. They are above all the paths of the priesthood, which begin, in a certain way, in a certain resemblance to the Master and end unfailingly in the identification with Him, as perfect Love demands.

For the disciple of the Lord —for the priest of Christ, so despised by the world and even, at times, so forgotten by the Church itself—, *home remains behind and the world ahead, for there are still too many paths to tread.* Go into all the world...! And even if the road runs *to the edge of night* (it could not be otherwise), the time will come at last when *all the stars will be all alight in the sky.*

At the end of it all, in the twilight of the night, when the end of the adventure approaches, *the world will be left behind and home will finally be glimpsed in the distance. That is when it will be time to return Home and rest.* Just as the Poet from Fontiveros thought:

> *I remained, lost in oblivion;*
> *My face I reclined on the Beloved.*
> *All ceased and I abandoned myself,*
> *Leaving my cares*
> *Forgotten among the lilies.*[42]

The time has also come for us to conclude. Someday, with the Lord at our side, we will have completed our task. In the meantime, it remains for us to listen with emotion to the call of the roads that still lie before us; those that are yet to be discovered and traveled. We can still follow them after the Master, together with Bartimaeus; those that lead us through the great Adventure of our existence, and that at the end will lead us

> *Towards the Moon or to the Sun.*

---

[42] Saint John of the Cross, *Dark Night*.

THE FEAST OF CHRIST THE KING

MEDITATION

(November 23, 2003)

It is difficult to explain the persistence of some of the Church's Feasts in the Liturgical Calendar overcoming the passage of time and adverse circumstances.[1]

But just because something is difficult to explain does not mean that it lacks reasons to justify it. It may simply be that the subject needs a deeper explanation; or a new clarification that makes the reasons for keeping it up to date more understandable, despite the

---

[1] The same difficulty arises, although now in the opposite direction, with some new Feasts being introduced in the Calendar. When Pope Pius XII instituted the Feast of Saint Joseph the Worker on the first day of May (profane Feast of Labor Day), as a First Class with Octave in the Liturgical Calendar, everything seemed to indicate that the purely Marxist character of Labor Day would be counteracted, or at least mitigated in some way. The passage of time has demonstrated the ineffectiveness of the Pope's good will, as well as showing that the profound vision of things of this great Pontiff were rather naïve. Today it has been reduced to the minimal liturgical category of Optional Memorial.

changes that the passage of time and new historical conditions may have introduced.

This is precisely what happens with the Feast of Christ the King, celebrated by the Church on the last Sunday of Ordinary Time, which precedes the first Sunday of Advent.

The approach to the problem could begin with a brief exposition of the feelings that present–day man, both adults and young people, experience with regard to Kings and Royalty.

It seems that most adults still have a more or less vague idea of the subject in question. However, ignorance, increasingly deeper and more widespread, as well as other circumstances that we will discuss later, are blurring and distorting the concepts as time goes by.

For the new generations, on the other hand, things look quite different. Within this field, the problem appears in a much more acute form and with more serious motives. If today's young people still retain any notion of royalty, it is undoubtedly to identify it with the anachronistic, the useless, and even the disastrous.

As is always the case, the causes of this situation are diverse and varied. We will try to summarize some of them, among those that seem to us to be the most important.

In the first place, there is the resounding failure of modern education systems.

Although, of course, it is possible that this statement is rather relative; and even, to a certain extent, not entirely in line with reality. We could rather say that it is a success of the System. Which has achieved, practically all over the world, that the present youth is anchored in a supreme state of ignorance, devoid of the ability to think, completely ignorant of History..., and therefore very easy to manipulate. In this regard, we could add, more concretely, that if the History that the System teaches to today's youth, as a learning subject, resembled reality in any way, it would be pure coincidence (something that, in reality, never happens).

It is then necessary to note the discredit that, at the cost of no small effort, the few members who still belong to this Institution have succeeded in bringing into disrepute (Europe is today almost the only point of reference that still remains).

Those who do not feel any kind of affective inclination towards the Monarchy or Royalty, who are many, think that the Institution today means nothing more than a useless and costly anachronism for the citizens, if not something even more harmful. And that it should, therefore, disappear.

Another large number of citizens, more or less indifferent to any form of government, are also convinced of the inoperability of the Institution, and of course of its discredit.

The supporters of Royalty, on the other hand, tend to be characters of a romantic tinge, deeply convinced, and rather clinging to traditions that many consider as obsolete and nostalgic. They are not very numerous in reality. Sometimes, however, they are simply individuals of a highly practical nature, dedicated to cultivating cronyism, which seems to yield them substantial benefits.

Personally, I am not a fervent enthusiast of the Monarchy. Although I do not consider it, in any case, a political system worse or better than the forms of government now called democratic, or even dictatorship. The Greeks, who were the pioneers and great architects of Political Law, unashamedly included dictatorship as another possible form of government. They were convinced that, for a given people and at a given historical moment, it could be the best form of government, and even necessary.[2] For my part, I have always believed that the forms of government as such are neither good nor

---

[2]The exclusively derogatory concept of dictatorship is relatively modern.

bad, but rather the men who govern them or the people who elect them. Since I was a child, I have been convinced that there is no perfect form of government, but only the least bad. And even then, I suspected that, as far as the world of politics is concerned, names and labels always conceal things different from what they proclaim: Can anyone believe, for example, that in the so–called Democracies it is the people who elect the rulers they truly desire?

In spite of everything, the Monarchy and the Royalty enjoyed for long centuries the esteem and respect of the Peoples (whether or not they always deserve that admiration is a different issue which we are not going to deal with here). And it is well known that, at least until the fall of the *Old Regime*, nobody questioned the charisma of the Kings or their Absolute Power. When Tolkien's epic speaks of the King's hands *as hands that heal*, the author is echoing an otherwise universal and popular sentiment of the quasi–sacred charisma of Kings. The great Empires amassed by the Peoples of the West who succeeded in making History, coincided in time with the Monarchic form of government, without this meaning that we are going to insist here on a cause–effect relationship. It is also known that the theologians of the Middle Ages, making their own a multi-secular tradition that goes back to times before Jesus Christ, were convinced of the divine character of the Monarchical Institution: *Monarchy, as a form of government of Divine Right*. Of course, today nobody believes in the latter, with the exception perhaps of a few fanatical dreamers whom nobody pays any attention to.

In any case, until the fall of the so–called *Ancient Régime*, as we have already said, one cannot doubt the immense prestige and the almost supernatural charisma which, for centuries, the Peoples gave recognition to Royalty. However, with the disappearance of the Absolute Power of the Kings, and even before the spread of *democratic* ideas throughout the world, a radical change took place in the mentality of the Peoples of the West. The Monarchies that subsisted to the new conceptions became democratic, representative, constitutional, guarantors of a simple unifying function, etc., according to many; merely decorative, or useless and discredited, according to others. In any case, the principle that *the King reigns, but does not rule*, has been accepted everywhere as indisputable. Thus, another new and important difficulty arises, which today's Christians have to face, if today's Feast can still be expected to make sense to them.

It is that the idea of Kingship as Absolute Power is not only unintelligible to modern mentality, but also absolutely unacceptable.

However, Jesus Christ is the Absolute King and Lord of the Universe. This affirmation is entirely contrary to what would mean Royalty as a mere decorative figure; and absolutely opposed, therefore, to the prevailing ideologies in today's world.

And so, strange as it may seem, we have not yet reached the thorniest part of the problem. The infiltration of *democratic* ideas within the Ecclesial Organism tries maliciously to subvert the Hierarchical and Monarchical structure of the Church, and, in an indirect but logical way, to distort and blur the figure of Christ as King and Lord of all creation.

If the Church possesses an unbreakable Hierarchical and Monarchical constitutional structure, as her Divine Founder willed and disposed, no human power can modify it. But it also happens *that its Hierarchical and Monarchical constitution is necessarily based on the fact that its Founder, the Word made Man, has been constituted as King, Master, and Lord of the whole Universe.* The Monarchical configuration of the Bride of Christ in all the interweaving of its Organism, and most of all in its apex, is not due to a mere arbitrary or random will of her Founder, but to what could be considered as a structural prolongation, *ad extra*, of the Person of the One *to whom God also hath exalted him, and hath given him a name which is above all names: that in the name of Jesus every knee should bow, of those that are in heaven, on earth, and under the earth: and that every tongue should confess that the Lord Jesus Christ is in the glory of God the Father.*[3] The Organism of which He is the Head was to be a reflection and manifestation of the Royal character of His Person.[4]

Because of this, when attempts have been made to blur, or at least mitigate, the constitutional structure of the Church (under the influence of ideological currents with *democratic* overtones), serious damage has been done to the faith and the spiritual health of the faithful. We will try to say something, as briefly as possible, about the way in which this situation has been brought about.

After World War II, the ideological wave of Democracy spread throughout the Western World. The fall of Nazism and the disappearance of the Berlin Wall years later also contributed to this. From that moment on, no political power or any other kind of legitimacy, was accepted as valid which did not pass through the sieve of Democracy and of the universally known *Human Rights*. As can be supposed, *Human Rights* have always been intimately linked to Democracy; and vice versa. There were —there are— no Human Rights without Democracy, and there is no Democracy without Human Rights.

As is often the case in the strange way human nature behaves, there were very few ho tried to define and clarify precisely what Democracy meant. It is not surprising, therefore, that absolutely opposite political ideologies have used the same name to designate

---

[3]Phil 2: 9–11.

[4]In the whole of Revelation all the dogmas are related, although some of them also have a special connection or interdependence among themselves.

opposite situations (each one pretending, as it is to be expected, to be the true possessor of the pure democratic essence). As for human rights, needless to say that each ideology, each country, and even each individual, have been enumerating and interpreting them differently.

Amazingly, however, none of this has seemed to worry the current currents of thought, which have continued their course as if nothing had happened. Everything seems to indicate that, just as the French Revolution enthroned the *Goddess of Reason*, the Contemporary Age has demolished *common sense*.

But even more astonishing is the fact that, throughout the second half of the twentieth century, these new ideas also found a place within the Church. From the time of the Second Vatican Council onwards, a group of ideologues headed mainly by the best-known German theologians (of markedly progressive tendencies, and even Neo-modernist according to some) managed to channel the thought within the Church along their own approach.

Through skillful handling of the media, clever distortion of theological data, subtle pressure (under the pretext of new needs and historical circumstances) on less prepared bishops and theologians, and an astonishing display of diplomatic skills, they achieved important concessions. The first of these was the fact that the discussions within the Council took place under their direction. Apart from that, already in the post-conciliar period, the conclusions reached by the Council Fathers were either ignored or interpreted in a rather distorted way.[5]

---

[5]The condemnations contained in the *Syllabus*, and the exhortations of the Encyclical *Pascendi*, were first ignored, and then practically abrogated. A more than dubious Ecumenism was successfully introduced in the Church, and all, or almost all, of the previous Magisterium was disregarded. To cite a few examples among the many that could be listed.

And this is not all. The new ideologues —*audaces Fortuna juvat*— achieved something paradoxical and curious. While the Movement has never cared to pay too much attention to the true Magisterium —ancient or modern—, it has never hesitated to hurl thunderbolts of anathemas against anyone who attempted the slightest resistance. They have played their cards very cleverly with a double game. On the one hand they skillfully undermined the authority of the Pope (and not least that of the Bishops), on the other they have pretended to impose on Catholics the obligation to accept, as dogma of faith, whatever the Pope thinks, speaks, or carries out; whether or not the conditions required for infallibility, or, in general, for the guarantee of the Magisterium, are met.

In this way, as we are about to see, the attempt to *democratize* the structures of the Church has been carried out, weakening her hierarchical and monarchical structure, and thus providing an easy field of action for the Progressive Pressure Groups. The way has been cleared for the winds of Modernism. Meanwhile, and thanks to the use of double–dealing by the new ideologues, the figure of Jesus Christ as King and Lord of the Universe, Head of the Mystical Body which is His Church, is also in danger of fading away.[6]

These new ideologies permanently permeated Europe during the time when the Second Vatican Council was inaugurated. The idea was circulated that the First Vatican Council had perhaps gone too

---

[6]Christian thinkers have always been particularly sensitive to new ideas that emerge (or that appear as new, even without being so at any historical moment). Pseudo-Dionysius, Saint Augustine, and Saint Thomas, for example, were able to make successful use of many of Plato's and Aristotle's ideas. In modern times, however, the phenomenon presents a quite different aspect. While it would seem that nothing at all usable could be extracted from the thought of Karl Marx, for example, we see with dismay, as incredible as it may seem, the appearance of *Liberation Theology* and the acute infiltration of Marxism suffered by Catholicism for more than half a century.

far in the attributions granted to the Pope.[7] If the previous Council had been that of the Roman Pontiff, the one to be held now was to be the *Council of the Bishops.* [8]

The new wave of democratic ideas flooded the Church at all levels: from the Papacy to the humblest parishes. Democracy, collegiality, solidarity, dialogue, and participation were some of the ideas that nourished the ecclesial organism from then on. To this must be added the untiring action of the Movements that advocated the *Promotion of the Laity*, the new ideas on the recognition of the *Rights and Participation of Women*, etc., which displaced the priests from their proper functions in order to insert them in a *second–class status of the faithful.*[9]

With regard to the Pope's own functions, well–known pressure groups circulated ideas like the need to emphasize collegiality; the necessity of obtaining the prior consensus, and even the approval, of the corresponding Sacred Congregations and Pontifical Commissions before the publication of Papal Documents; the convenience to obtain the consent of the Bishops; the suitability to use consultations and dialogue with the various Episcopal Conferences or to iron out *doctrinal differences* that could hinder understanding with *other Hierarchs of the Separate Churches*, etc. All of this without ceasing to use, as a condemnatory argument and whenever necessary —as a

---

[7]Although such a thing was not openly and unabashedly proclaimed, an honest examination of the historical facts would prove the truth of this assertion.

[8]Once again the irony of History. The reality, of which we will speak later, is that the authority and the role of the bishops was considerably curtailed after the Council. And not precisely in favor of the Pope but of the rise and tremendous influence granted to the new figure of the Episcopal Conferences.

[9]With regard to the vocabulary–jargon made up of terms such as democracy, collegiality, solidarity, dialogue, participation, etc., it is curious to note, and therefore worthy of note, the almost total absence of terms or concepts of supernatural content. There seems to be no doubt: Sociology has gradually displaced Theology, just as Human Rights have displaced the Rights of God.

double–dealing maneuver— the lack of fidelity to the Roman Pontiff against any attempt to denounce such proceedings.[10]

The role of the Pope, who until now had always been recognized as the Supreme Pastor of the Universal Church, was fading away. And with it the concept of the Church as a Monarchical Institution built on the Rock of Peter.[11]

---

[10] The move is clever and not easy for the naive to discover. What happens here is similar to what is explained in the physical theory of the sensory threshold: If the intensity of the received wave exceeds the threshold of the receptive capacity of the human sense (sight, hearing, taste, etc.), the signal is no longer perceived at all. To pretend at all costs to exaggerate the Authority of the Pope, to the point of considering it as absolute, including his deeds or opinions in or on matters that are not his concern (or considering as Solemn Magisterium, for example, opinions expressed in passing to journalists during an air trip or anywhere), is an effective way of destroying his authority and his prestige.

[11] The new ideas were introduced into the Church in a gradual way immediately after the end of the Second Vatican Council. What was the real meaning of the suppression of the *Anti–Modernist Oath*? Juridically it could have no other meaning but what it is: an abrogation. But the facts, once consummated, possess in themselves an intrinsic content whose meaning cannot be concealed. An attempted murder, a pernicious lie, or a swindle, for example, never manifest charitable intentions; just as an act of true love cannot indicate anything other than the desire for the good of the beloved. Was such a suppression perhaps due to the conviction that the condemnations of the *Syllabus* were no longer pertinent? And if not, to what did it really respond? Perhaps the conviction had gained ground that the new historical conditions had given modernist ideas a legal status? Whatever the case, one way or the other, it is clear that many would have welcomed an explanation here. It is often said now that the era of condemnation has passed and the era of *rapprochement* has arrived. But no one knows what would have happened if the Fathers and theologians of the Church, throughout twenty centuries, had not condemned the heresies and fought fiercely against them. And what should we say about the numerous imprecations and condemnations contained in the New Testament; would they have been meaningless? (cf. Mt 18:7; 23: 13–39; Lk 6: 24–26; 10: 13–15; 11: 42–46; 17:1; 1 Cor 16:22; Gal 1:8; Rev 22:15; etc.). It is as if the Word of God had ceased to be *living and effective* (Heb 4:12). The results, however, are shown to be rather bleak; for all seem to indicate that it was not the mountain that came to Muhammad, but Muhammad to the mountain.

As for the Bishops, contrary to what might have been expected, their functions and authority were also diminished by the importance that the Episcopal Conferences acquired after the Council. True, all the Documents and Declarations insist that each Bishop is independent within his own diocese —although integrated into the Episcopal College, itself subject to and presided over by the Authority of the Pope—, and that he is not subject to the decisions of the Episcopal Conference itself, in theory; but unrealistic and utopian in practice, since any Bishop knows the consequences that could befall him if he disagrees with the whole. The decisions of the Episcopal Conferences are taken by the voting system, as provided for by collegiality, solidarity, consensus, democratic doctrine, etc., etc. However, reality shows us that it is not rare that Pressure Groups always end up imposing their opinion, for it is difficult to maintain one's personal criteria when inserted in a collectivity like Episcopal Conferences.

Thus, the figure of the Bishop, until now Father and Pastor of his own Diocesan Church (always submitting to the Authority of the Supreme Pastor or Pope), is practically obliged to govern under the rule of the vote and the *consensus* of the majority. This is how the democratic system, gradually and almost insensibly, continues to displace the monarchical system.

But it is perhaps in the parishes that this phenomenon is most ostensible to the simple faithful, even though it often goes unnoticed by them. In this way, the lowest stratum of the Organizational Chart, although also the most popular and most numerous, is not excluded from suffering the harassment of manipulations that try to change the structures of the Church.

From the moment that parishes have become macro–organized and organizational structural entities, forgetting their former character as a place of family gathering of sanctification —*ecclesia*—, they have seen a swarm of Ministers,[12] Commissions, Parish Councils, etc., all run by the laity and sometimes also with the intervention of nuns. Once these entities have taken over the management and direction of almost all parish functions, the age–old figure of the Parish Priest, as spiritual Pastor of his flock of faithful, has been practically relegated to that of a simple bureaucrat under their orders.

The problem as a whole, considering all the circumstances, presents a doubly serious aspect.

In the first place, because the Church being hierarchically structured by divine institution —the Pope as the only Supreme Pastor, not subject to any other form of authority; the Ecumenical Council presided over and approved by the Pope; the Bishops; the Presbyters and Deacons; all in that order—, such foundations cannot be modified by any Authority of this world. The simple faithful who have received only Baptism or Confirmation, or those who have not been invested with the sacrament of Holy Orders, in spite of their immense dignity as authentic Christians and true children of God, *do not constitute authority in the Church.*

On the other hand, *Democracy* is a political figure, or form of government, whose existence is more located in the world of speculation than in reality. Although it is not accepted, Democracies are also governed by oligarchies.

At this point, after this brief exposition of the state of the question, we can better understand the timeliness of the question: Does the Feast of Christ the King still retain meaning for Christians to-

---

[12]The number and types of the various ministries existing in the parishes are as yet unknown. There are parishes in which the number of Eucharistic Ministers is greater than that of the simple faithful.

day? And if it has kept its meaning, as it had in the past, are Christians today able to understand it? It is necessary to recognize that the question would not be easy to answer given the disappearance of the condition of the Absolute Power of the Kings, the disrepute brought upon the Institution of Kingship by its own representatives, the distortions and falsehood suffered at the hands of modern History, and the new historical circumstances.

However, Revelation is clear and forceful on this point: Jesus Christ is the Absolute Lord and King of the Universe: *Dominus dominorum et Rex regum.*[13] Saint Paul glories in proclaiming of Him: *To the King of eternity, incorruptible, invisible, the only God, honor and glory forever and ever.*[14]

But the Mystery of the Kingship of Christ cannot be well understood except within the Mystery of the Church, of which He is the Head. Although the Church, in turn, together with the structures that constitute her, is also a Mystery of Faith, contained as such within the Articles of the Creed: *I believe in the Holy Catholic Church.* Only in this perspective can we take a look at her history and to the issues of the present, without the danger of scandalizing ourselves.

Both themes —the Mystery of the Kingship of Christ and the Mystery of the Church— are closely linked. For the ultimate reason that the Church has been instituted under a monarchical form of government, not a democratic one (especially from its apex), lies in the fact that Christ —the Word made Man— has been constituted as the Only King and Lord of the Universe.

If we forget that the Church is a Mystery of Faith, it becomes unintelligible to us. At the same time, it must be kept in mind that

---

[13] Rev 17:14.
[14] 1 Tim 1:17.

any Mystery of Faith is already in itself, and therefore, a mystery. This means that it can be open to the deepening of its content, but that, by definition, it will always remain something mysterious and impossible to fully know (understand or comprehend).

In this way we can already admit, without silly scruples, the fact that the Church is divine and human at the same time. This is equivalent to saying that it is also, at the same time, holy and sinful: *Ecclesia semper reformanda.* Neither the Christians of the apostolic age, nor the Fathers of the Church, nor the theologians of the Middle Ages, were unaware of this fact, much less would they ever have admitted it as an object of scandal. This is recognized, without palliation, by a magnificent text by Bernanos: *A parish is bound to be dirty. A whole Christian society's a lot dirtier. You wait for the Judgement Day and see what the angels will be sweeping out of even the most saintly monasteries... Which all goes to prove, boy, that the Church must needs be a sound housewife–sound and sensible... a real housewife knows her home isn't a shrine. Those are just poets' dreams.*[15]

In spite of all this, or if one wants to keep it in mind, any Catholic is aware that he is part of the Church; in which he was born to supernatural life and within which he has to live and die. He knows that the Church is the exclusive means of sanctification for him, and the only way to reach Heaven. He will never feel entitled to rebel against a Mother through whom he was granted the life of grace. *Extra Ec-*

---

[15]Bernanos, *The Diary of a Country Priest*, I. There are also, for example, the harsh *Sermons* of Saint Augustine against the bad Shepherds; or the harsh exhortations of Saint Catherine of Siena to Popes Gregory XI and Urban VI. These are just a few of many possible examples.

clesiam nulla salus.[16] A true Catholic is not ignorant of reality and knows that there may be occasions when the Hierarchy forgets, and even betrays, its sacred duties of shepherding. To think otherwise would be, for a Catholic, to abandon the world of reality to walk in the world of utopia and fiction. Hence, a faithful son of the Church, fully aware that there are bad Shepherds (Jn 10: 10.12–13),[17] must be prepared to bear such a sad and heavy cross, which, of course, will make his existence as a disciple of the Lord much more difficult, since his duty of fidelity to the legitimate Hierarchy will always remain in force.

Together with all this, the Catholic knows that it is not licit for him to lend himself to the *double game* maneuver, set in motion by avant–garde theology. He is not unaware of the doctrine about the Magisterium of the Church; and hence he is able to distinguish between the Magisterium of the Pope and that of the Bishops, as well as between Ordinary and Solemn Magisterium. Aware of the conditions that must be met for the Magisterium to enjoy the guarantee of infallibility, he does not allow himself to be deceived by abusive pretensions of assent to actions that are presented as magisterial, when in reality they are not. Finally, he knows that in the Church there is only one Magisterium and that, consequently, it is

---

[16] Yet another expression that modern progressive theology has been emptied of meaning. There is no salvation, indeed, outside the Church. But the progressive concept of the Church is now broad enough to include everyone, including those who in no way wish to belong to it.

[17] It should be noted, with regard to this text of Saint John, that Jesus Christ does not refer to hypothetical beings, but to tangible realities who, because they are tangible, are there. The text is abundantly clear in this sense. Mere possibilities, being mere essences that have not received the act of existence, do not belong therefore to the world of realities. What is the true meaning of the expression *mere real possibility*, referring to Hell, and now so fashionable in progressive thought? Logic seems to be able to attribute to it only one: unbelief in its existence.

not possible to contrast teachings that claim to be *up to date* with others that are said to be *òbsolete and that respond to historical circumstances different from the current ones.*

In short, and to express it briefly, there is no incompatibility for a Catholic between the duty to feel bound to the legitimate Hierarchy, on the one hand, and the no less firm duty of fidelity to the immutable principles, on the other; the latter coinciding, moreover, with those proclaimed, through the Hierarchy, by the authentic and unique and perennial Magisterium. Hence the true Catholic cannot accept, among many other things that some now pretend to admit more or less openly, a certain democratization of the Church; not even under the threat of blackmail for lack of fidelity to the Hierarchy. There is only one Hierarchical Church, ultimately governed by the One Who is the Head of the whole Ecclesial Organism; Who is the Beginning, the Firstborn from among the dead, and the One Who possesses the Primacy in all things (Col 1:18): Christ Jesus, King and Lord of the Universe.

It is not our intention here to carry out an exegetical study of a subject which, moreover, is not the object of any theological polemic. For this reason, we will limit ourselves to bringing up two important texts, one from the Old Testament and the other from the New Testament, in order to use them, at least as a starting point, for the consideration of some interesting questions that the Kingship of Christ raises for the Christian of today (and for the Christian of all times, in fact).

The Lordship of Christ over the entire Universe was already solemnly foretold by the prophet Daniel: *I beheld therefore in the vision of the night, and lo, one like the son of man came with the clouds of heaven, and he came even to the Ancient of days: and they presented him before him. And he gave him power, and glory, and a kingdom: and all peoples, tribes, and tongues shall serve him: his power is an everlasting power that shall not be taken away: and his kingdom that shall not be destroyed.*[18]

The New Testament text to which we refer, though told by all the Evangelists, is recounted in its clearest and most complete way by Saint John: *Pilate said to him: "Art thou a king then?" Jesus answered: "Thou sayest that I am a king. For this was I born, and for this I came into the world; that I should give testimony to the truth."*[19]

We have considered inoperative the problems that, for the present-day Christian, the Kingship of Jesus Christ seemed to present. However, the subject still offers an apparent antinomy that may deserve deep attention.

Having recognized the fact of the Universal Lordship of Jesus Christ —*You have called Me Master and Lord, and you are right, because I am*[20]—, it still remains to explain the fundamental reality of the intimacy of love offered by God to man in Jesus Christ. Everything seems to point to the immense distance that mediates between His condition as King and Absolute Lord, on the one hand, and the proximity, reciprocity, bilaterality, and equality of conditions, that imposes the *one-on-one* relationship that in fact exists between Lover and Beloved, on the other.

To achieve this intimacy of love, the Word became Man: *No longer do I call you servants, but friends...*[21] Jesus, having loved his

---

[18] Dan 7: 13–14.

[19] The text is from Chapter 18 and covers verses 33–37. The trite textual difficulties of verse 37 are meaningless, and do not take away at all from the clarity or the strength of its meaning, quite forceful at that.

[20] Jn 13:13.

[21] Jn 15:15.

own who were in the world, loved them to the end.[22] The revelation and fullness of this ineffable reality have their fulfillment in Jesus Christ, although it existed already in the lost ages and the most remote times of the Old Testament. The King–Husband dichotomy, for example, offered in the *Song of Songs* is well known:

> *Draw me: we will run after thee*
> *To the odor of thy ointments.*
> *The king has brought me into his storerooms:*
> *We will be glad and rejoice in thee...*[23]

A dichotomy that also runs throughout the pages of the New Testament, in which the antithesis King —Husband, Lordship— Friendship and Intimacy of Love is played with.[24] A fact whose ultimate foundation is the dual nature of Jesus Chris, divine and human, derived in turn from the mystery of the Incarnation of the Word. Saint Paul explains it with concise exactitude: *Christ Jesus, who, having the form of God, did not consider it a coveted prey to be equal to God. On the contrary, he emptied himself, taking the form of a servant, being made in the likeness of men; and being found in human form, he humbled himself and became obedient unto death, even death on a cross.*[25] Since perfect Love supposes perfect bilaterality, equality, and reciprocity, God wanted to be loved by

---

[22] Jn 13:1.

[23] Song 1: 4. Cite also 1:12; 3:11. In reality the entire sacred Poem is the poetic narration of the battle of love (Song 2:4) that takes place between two types of Lovers: that of the King–Husband, on the one hand, and that of the Bride, on the other.

[24] Cf. Mt 9:15; 17: 25–26; Lk 5:35; Jn 3:29; 1 Tim 6:15; etc.

[25] Phil 2: 6–8.

men with a human love, but perfect as such love. Love of total self-giving on the part of God; response of Love in totality on the part of man. That is why He became Man in Jesus Christ, without ceasing to be God. And from that moment, man can love Him, in turn, as his Lord and as the Spouse and Friend of his soul.

The divine–human love that follows from this is one and only one. For the condition of bilaterality and perfect reciprocity is resolved in a situation of total oneness:

My beloved to me, and I to him.[26]

One heart and one soul. Taking into account the uniqueness of the (divine) Person of Jesus Christ, as well as the uniqueness of the Bride. It should not be forgotten that the Good Shepherd calls *each of his sheep by name* (Jn 10:3). Divine–human love, like all true love, is always consummated in the relationship *of one to the other*.[27]

---

[26] Song 2:16.

[27] In divine–human love man loves God as *the Other*. Without excluding the Trinity of Persons, what the act of love considers of first intention is the unicity of the divine nature, although *previously known and contemplated through the Person of Jesus Christ*. This is what happens also in the purely human relationship, in which the reference is always to the person (which in no way means the exclusion of the body or the soul); and, since it is a question of a relationship, it always occurs in reciprocity. In divine-human love, the creature loves God through the Person of Jesus Christ. Flooded in the Love of the Spirit, and through the divinity of the Person of the Lord, is how the creature finds the Father; through Christ, in the Spirit, to the Father: *No one comes to the Father except through Me* (Jn 14:6). Hence the error of certain mystics, who thought that, once the soul had been *divinized* (once the mystical union has been achieved in its highest degree, known by the name of *mystical betrothal, spiritual marriage*, or any other name), one could safely dispense with the Humanity of Christ. A grave error, inasmuch as to dispense with the Humanity assumed by the Word would be to dispense with the Person of the Word made Man (the hypostatic union no longer admits separation); which would be equivalent to dispensing with the divinity.

One is my dove, my perfect one is but one.[28]

The solution to the (apparent) problem raised by the Kingship of Christ in the relationship of divine–human love requires recourse to analogy. Something similar to what theology does with the divine attributes, for the knowledge and explanation of which the so–called *via remotionis and via eminentiæ* are used. It is simply a matter of eliminating in the corresponding attribute everything that implies imperfection, while at the same time predicating of them the highest degree of perfection.

The difficulties that the faithful of any historical moment might feel, with respect to the figure of Christ the King, would have their ultimate foundation in the illegitimate extrapolation of the human concept of Kingship to its divine concept.

Jesus Christ knew well the sensitive points through which the weaknesses of human royalty become evident. And hence He took great care to distinguish it from His own: *The kings of the Gentiles lord it over them; and they that have power over them, are called beneficent. But you not so.*[29] Hence His clear statement before Pilate: *My kingdom is not of this world.*[30] Which, rather than referring to the fact that He does not belong to the present eon, seems to mean rather that his Kingdom does not conform to the parameters of purely human measurements; as suggested by the

---

[28] Song 6:8.

[29] Lk 22: 25–26. It is to be noted the gentle irony enclosed in the phrase that those who have power over the nations *are called benefactors*, which speaks for itself. It is the same here as with other themes, as that of peace, for example; about which Jesus Christ took exquisite care to warn that His peace —which He left forever to His disciples— has nothing to do with that which the world provides, and of which it is always speaking (Jn 14:27). This last warning the current Official Catechesis seems to have forgotten, inasmuch as it focuses its insistence on worldly peace and forgets to do the same with that of Christ.

[30] Jn 18:36.

clear statement *that the kingdom of God is among you.*[31] Saint Paul, for his part, also clearly apostrophized the Master's words: *For the kingdom of God is not meat and drink; but justice, and peace, and joy in the Holy Spirit.*[32]

Clear proof that the Kingship of Christ has little to do with human Kingship. In addition to the fact that —Oh, wondrous thing!— it is seldom realized, as is also demonstrated by the Master's categorical affirmations: *Suffer the little children, and forbid them not to come to Me, for theirs is the kingdom of heaven.*[33] Or the even clearer statements of the Beatitudes: *Blessed are the poor in spirit, for theirs is the kingdom of heaven.*[34] But the Children and the Poor, as the New Testament understands these concepts, do not belong to a future eon, but to the present.[35] And it does not seem in any way to follow from the context that the beatitude spoken of is to await a future Kingdom.

It is quite clear, according to what has been said, that the Kingship of Christ is not exercised on the plane of submission and obedience, even though these realities seem to be constitutive and charac-

---

[31] Lk 17:21. The translation *among* you seems more in line with the context than the alternative *within* you. In any case, it is clear that the Kingdom is already present and that it is not according to the measure of this world, nor is the Kingship exercised in it in the way men have always practiced it and felt it: *The kingdom of God shall not come with spectacle* (Lk 17:20).

[32] Rom 14:17.

[33] Mt 19:14.

[34] Mt 5:3.

[35] The only Poor, for the New Testament, are the *poor in spirit* (those who live in a state of misery are not necessarily identified with the Poor according to the Bible). The distinction between the one and the other, in the New Testament context, does not make sense if one has a clear idea of the virtue of Christian poverty. Hence, the already old exegetical discussion between the text of Luke 6:20, opposed by many to that of Matthew 5:3, is trivial and inconsequential.

teristic notes of the Royal Institution;[36] but rather, as the Apostle said, it is actualized in the sphere of justice, peace, and joy in the Holy Spirit.[37]

A logical conclusion of what has been said is that in the Kingdom of the Children and the Poor —of Spiritual Childhood and Poverty— the King will surely be the most Childlike and the Poorest of them all. As it is, in fact; although the idea will be strange to those who do not have a clear notion of the excellence of Spiritual Childhood and Christian Poverty. However, since Spiritual Childhood and Poverty are realities so intimately linked to Love, we can then conclude that we have found the main characteristic of the Kingdom whose Lord is Christ. Yet another confirmation that the Kingship of Jesus Christ, although similar to Human Kingship in some respects, has little to do with it in reality.[38]

We must now see, in fact, that both Spiritual Childhood and Poverty are exclusive qualities of those who are truly in Love.

The One in Love —the Bridegroom—, insofar as He is truly in Love, is an authentic Child. For His pure heart, for His simplicity and ingenuousness, for His candor, for His nobility, for His trust, for His tenderness, for His sympathy, for the beauty of His face not stained by concupiscence..., and even for His language which Love seems to make childish, candid, and excessive to the point of exaggeration and absence of logic:

---

[36] Something completely different is what will happen to the enemies who refuse to recognize and accept it (Cf. 1 Cor 15: 24–27; Rev 19: 15–16.20–21).

[37] Here we must make no mistake either. Justice and peace should be understood in their New Testament sense.

[38] As is evident, as far as analogy is concerned, both the *via remotionis* as well as the *via eminentiæ* must be used throughout in the study of the problem. There is in it much to take away and also much to put in.

> *How beautiful art thou, my love, how beautiful art thou!*
> *Thy eyes are doves' eyes, besides what is hid within.*
> *Thy hair is as flocks of goats,*
> *Which come up from mount Galaad.*
> *Thy teeth as flocks of sheep, that are shorn,*
> *Which come up from the washing, all with twins,*
> *And there is none barren among them.*
> *Thy lips are as a scarlet lace...*[39]

But the Kingdom of which Christ is King is the Kingdom of Children, which is the same as saying the Kingdom of Lovers. To which it only remains to add —in order to avoid possible confusions of the language— that Spiritual Childhood, in addition to being entirely opposed to immaturity, is the only thing capable of turning human beings into authentic Men and true Women.[40] In the love story, on which the warp and weft of the *Song of Songs* is woven, the Lover who passionately seeks the Bride possesses the heart of a Child; at the same time He is also the King and the Bridegroom Who shows Himself to be in love as only a true Man would know how to be in love with a true Woman. As the Bride rejoices in recognizing:

> *My beloved is white and ruddy,*
> *chosen out of thousands.*
> *His head is as the finest gold:*
> *His locks as branches of palm trees,*
> *Black as a raven...*

---

[39] Song 4: 1–3.

[40] In the language of the Gospel, the child who as such is destined for the Kingdom, rather than being born, *is made*; as if it were a marvelous quality that must be acquired: *Unless you become as little children, you will not enter the kingdom of Heaven* (Mt 18:3).

> *His legs as pillars of marble,*
> *That are set upon bases of gold.*
> *His form as of Libanus,*
> *Excellent as the cedars...*[41]

And His Kingdom is also the Kingdom of the Poor (Jas 2:5). Which is so because, as we have said before, it is also the Kingdom of the Lovers. And can there be anyone Poorer than the greatest of Lovers, Who in His total love *has given everything* to the one He loves? According to Saint Francis of Assisi, Jesus espoused Poverty on the Cross in order to be the Poorest of the Poor. The truth is that no one has given more than He since no one has loved more than He has loved. That is why, in the combat of love that He sustains, not being able to give more because He has nothing left, He finds Himself in need of asking. Thus, we arrive at the most surprising of realities: neither the human mind nor the human heart could ever have imagined the figure of a King who goes so far as to beg for love:

"I had gone, begging from door to door in the village path, when thy golden chariot appeared in the distance like a gorgeous dream and I wondered who was this King of all kings!

My hopes rose high and I thought my evil days were at an end, and I stood waiting for alms to be given unasked and for wealth scattered on all sides in the dust.

The chariot stopped where I stood. Thy glance fell on me and thou leanest down with a smile. I felt that the luck of my life had come at last. Then of a sudden thou didst hold out thy right hand and say "What hast thou to give me?"

---

[41] Song 5: 10–11.15.

Ah, what a kingly jest it was to open thy palm to a beggar and to beg! I was confused and stood undecided, and then from my wallet I slowly took out the least little grain of corn and gave it to thee.

But how great my surprise when at the day's end I emptied my bag on the floor to find a least little grain of gold among the poor heap. I bitterly wept and wished that I had had the heart to give thee my all." [42]

We must notice reciprocity and bilaterality in the poem as fundamental notes of Love. For in Love there is no I without you, nor surrender without donation. Love expects everything because it has previously given everything. It asks and begs because it cannot do otherwise from the moment it has been left with nothing. But it asks and begs, above all, because it cannot give without receiving; and even more than that, because it craves and desires to the death the love of the Bride. However, in the combat of divine–human love, it is Jesus, the Lord, Who has taken the initiative: He made Himself poor first, because He also loved us first:[43]

> *Open to me, my sister, my love,*
> *My dove, my undefiled:*
> *For my head is full of dew,*
> *And my locks of the drops of the nights.*[44]

The Bridegroom humbly begs the Bride to open up to Him, given the precarious situation in which He finds Himself and which only she can remedy: His head is covered with dew, and His hair is damp and sprinkled with the frost of the night.

---

[42] Rabindranath Tagore, *Song Offerings*, 50.
[43] Cf. 2 Cor 8:9; 1 Jn 4:19.
[44] Song 5:2.

And such are the subjects of this Kingdom whose King and Lord is Christ: the true Children and the true Poor. Without them, neither the Kingdom, nor even the Church, could subsist. Hence the evils that can result if this perspective is lost sight of. Too much time and too much energy would surely be wasted in order to banish Poverty from among men. If the attempt to do away with the poor refers to situations of material misery, we are pursuing a utopia; but if it is aimed at the Poor in spirit, we are thinking of committing a crime. For twenty centuries the Church has striven to mitigate human suffering and also to sanctify it; but she has never suffered the illusion of eliminating it. As for the Poor in spirit... they are the true aristocracy of the Church and the true subjects of the Kingdom of Christ. The effort to establish social justice in the world cannot be a priority or even a principal objective for the Church. To anxiously seek horizons of material well-being for men, besides the danger of setting aside and dispensing with true well-being, would mean forgetting the Children and the Poor, without whom there would be no reason for the World, nor indeed the Church, to continue to exist.

We have already said that in the Kingship of Christ, unlike what happens in purely human Kingships, there is no room for the categories of submission or obedience. Therefore, it would not be an exaggeration to say that we are faced with one of the most important, and even most surprising, of the findings provided by the *via remotionis*.

The surprise vanishes, however, as soon as we consider that the Kingdom of Christ is the Kingdom of Love. And Love, by definition, excludes submission inasmuch as it places those who love each other on an equal footing, on the one hand, and insofar as it makes the hearts and souls of both one heart and one soul, on the other. More still, inasmuch as the Supreme King in no way desires to maintain with man a relationship of lordship–servitude, but exclusively the only one that knows of nothing else but friendship, intimacy, and mutual love: *I will no longer call you servants, but friends.* For this purpose and for this reason God became Man. A reality —the face-to-face relationship— which, more than being based on the infinitely generous and loving will of a God, finds its ontological explanation in the plane of similarity, or equality, in which Love places the lovers: *It is enough for the disciple that he be as his master, and the servant as his lord...*[45] *Each one who is well formed shall be as his master.*[46]

> *My dove is in the clefts of the rock,*
> *In the hollow places of the walls,*
> *Show me thy face, let thy voice sound in my ears:*
> *For thy voice is sweet, and thy face comely.*[47]
>
> ....
>
> *I am come into my garden, O my sister, my spouse,*
> *I have gathered my myrrh, with my aromatical spices:*
> *I have eaten the honeycomb with my honey,*
> *I have drunk my wine with my milk.*[48]

Perhaps it would be appropriate to point out, at this point in our reflection and as if in parenthesis, that the same thing happens in the Sacred Poem of *The Song of Songs* as happens with all poetry. Either it is a series of metaphors and beautiful expressions, whose

---

[45] Mt 10:25.

[46] Lk 6:40. According to the Neo Vulgate version of the text: *Perfectus autem omnis erit sicut magister eius.*

[47] Song 2:14.

[48] Song 5:1.

meaning is as mysterious as it is hermetic and even esoteric; or else such expressions mean nothing at all, apart from the play of the beauty of language. But when it is true poetry, it must necessarily possess real content, inasmuch as it always refers to the splendor of being (reality), which is beauty; the same which, because it is splendorous, is also lovable. The Sacred Poem *The Song of Songs* has known an infinity of interpretations throughout the centuries, both of mystical or religious dye and of merely profane character. Of course, they have all referred to love; but almost always of such a puerile character, so childish, so sweetened, and sometimes even cloying, that almost all of them have contributed to diminishing the marvelous content of the Sacred Poem. Which, if interpreted seriously and conscientiously, banishes all appearance of cheesiness, as referring to the relations of divine-human love, of Bridegroom–Bride; since for what other purpose could this Sacred Book have been inspired and written?

But the most important biblical text on this subject, and even the most clarifying, is surely the one that narrates the event of the Washing of the Feet, which took place on the night of the Last Supper. When the feet of the Apostles were washed, and Peter's turn came, the soon–to–be Head of the Apostolic College refused to allow his Master to humble Himself before him in such a way. Peter is still far from understanding the true demands of Love, and that is why Jesus Christ warns him gravely: *If I wash thee not, thou shalt have no part with me.*[49] An all too graphic example of the disciple not being above his master... nor the master over the disciple: *It is enough for the disciple to be like his master.* Like his Master Who loves to the end, of course; and that, when it is impossible for the one below to rise to the condition of the one above, things are simply

---

[49] Jn 13:8.

made feasible by making the one above come down to the inferior condition of the one below. In short, because *the Son of Man came not to be served, but to serve.*[50]

Of course, the man whom Saint Paul would call carnal —as opposed to one being led and animated by the Spirit— would not understand any of these things and would even consider them to be another form of madness, as the Apostle himself warns. Which is, in the final analysis, what is happening with our world today. Paganized to its roots and having even turned its back on God and against God, it is incapable of understanding them. And hence the meaning of true kingship, even if it were to be well understood and correctly interpreted by the men of today, would be strangely alien to them, while the Feast of Christ the King would continue to have no meaning for them.

All this contributes —who can doubt it?— to nourishing the hope of Christians. To make them live more and more the nostalgia and the certainty that someday the Better World that has been firmly promised to them will be made present. Because it is true that everything seems to indicate that the World is not willing to listen again to the teachings of the Galilean. And even we ourselves, His small and weak disciples who struggle day after day to remain faithful to an ever more difficult testimony, are sometimes assailed by the horrible temptation to think that things will not change. Simply because men do not wish it in any way.

But it is then, and only then, that we perceive and feel clearly the enormous beauty of the theological virtue of Hope. Sister in turn of Faith and Charity, it is she who keeps us on our feet without falling in the struggle, and without giving way to despondency. For it is she, the sublime virtue of Hope, that teaches us and leads us

---

[50] Mt 20:28.

to Perfect Joy, while at the same time making it a reality for us in advance. What would it matter, even if it seems to us —*seems* indeed, because it would be nothing more than an illusion; in the end, *if they heard my word, they will also hear yours*— that men refuse to hear us, that the World despises us and persecutes us..., if we know with certainty that, at the end of the road, having left all things behind, it is He Who awaits us?

> *From the high, snow-capped summit,*
> *Down lofty mountains through chasms of granite,*
> *The river is falling fast.*
> *Leaping and repeating with a noisy blast*
> *The songs of brisk waters, crystalline, icy,*
> *With quicker pace now through the hills and valley,*
> *For he feels the great need in the land below*
> *To swiftly reach the plains where the grasses grow.*
> *But he sees that his refrain*
> *Goes unheeded; greatly saddened and in pain,*
> *His course now more sinuous,*
> *More tired, more sad, lazy, and more languorous,*
> *He forlornly seeks the sea;*
> *And as he descends slowly,*
> *To wheat fields, that grain may be gleaned in the spring,*
> *Vital waters imparting,*
> *Now the river flows and flows.*
> *With dreams that he joins the sea, onward he goes.*

TO EVERY MAN A PENNY

(PARABLE OF THE WORKERS SENT TO THE VINEYARD)

MEDITATION

(Mt 20: 1–16)

The kingdom of heaven is like to an householder, who went out early in the morning to hire labourers into his vineyard. And having agreed with the labourers for a penny a day, he sent them into his vineyard. And going out about the third hour, he saw others standing in the market place idle. And he said to them: Go you also into my vineyard, and I will give you what shall be just. And they went their way. And again he went out about the sixth and the ninth hour, and did in like manner. But about the eleventh hour he went out and found others standing, and he saith to them: Why stand you here all day idle? They say to him: Because no man hath hired us. He saith to them: Go you also into my vineyard. And when evening was come, the lord of the vineyard saith to his steward: Call the labourers and pay them their hire, beginning from the last even to the first. When therefore they were come, that came about the eleventh hour, they received every man a penny. But when the first also came, they thought that they should receive more: and they also received every man a penny. And receiving it they murmured against the master of the house, saying: These last have worked but one hour, and thou hast made them equal to us, that have borne the burden of the day and the heats. But he answering said to one of them: Friend, I do thee no wrong: didst thou not agree with me for a penny? Take what is thine, and go thy way: I will give to this last even as to thee. Or is it not lawful for me to do what I will? Is thy eye evil, because I am good? So shall the last be first, and the first last.

Many of the popular situations and customs contained in the Gospel parables have already disappeared. Because of which, today's young people are acquainted with none or almost none of them. I, on the other hand, who am old and carry on my shoulders the weight of many more years than you, have experienced some of those that make up the small existing remnant. For example, the picturesque depiction described in the parable of the Workers sent to the Vineyard.

The scene of the day laborers, congregated since dawn in the town's main square waiting to be hired,[1] was for me a routine image to which I was accustomed since my childhood. Now life has changed too much, and towns have become much bigger: taken by storm by immigrants and strangers, full of tall buildings, avenues, and new

---

[1] Mine was then a small, quiet, and sleepy town, where we were all relatives, friends, or acquaintances, and where life passed in a happy peace which I now remember with nostalgia.

squares, they are now places where nobody knows anyone anymore and where memories and recollections of a better past that will never come back wander around, like fleeting shadows. That is why, when I read and reread this parable, I cannot avoid feelings of bittersweet longing which, on the other hand, help me make better use of the famous *composition of place* of which Saint Ignatius of Loyola spoke in his meditations. There they still are in the parable, without time having been able to do away with them and just as I remember them from my childhood, the day laborers gathered in the square; impatiently and anxiously waiting for the possibility of being hired for a job that will, at least, provide them with a meal for the day.

The thing is that, ever since my younger days, whenever I reread this intriguing parable, it seemed to me that the complaining workers were right. After all, they had worked all day long, while the others, who arrived at the end of the day and therefore had worked less, received the same remuneration. And, of course, it must be recognized that, at least at first glance, this is the first thing that comes to the mind of anyone who looks at this situation.

It seems as if Justice suddenly appears energetically claiming, and even shouting, its trampled rights. To which all of us humans react as everyone knows: readily willing to stand up for the just (at least at first glance) claims of others... as long as, above all, they do not adversely affect our own interests. In those days of my youth, just as concerned for social justice as we are now, the tirade of just rights had been repeated so often as to have been engraved in all our minds: social justice, wage claims, workers' rights, intolerance of corporate abuses, etc.; as well as everything that, according to the world, cannot be allowed. It is already understood that the day laborers of the first hour would not have needed to go to the Union; and not even to use the resource of summoning mobilizations with placards, in order that their rights were recognized to them. Even we ourselves would have taken their side.

Which proves, once again, that the human race is not too prone to do deep analyses of important issues. And yet, rarely, if ever, will we find one matter which does not need to be considered seriously and slowly. As happens precisely in the case we are now contemplating: the one posed by the parable of the Laborers sent to work in the Vineyard.

Since it is evident that the global sense of the parable, with its final teaching, has nothing to do with the claims of left–wing trade unionism (the only ones that exist in Spain), it will be necessary to find out the true didactic intention that Jesus Christ proposed with this apologue. And, for starters, we can say that the task does not seem to be easy.

This raises a previous problem. Given that parables are supposed to be brief narrations, by way of example, whose purpose is to facilitate the understanding of the doctrine being expounded,[2] how can it be that sometimes their intellection is not too easy, and even poses profound questions, as in this case? Even more: how can we explain that sometimes parables can be used–at least so it seems–in order to not offer openly to everybody the complete truth?[3]

---

[2] All readers are aware that the parable does not pretend to attribute historical reality to the event narrated. It coincides with the fable in that it aims to lead to a moral or practical teaching; although it differs from it in that the parable departs from fantasy to immerse itself in the real world. Although the purpose of both genres is didacticism, their diversity is evident: while the fable uses the world of the imaginary and fiction as a framework, the parable, on the other hand, elaborates its teaching through the simple realism of everyday life.

[3] With reference to this subject, there is a text whose meaning might seem ambiguous: *And his disciples came and said to him: Why speakest thou to them in parables? Who answered and said to them: Because to you it is given to know the mysteries of the kingdom of heaven: but to them it is not given* (Mt 13: 10–11).

It is evident that some parables contain a meaning that, although profound, is clear and simple to understand; like that of the Prodigal Son, for example. While others, on the contrary, are presented as disturbing, apparently enigmatic, or at least not easy to understand;[4] like this one, of which we are speaking, or that of the Unfaithful Steward (Lk 16: 1–8).

Why do you speak to them in parables? And it would not be fair to pretend that the question is idle. If it is admitted that the function of example in language is to facilitate the understanding of discourse, why use obscure or difficult language?

It should be said, both with regard to the language of the parables and that of Sacred Scripture in general, that the Word of God, addressed to all men for their salvation, cannot be formulated in hieroglyphic form, which would make it incomprehensible to many. It is true that Saint Peter warns of the difficulty of some points in the writings of Saint Paul, but he adds that the key to the problem must be found —according to the Prince of the Apostles—, not in a supposed impossibility of understanding, but rather in the fact that many ignorant and unconscious people *misrepresent* the Scriptures to their own perdition (2 Pet 3:16).

In reality, the key to the language, the meaning of the parables, and the opportunity to use them, is provided by the Lord Himself, with the help of a text from Isaiah. It would be enough to read it carefully to understand the situation and what the Master intends: *Therefore do I speak to them in parables: because seeing they see not, and hearing they hear not, neither do they understand. And the prophecy of Isaias is fulfilled in them, who saith: "By hearing you*

---

[4]The disciples themselves sometimes asked the Master to explain to them the meaning of certain parables: *Then having sent away the multitudes, he came into the house, and his disciples came to him, saying: Expound to us the parable of the cockle in the field* (Mt 13:36).

shall hear, and shall not understand: and seeing you shall see, and shall not perceive. For the heart of this people is grown gross, and with their ears they have been dull of hearing, and their eyes they have shut: lest at any time they should see with their eyes, and hear with their ears, and understand with their heart, and be converted, and I should heal them."[5] It follows that, according to the Lord, if He speaks to them in this way, it is *precisely because they have voluntarily closed their hearts and embraced the lie.* So, the darkness does not lie in His words —which anyone of good will could easily understand—, but in the hearts of the hearers who have adopted an attitude of hostility towards them. Yet He speaks to them, as a form of testimony against them (accusatory pleading): *If I had not come, and spoken to them, they would not have sin; but now they have no excuse for their sin.*[6] In short, I think we can take for granted the following summary, perhaps valid as an initial explanation of the object of the parables: It happened that a copious rain had to fall from heaven, like an abundant torrent of clarity and light, on those who made their choice for darkness because they loved lies more than the truth; and this, so that the wickedness of their heart would be made more evident in this way: *And the light shineth in darkness, and the darkness did not comprehend it...*[7] *For every one that doth evil hateth the light, and cometh not to the light, that his works may not be reproved. But he that doth truth, cometh to the light...*[8] The sun may abound in fiery rays of heat and light; but if the shutters of the window are closed, no luminous flash will penetrate into the room.

---

[5] Mt 13: 13–15.
[6] Jn 15:22.
[7] Jn 1:5.
[8] Jn 3: 20–21.

Now we can begin a first approach, with emotion and trembling, to the content of today's parable. With curiosity and excitement filled with emotion, in fact, because the parables are like pearls scattered throughout the Gospel, well able to cause us joy when we notice them. For example, almost all of them begin with a strange, charming, and sublime reference that usually goes unnoticed: *The Kingdom of Heaven is like unto...* Which makes us think that the content of the parable contains something that resembles, in some way, the Kingdom of Heaven; and that it is enough, by itself, to provide the parable with a tone of intoxicating and fascinating seduction. Undoubtedly, something proper to Heaven is enclosed, more or less hidden, in its content. Even parables such as that of the Importunate Friend,[9] or that of the Unjust Judge,[10] based on normal events of ordinary life but somewhat difficult to explain, contain teachings of sublime beauty and profound meaning. Both parables, for example, once read attentively and beyond their apparent somewhat harsh overture, easily manifest their clear reference to prayer, viz: to the ineffable loving dialogue between God and man.

Today's parable begins by saying that *the Kingdom of Heaven is like a landowner*[11] *who went out early in the morning to hire laborers for his vineyard.* And the first thing that calls our attention is the contrast that appears with respect to the parable of the Wedding Guests.[12] In the latter, emissaries are sent to summon the guests; while in the one we are commenting on, it is the owner himself who

---

[9] Lk 11: 5–13.

[10] Lk 18: 1–8.

[11] The classical term, already outdated, was that of *Head of the family*, which is a bad transcription of the *paterfamilias* of Roman law (a legal term that has disappeared and therefore difficult to translate into modern language).

[12] Mt 22: 1–14; Lk 14: 16–24.

goes out personally to hire the laborers. First point to consider, therefore.

The reason for the owner's behavior in this case does not seem difficult to explain, although it is necessary to go deeper than it may seem at first glance. The parable of the Wedding is intended to proclaim the universal summons for all to come to the Nuptials of the Lamb; which is equivalent to the general call to holiness. While that of the Laborers sent into the Vineyard, refers to a much more peculiar and particular invitation; which is the call to the specially chosen, namely, to those who are to follow the Lamb more closely (Rev 14: 1–4). This parable of ours today deals, in reality, with those who have been destined to become *other Christs* and, by extension, those who have always been designated as *consecrated souls.* In other words, those whom the owner, or Father of families is looking for here are precisely his own, who are the ones who will be in charge of tilling his vineyard in order to provide good pasture for the rest of the sheep. Generally speaking, the parable encloses in its meaning the whole group of men and women who have had no qualms, out of love, in making of their lives a complete donation to Jesus Christ. This is precisely the group of the elect of whom Saint Paul would have felt no shame in proclaiming today what he already said in his well–known text: *But I would have you be without solicitude. He that is without a wife is solicitous for the things that belong to the Lord, how he may please God. But he that is with a wife is solicitous for the things of the world, how he may please his wife: and he is divided... And this I speak for your profit: not to cast a snare upon you; but for that which is decent, and which may give you power to attend upon the Lord, without impediment.*[13] Of course

---

[13] 1 Cor 7: 32–35.

some will be disposed to say that we are not here confronted with the inflexible rigidity of the revealed Word; but that, since the text was written at other times, and under different circumstances, the teachings of the Apostle have no application now. Nevertheless, we continue to maintain, on the one hand, that revealed truths never pass away (Mk 13:31); and that the meaning of the parable is very clear and forceful, on the other: since those whom the owner seeks in this case —He personally— are those who are to be entrusted with the care of his vineyard.

It is evident that the Good Shepherd loves all His sheep; He calls each of them by name, and for all of them He gives His life. But it is also obvious, whether or not one wishes to recognize it, that it is *His own* to whom He professes a special devotion, which Saint John does not hesitate to describe as a *love to the end* (Jn 13:1).[14] And it is also true, consequently, that, taking all this for granted, we place ourselves at the antipodes of the doctrine called *the promotion of the laity*. It is impossible not to admit that, according to both Scripture and the unanimous Tradition of twenty centuries, consecrated life is more perfect, in the sense of Christian living, than the merely lay life.[15] The Pauline doctrine on this subject (1 Cor 7) is categorical and clear, even though efforts are now being made to ignore it. The truth is that *the promotion of the laity* has uprooted, perhaps

---

[14] The expression *his own*, referring to some of His sheep, is from the Evangelist himself in the text I just mentioned. Although the expression could be extended, in a broad sense, to all the members of the Mystical Body, it is unquestionable, if one wants to make a serious exegesis considering the context, that it refers in a strict sense to the specially chosen ones.

[15] Consecrated life has always been considered within the framework of what has always been called *states of perfection*, according to a terminology that speaks for itself.

unintentionally, the feeling that Christian people had about such things as virginity, religious life, the states of perfection, priesthood, and, in general, everything that implies a total dedication to God within the framework of Christian spirituality.[16]

Saint Josemaría Escrivá, founder of the Personal Prelature *Opus Dei,* had the audacity in his time to write that *marriage is for the troop class, and not for the general staff of Christ.*[17] This is absolutely true, and for that very reason deserves to be maintained. Although it is quite possible that the expression, after all the fruit of his time, was not very fortunate, nor does it enjoy the esteem of modern ears; and hence it has caused the displeasure of many, including some of his own spiritual children, who have even tried to disguise it. But the truth is always the truth, and it does not cease

---

[16] I am aware that I will be accused of exaggeration, at best. However, no one can deny that the so-called *promotion of the laity* has been a peculiar phenomenon, the results of which have not always been satisfactory. In fact, although everyone talks about the famous promotion, hardly anyone tries to explain seriously what it consists of. Is it perhaps a matter of the laity taking a few steps forward *(promotion)*? If so, what exactly does this forward movement translate into? Does it refer, as many think, to a certain progress or rise in status —rise, but to where?— which is concretized, in turn, in a participation in the hierarchical function of the Church? We will have to be careful on this point, inasmuch as the tasks of worship now carried out by the laity can contribute to making them sacristans. This cannot be considered as the proper charism of the laity. On the other hand, it has been demonstrated that, when one wants to promote one of two things of opposite nature, he usually resorts to the method of undervaluing the opposite one. Consequently, *the only thing that is achieved is to lower the nature and value of both, if not to destroy them* (something like the Socialist theory of social equalization: lowering those who are above instead of raising those who are below, in order to keep them all at the same level; that is, ground level.

[17] Escrivá de Balaguer, *The Way,* 28.

to be so no matter how much it is expressed in such a way that at present, and for some, it does not sound correct.[18]

However, we have not yet arrived at the ultimate reason that explains with definitive clarity what is said at the beginning of the parable. I am referring to the fact that it is the owner of the estate himself who is *personally* in charge of hiring possible day laborers.[19]

For since we are dealing here with a question of love, and *even the finest and most delicate of all love affairs*, it is undoubtedly a matter to be dealt with in a personal way, solely and exclusively, namely: from lover to lover, from Lover to the Beloved Person; where once again the reciprocal *thou and I* appear; that which always constitutes the fabric of the love relationship.[20] For we are dealing here with not just any love, but with a call or invitation —*vocation*—

---

[18] This should not be the case, if the statement, as in this case, is strictly real. The heart of the problem lies, however, in the fact that today's progressives are unwilling to recognize the superiority of virginity over marriage. Additionally, many prudish people, too attentive to the winds of the times, suffer from what is usually called the *scandalum pusillorum*. Neither should we forget those who pay more attention to what sounds good or bad than to the reality of things. Of course, lie frequently sounds better than truth; which is not surprising when one thinks that the lie, in order to survive, needs to load itself with adornments and beads, as the servant it is of appearances and even of truth itself. It is not by chance that adjectives such as *naked*, or *mere*, are reserved instead for truth: mere truth, or naked truth, as it is often said. Indeed, modern thought has made its choice for appearance rather than for being, convinced as it is that reality (or being, or entity) has no other existence than that which is provided by the mind of man. For today's world is, in fact, the world of Idealism; in which, once God has been suppressed as useless, being has also evaporated.

[19] In contrast, it should not be forgotten, with the parable of the Wedding, where emissaries are sent to call the guests.

[20] Among the many texts that could be quoted, the one from Saint John is very expressive: *Manete in me, et ego in vobis* (Jn 15:4), where the reciprocity in the relationship of love is once again underlined. Cf. Jn 6: 56–57; 14:20; Rev 3:20.

which the most loving of Lovers addresses to a particular creature for a reciprocal, mutual, and totally perfect falling in love: *If you would be perfect, go and sell all you have and give it to the poor; and you will have treasure in heaven. Then come and follow me.*[21] And Love being the most personal thing that exists in the Universe, and its expression being here the most subtle and delicate that can be given or imagined, there is no room whatsoever for the intervention or participation of third parties. The third party is reserved for merely human and profane relationships which the world, without anyone having yet explained the reason, continues to call amorous. It is not so in true love, in which intimacy with the other, dialogue in solitude, and the Lovers being forgetful of anything else takes place:

> *Ah, who will be able to heal me!*
> *Surrender thou thyself now completely,*
> *From today do thou send me no other messenger,*
> *For they cannot tell me what I wish.*
>
> ....
>
> *In solitude she lived,*
> *And in solitude now has built her nest,*
> *And in solitude her dear one alone guides her,*
> *Who likewise in solitude was wounded by love.*[22]

The same is true of the *Song of Songs*. For the Bridegroom and the Bride each one of them is unique, so that the idea of a collective

---

[21] Mt 19:21. As we can see, the Master is speaking here about perfection.
[22] Saint John of the Cross, *Spiritual Canticle*.

type of love has no place here. Love —perfect and true love—, rather than along the line of the *I–you all*, runs along the line of the *I–thou*.[23]

> *As the lily among thorns,*
> *so is my love among the daughters.*[24]
>
> ....
>
> *One is my dove, my perfect one is but one,*
> *she is the only one of her mother,*
> *the chosen of her that bore her.*[25]

Says the Bridegroom, speaking of the Bride. And the Bride thinks the same with respect to the Bridegroom, Who is for her the only one among all:

> *As the apple tree among the trees of the woods,*
> *so is my beloved among the sons.*[26]

The call to total discipleship is the summons to perfect and total love: the greatest gift of love that God is capable of giving to a

---

[23] Love for others is not excluded. It happens, however, that here we are talking about perfect love, which is always resolved in the interpersonal relationship from the *I* to the *Thou*. In reality, something similar happens, in one way or another, although on another level, in the love of collectivities (neighbors, enemies, etc.); since it always ends up being concretized in the love of each of the persons who make them up. The Good Shepherd is the Great Shepherd of all the sheep (Heb 13:20); although he knows them personally and *calls each one by name* (Jn 10:3).

[24] Song 2:2.
[25] Song 6:8.
[26] Song 2:3.

human being. Hence, the call has a peculiar and intimate character, as it is addressed to a special and particular person, whom God calls by name; but with a loving whistle that only the person alluded to is able to hear and understand: *Ego te vocavi nomine tuo...*[27] *And I will give him a white counter, and in the counter, a new name written, which no man knoweth, but he that receiveth it.*[28] This has a singular application in the priestly vocation, where it is no longer a matter of a mere fusion of hearts, but of a quasi-personal identification.[29]

The problem now lies in the fact that, as the world has dispensed with God and society has become more profane, the constant increase in wickedness has been matched by a consequent decrease in charity. It was the Lord Himself Who expressly pointed out this proportional relationship (Mt 24:12). It happens, however, that, as charity cools, the idea of perfect love fades away; and with it the pos-

---

[27] Is 45:4.

[28] Rev 2:17.

[29] Cf. Jn 20:21; Lk 10:16. This is the reason for the failure of so many vocation campaigns, which produce no results. The authentic priestly vocation is configured *necessarily* and *exclusively* through the love of Jesus Christ on the part of the one called. It is in no way a matter of getting young men enthusiastic about the priesthood (even less so if this is attempted through programs with little or no supernatural content), but rather of getting them to fall in love with Jesus Christ. This, in turn, is impossible to achieve without using supernatural means, of which prayer is the first and foremost (Lk 10:2). The grace of the priestly vocation —the grace of graces— begins with a mutual falling in love, develops and grows through an ever more perfect and mature love, and is consummated in the amorous apotheosis of two lovers who, while preserving their personal and proper character, nevertheless identify themselves, as if they were one being, totally and for all eternity: *And I live, now not I; but Christ liveth in me* (Gal 2:20). Just as the Master promised: *And if I shall go, and prepare a place for you, I will come again, and will take you to myself; that where I am, you also may be* (Jn 14:3).

sibility of mutual infatuation between persons. Therefore, once the *feeling of tender and emotional love for the Person of Jesus Christ* —which is ordinarily known as being in love— has disappeared from the horizon, the priestly vocation has lost its guiding compass. The illusionary goal of being madly in love with Jesus Christ has been replaced by *programs* whose content and orientation are not usually supernatural. This is how the Gospel, until now considered as a Proclamation of the Love of God towards man (with its peculiar and personal calls to follow the Master through total surrender), has been relegated to the attic of useless things to be replaced by Programs of Social Reforms. With a clear result that can be considered as alarming and shocking: mass desertions from the consecrated life, scarcity of vocations, identity crisis in the priesthood... and a disoriented Christian People hungry for true Shepherds whom they are anxiously searching for, but who are nowhere to be found.

The crisis of Pastors for the Christian People today is a cruel and frightening reality.[30] But if it is admitted, according to the doctrine of all times, that the vocation or call depends primarily on God (Heb 5:4), how is it possible that this situation has come about? And the explanation is not difficult if one takes into account, above all, that *primarily* does not mean *exclusively*. The vocation or call, by which someone is invited to become *another Christ*, is a fine and delicate act of love, according to what we have already said above. And the act of love, as is well known, is always a matter of two: one who proposes his love and another who responds with his acceptance; or one who goes out of himself to the other and who is reciprocated in turn in the same way. But it is always a

---

[30] As far as the lack of Pastors is concerned, it is something that cannot be denied by the triumphalist propaganda, so skillful in downplaying and disguising the facts. How could one otherwise explain the establishment of the permanent diaconate?

bilateral, reciprocal, and mutual act, to the point that it cannot exist otherwise. Without two who mutually call and respond to each other, and at the same time reciprocate, there is no love. Of the Holy Spirit, to Whom in the Trinity Love is attributed, it is said in the Creed *qui ex Patre Filioque procedit*. The parable of the Workers sent to the Vineyard, as it must, addresses this issue and provides an adequate response.[31]

The concern of the owner or father of the family to attend to the tilling of his vineyard is evident. The parable begins by alluding to the concern that moves him to go out diligently, *very early in the morning*, to hire laborers; then it goes on to speak of various other departures, at different times and for the same purpose. Circumstances that have often been understood, by the authors of Spirituality, as the diverse moments of his life in which the man can be the object of the call or vocation on the part of God. A pious interpretation that we would not have any inconvenience to accept.

However, in a more serious and well–founded exegesis, what appears clearly in the text seems to point rather to the divine care for vocations to the consecrated life. It is quite clear that God intervenes, with the necessary diligence and means, in order to provide Laborers to work in His vineyard; or Shepherds to lead the rest of the sheep, if one wishes to express it in this way. He goes out at various times of the day, including those that are almost immediately after the end of the day, talks to and strikes an agreement with the

---

[31] The parable, considered directly, is above all a clear exposition of God's care and concern with regard to the problem, of course in the part that corresponds to Him. A fundamental complementary text, which attends to its solution, is that of Mt 9: 37–38 (cf. the parallel Lk 10:2).

laborers, calls upon those who are idle so that they will also come to work, etc. No one could say that God has not fulfilled His part of the task.

Nevertheless, as we have already said, God works in such a way that, in all the affairs that He undertakes with man and in which love is involved,[32] He expects the collaboration of His creature. As it could not be otherwise. For love being a bilateral and reciprocal relationship —a *product* of two—, it cannot be fulfilled *without the one and the other*, jointly and at the same time. On the other hand, having been originated also —love mutually offered and reciprocally accepted— as an act of two wills entirely devoid of any shadow of coercion, it cannot exist, therefore, without the mutual assent and free action of the two opposites who love each other: *Ubi autem Spiritus Domini, ibi libertas*.[33] In other words: regarding the vocation to the life of total discipleship or evangelical perfection, although the indispensable grace and collaboration from on High are always present, the necessary human cooperation is in fact often lacking, as expressly recognized by the Lord Himself; hence the distressing shortage of laborers to work in the Vineyard (Mt 9:37).

This problem is currently one of the most serious challenges of the Church.[34] The need for a reform of the *Tridentine Seminaries*

---

[32] All the actions God carries out, through man and for man, are nothing more than a pure and exclusive exchange of love.

[33] 2 Cor 3:17.

[34] Although the advocates of false triumphalism are not willing to admit it. They are determined to spread progressive ideas within the Church that are quite akin to Modernism, and they strive to present what is an obvious catastrophe as if it were a fortunate phenomenon from Heaven.

existed long before the Second Vatican Council.[35] It is painful to say, however, that there is no hope whatsoever of the long-awaited and much–needed reform. The Church is immersed in a grave crisis of faith and discipline which has led her to dangerous anarchy. Imbued with worldly criteria; influenced by Marxist philosophies and Protestant theologies; touched by Modernism in many of its theologians and Hierarchs; and engaged in an enterprise of dubious Ecumenism... the Barque of Peter does not seem to be aware of the problem. She does not talk about it, which seems to indicate that she is not even thinking about it. It is to be feared that the twenty–first century will pass without the problem being seriously addressed and, consequently, by then no solution will be necessary.

---

[35]The subject is treated at greater length in my *Notes on the Spirituality of the Society of Jesus Christ The Priest*, Shoreless Lake Press, New Jersey (USA), 1994. There was considerable deficiency in both the human and intellectual formation of future priests, to which must be added the serious lack of focus on the spirituality that was imparted to them. With regard to the former, the formators did not attach much importance to the cultivation of human qualities in the students, nor did they pay much attention to the secular sciences, with the result of an extraordinary poverty on this point. As far as the preparation for theology was concerned, the little philosophy that was taught was partial to Duns Scotus and Francisco Suarez, and practically ignored Thomism. As incredible as it may seem, for example, I personally had to discover Saint Thomas when I was already a priest, after having passed the seminary stage.

Even more serious, however, was the problem of spirituality. Focused exclusively on religious life, there was an urgent need for an authentic secular spirituality, which would have corresponded to secular priests who were going to live in the midst of the world. It is fair to say that although intense (I would say rather pious), orthodox, and animated by authentic Faith, it all revolved around the methods, modes of prayer, customs, and even vocabulary proper to religious life.

In spite of all the problems, what survived of the Seminaries after the devastation they suffered from the time after the Council was much worse than what had existed up to that time. The expected reform did not translate into steps forward, but rather into a swift race backwards.

But let us return to the main content of our parable. After a first reading, even superficially and without excessive attention, it is impossible to avoid the idea that a possible injustice is being committed; or that it points at least to a certain lack of logic. The workers who appear in it worked, according to the narration, in very different degrees of dedication and intensity, to end up receiving all exactly the same salary. But bearing in mind that the parables, as is always the case with the Word of God, have been pronounced and written for our instruction, what exactly is the lesson that our Lord intends for us to learn from this one?[36]

It is not difficult to understand why there have been so many interpretations of the meaning of this parable, which seems to indicate either that none of them is fully satisfactory or perhaps that the content of the narration lends itself to different layers of depth, as far as the explanation of what is said in it is concerned. And it is even possible that prudence might advise taking into consideration both possibilities. Of all those I know, I confess that I was pleasantly impressed by Bruce Marshall's original interpretation, contained in *To Every Man a Penny*, one of his novels.

According to this interpretation, the complaint of the workers who arrived early in the morning, thus being forced to bear the brunt of the work, was unjustified. A point on which everyone agrees, as could not be otherwise, since the very general tone of the parable reproves the attitude of such laborers. The problem lies in elucidat-

---

[36]Everything seems to indicate that, at least in some of His parables, the Lord intentionally sought an ambiguous meaning, or at least a somewhat obscure one, if one wishes to qualify in this way what is simply profound. Admitting this, we would have to conclude that what the Master intends to do is to place at our disposal a wealth of teachings; which, however, because of the richness and depth of their content, do not lend themselves to being formulated by means of a merely simplistic enunciation and meaning.

ing the exact reason capable of disqualifying such complaints. Can it be affirmed with certainty that they were absolutely groundless? In fact, since the laborers received their wages in the exact amount that had been agreed on, there is no room for controversy on this point. Nor can the right of the owner to dispose freely of his own money be disputed, especially if the interests of third parties are not injured.

However, if one considers the demands of justice from a broader and more flexible point of view, it seems that, since they had worked much harder, perhaps they could have expected a more generous and understanding attitude from the owner; if not out of justice, at least out of fairness.[37] In any case, and in spite of anything that may be said, the protest of the workers of the first hour must be maintained as unfounded, as is established by the general tone of the parable. *But not for the reasons ordinarily considered.*

According to Bruce Marshall's original theory, the first shift workers complained unduly and unwisely because, *in reality and compared to the others, they had received the best,* namely: the privilege of having carried the heaviest burden, of having made the most difficult effort, of having been considered the last in this sense... and, in short, from the Christian point of view, to have shared more than others in the sufferings, the burdens, and the Cross of the Lord. And of course, what cannot be doubted is that the parable *must be considered from a Christian perspective.*

This brings us to the climax, not only of the parable, but also of Christian existence and even of human life itself. I am referring to the supreme value of suffering and even of the so-called passive

---

[37]Roman jurists thought that the strict application of Justice could degenerate into cruelty in some cases. The principle *summum jus, summa injuria* was well known in Roman Law.

virtues, seen from the perspective of the Cross. In this way, the mysterious verse that closes the parable, which is not always well understood, acquires meaning: *Thus the last shall be first; and the first shall be last.*[38]

In this way the parable, almost without our realizing it, has led us to the very center of Christian existence. To that for which we were baptized: *Do you not know that as many of us as were baptized into Christ Jesus were baptized into his death?*[39] We were baptized in order to make the life of Jesus our own, above all through participation in His Passion and Death. To share closely in the Master's existence, carrying with Him, like a modern-day Cyrenean, the greater part of the burden, —*the weight of the whole day and of the heat*—, means nothing other than having received from on High the grace of graces: *Whoever does not take up his cross and come after me cannot be my disciple.*[40]

The great tragedy of modern Christianity is that it has forgotten this fundamental truth. The Word became Man to make this Earth a better world, which is not the same as a comfortable one, although many have believed it to be so. But to do without the Cross of the Lord is to reject the Love that God offers us, which is precisely the axis around which all Christianity revolves. Who could sincerely think that things like the greater comfort of life, the

---

[38] If considered carefully, the verse seems to admit different readings. Those who came last, for example, will be the most graced; while those of the first hour, because of their clumsiness, will be relegated to last place. Or the verse can also be read: those who, according to purely worldly or profane criteria, are considered last will be the first for God; while those who occupy the first place for the world will be confined, on the contrary, to the last place. Everything seems to indicate that this second reading is the more correct one and the one more in accord, therefore, with the lesson that emerges from the parable.

[39] Rom 6:3.

[40] Lk 14:27.

pretended establishment of world peace, the universal recognition of human rights, or the general establishment of democracies would bring us closer to God and could build a better world for all?[41]

The Christian Message is not a UNESCO program to build a world in which people live better and more comfortably. If we are thinking of a better and more comfortable life, the slogan is well pointed out and very clearly delineated: *How narrow is the gate and strait is the way that leads to Life, and how few there are who find it!*[42] On the other hand, since the Word became Man, there is no other way to follow but the one that He Himself represents (Jn 14:6). And he who decides to follow it (it is important to insist that there is no other) also knows with certainty what awaits him: *all those who want to live piously in Christ Jesus will suffer persecution.*[43] Where is the better world, universal peace, human rights recognized and respected by all, social justice finally implemented, the United Nations as the undisputed Authority and guarantor of the World Order, etc., etc.? Utopias play an adequate role in the realm of Literature, or at most as a dreamy desideratum; but they are not capable of going beyond that. Christians, however, certainly know that the Kingdom of God will one day be a full reality, including a new heaven and a new earth (Rev 21:1). But the same will never be

---

[41] One might ask whether it is our intention to throw these values overboard; although such an accusation would be far from what is being said here. Such aspirations are indeed desirable and worthy, therefore, of the consequent effort to achieve them. However, we must always bear in mind that some of them, if not most of them, are reduced to mere utopias. What we are trying to denounce here, echoing the content of the parable, is the falsity and malice of the pretension of making a better world *without worrying first and foremost about making a better man.*

[42] Mt 7:14.

[43] 2 Tim 3:12.

true of the Kingdom of Man, since the gates of the Earthly Paradise were closed forever.

The complaints of the workers of the first hour were unjustified because they did not know how to truly see the gift they had received. Just as those who pretend to live Christianity without fully accepting the way of the Cross are equally mistaken. A way that, *far from being a lesser evil to be accepted with resignation*, is already a pledge of definitive glory and future beatitude. Saint Paul put it in timely words that today seem to have been forgotten: *Gladly therefore will I glory in my infirmities, that the power of Christ may dwell in me. For which cause I please myself in my infirmities, in reproaches, in necessities, in persecutions, in distresses, for Christ. For when I am weak, then am I powerful.*[44]

Perhaps this is the way to explain the failure of the *reforms* undertaken in the Church after the Second Vatican Council. A careful examination would surely reveal that the emphasis was placed on the change of *structures* rather than on the reform of *persons*. New Pontifical Commissions were erected; Episcopal Conferences and Presbyteral Councils were created; innumerable Diocesan and Parish Commissions flourished rapidly everywhere, as if by incantation, with a multitude of attributions that reduced to a minimum the functions of the Parish Priest as Pastor; the Permanent Diaconate was imposed, or reestablished (where it was necessary and even more so where it was not); lay ministries were created, in a variety of classes and functions known only to God;[45] new paths of dialogue with the separated Churches were opened; the celebration of Mass in the vernacular was declared obligatory; *the rights of*

---

[44] 2 Cor 12: 9–10.

[45] The term *lay Ministry* is abhorrent both canonically and theologically since the ministerial charisma is something completely foreign to the laity.

women were emphatically proclaimed, once their admission to the functions of worship was also permitted;[46] old condemnations which warned Catholics of the dangers of modern rationalist thought were abolished; the causes for the nullity of marriage were facilitated and broadened, with a criterion as broad as it was generous...; and a long etcetera in which the only thing missing was the updating of supernatural means: precisely those necessary for the improvement of the Christian life of the members that make up the People of God. Nor is it necessary to say that the greater effort that the workers of the first hour had to bear —*the burden of the whole day and the heat*— seemed to be valued negatively; while everything induced to overestimate, as preferable and valuable, the more comfortable labor facilities obtained by those of the last hour. In short, the complaints of those who considered themselves the object of a possible injustice seemed justified; since they had been obliged to bear the burden of the most fatiguing work.[47]

Saint Paul was defending himself against some who accused him of continuing to preach circumcision. If that were true, the Apostle

---

[46] Up to that time no one had noticed the lack of women's rights, nor has anyone since explained satisfactorily exactly what these prerogatives consist of. It had always been thought, without anyone allowing himself the slightest doubt — apparently naively— that women possessed the same dignity as men; and that they also enjoyed within the Church a special status that allowed them to carry out functions of their exclusive competence and worthy, on the other hand, of high recognition and sublime admiration. For Saint Paul, the highest mission of women is motherhood (1 Tim 2:15), a sacred and quasi–divine office that not only includes the generation and carnal upbringing of the offspring, but also their education and complete formation (without forgetting that spiritual motherhood possesses an immensely higher dignity than the merely carnal).

[47] Karl Marx also sought to improve the order of the world, putting a definitive end to social injustices by means of violent change of structures. But by forgetting, however, man as a person, this led to the results we all know.

came to say, *the scandal of the Cross would be liquidated* (Gal 5:11). Scandal that he tried, with extreme care, that it was always in the first line of his preaching since it was the only thing that mattered; to the point that everything else was superfluous as a hindrance (1 Cor 1: 17.22–23). The Cross was for him, therefore, the standard-bearer of his catechesis and the principal and only means of salvation; without mattering too much that it seemed madness for some and scandal for others. Today, however, there are many who are unwilling to offer the world a Message that scandalizes it and in which it does not wish to believe. The men of today, besides worshiping hedonism, do not seem to be willing to admit anything that does not pass through the narrow filter of their mentality. Everything seems to indicate that both the World and today's Christians are rebelling against the possibility of bearing the burden of the Cross —*the weight of the whole day and of the heat*— hoping rather to receive their denarius with the minimum effort involved in having reached the end of the task. He would be mistaken, however, who would naively believe that modern Society does not accept the Cross simply because it is not capable of understanding it. At the bottom of this attitude there is an unconfessed hatred of God and all that He signifies. While Perfect Love is far beyond the capacity of human comprehension, the fact remains that man has been given, by grace, the possibility of understanding It... and of sharing It if he so wishes.

They say that Satan, besides hating God's ways, is incapable of understanding them. His twisted mind, now petrified forever in lies, compels him to be continually in error and to distort the Word of God, even to his own regret and to his own detriment. It is not strange, therefore, that many interpret the meaning of this parable in a sense different and even opposite to the true one. In such a way that, seen from a certain point of view, they would even be ready to justify the workers who arrived at the beginning of the day, in spite of the teaching of the parable.

Before entering into a more detailed examination of the complaints made by the workers who had arrived at daybreak, it is necessary to add one observation. Certain situations are too complex to be reduced to a simplistic explanation, even if they contain elements that accurately reflect reality. With regard to our subject, it is quite possible that the situation of the Church, as a result of the reforms that were introduced after the Second Vatican Council, cannot easily be reduced to a simple and excessive accentuation of structures to the detriment of the person. Such an interpretation, while containing sufficient fragments of the whole truth, would surely err in its simplicity; it would probably prove to be inaccurate under objective scrutiny, inasmuch as it would soon appear incapable and insufficient to provide a convincing explanation of the facts. We believe that what we are dealing with here is nothing more than the eternal return of gnosis:[48] the attempt to make Christianity more *rational* and accessible to human understanding which, besides having set itself up as the only god and arbiter of everything, is incapable of understanding the grandeur and sublimity of the ways of the Highest. Once again, the usual: if the mountain does not come to Mohammed, Mohammed will worry about going to the mountain. If the World is not willing to accept the Church, the

---

[48] It is appalling to see the coercion exerted against those who insist on maintaining their fidelity to principles which have always been considered as unbreakable, precisely because they have been upheld by Tradition and the constant Magisterium of the Church for centuries and centuries. At a time when a complete doctrinal, liturgical, and disciplinary anarchy is spreading everywhere, as well as an open license to attack even dogmas, there is rather little freedom for those who claim to denounce such activities.

Church is determined to come to the World.[49] In this way, suicide is finally served on a silver platter, ready and waiting to be carried out.

With regard to the protests of the workers arriving at the beginning of the day, it should be noted first of all that, at least in most cases, the *complaints are never justified*. This is not difficult to admit if we bear in mind that to speak of complaints is not the same as to speak of lamentations. For while the latter usually express tender and deep feelings of the human heart, complaints, on the contrary, are almost always tinged with a certain shade of protest. Moreover, even the Bible contains a *Book of Lamentations*; and it is not uncommon for mystics to use them to express their relationships with God, often also tormented and heartbreaking:

> *Oh! who will be able to heal me!*
> *Surrender thou thyself now completely*
> *From to-day do thou send me now no other messenger,*
> *For they cannot tell me what I wish.*[50]

Complaints, on the other hand, as we have said before, are almost always wrapped in the spirit of protest, distrust, and dismay at the wrong suffered. And it is really difficult for the offenses inflicted on us to surpass those we ourselves have committed against

---

[49] But not to fight to conquer it, but to show the world that she is like it, that she is with it, and that she accepts its approaches. A desperate, if not erroneous, attempt to achieve a constructive dialogue acceptable to all. Senselessly forgetting that, faced with the offer of a dialogue, the Devil, no matter how much he pretends to accept it, *never gives in, not even with respect to the whole, and not even in the smallest of details.*

[50] Saint John of the Cross, *Spiritual Canticle*.

others.[51] According to Bernanos, after the offense that we men committed against God, putting His own Son to death on the Cross as if He were a criminal, no one, absolutely no one, would have the right to complain of having suffered wrongs.[52] It is said of Saint Vincent de Paul that, when the hour of his death arrived, the prayers for the dying were recited to him as was the custom. When asked, he replied that he humbly asked forgiveness of all those whom he had offended; but that he, in turn, had no need to forgive anyone, since he had received no offense from anyone. In an interesting text, Bernanos transcribes some of the words uttered by the Country Priest near his death: "It greatly comforts me also, to think that nobody has been guilty of real harshness towards me —not to say the great word: *injustice*. I certainly respect those victims of iniquity who are able to find in that knowledge some basis of strength and hope. Somehow, I should always hate to think myself —though unwittingly— the cause, or merely the pretext of another's sin. Even from the Cross, when Our Lord in His agony found the perfection of His saintly Humanity; even then He did not make Himself a victim of injustice: *Non enim sciunt quod faciunt*. Words that have meaning for the youngest children, words which some would like to call childish, but which the spirits of evil must have been muttering ever since without understanding, and with ever growing terror. Instead of the thun-

---

[51] It is convenient to remember Jesus' expression regarding the splinter in the eye of our neighbor and the log in our own.

[52] The modern claim to exempt the Jews from responsibility for the death of Jesus is truly ridiculous. Of course, His death is imputable to the whole of mankind... including the Jews; and it does not seem likely that we are about to discover, as some seem to claim, that the Chosen People are the only ones innocent in the deicide. What is certain, however, is that the Chosen People, precisely because they are the Chosen People and for other reasons, are imputable for a certain degree of greater culpability.

derbolts they awaited, it is as though a Hand of innocence closed over the chasm of their dwelling."[53]

It is important to note that the workers of the first hour, by deciding to raise their complaints to the Paterfamilias, introduced a radical change in the tone of the situation. It was they, in fact, who had borne the brunt of the day and the heat; and yet they were unable to realize that, contrary to all appearances, they had received much more than the others. They made the mistake of forgetting that the case had nothing to do with what might be considered a mere labor contract, but that it pointed to something much loftier. As is always the case in the relationship of divine–human love, in which, although governed by a sense of totality that encompasses bilateral and reciprocal relationships, man receives much more than he gives.[54] Unfortunately, the first arrivals did not know how to understand things. They interpreted what would have been an act of special trust, the consequence of a peculiar love for them, as a terse and arid contract of employment; in such a way that everything was reduced to a mere *do ut des*, or *facio ut facias,* legal business.

It is true that God, in His overwhelming Love, has granted man the possibility of returning to Him more than he has received, as is

---

[53] Bernanos, *The Diary of a Country Priest.* As a note of curiosity, for example, we might recall here the verse of Ovid in which the poet, with his customary literary elegance, asks his Muse to cease her sad complaints:

Tam longas sed supprime, Musa, querelas.

[54] Interpreting the parable as something other than a mere contract or legal business imposes itself as the most obvious and the only legitimate thing to do. The didacticism of the parables could not be absent and is always oriented to salvation and the Love that God offers to man; and in no way admits to being reduced to what would be a mere code of social or commercial conduct.

clear from the parables of the Talents and the Mines.[55] But this, in turn, is but another gesture of the infinite divine liberality, which is capable of converting, out of pure love, what is nothing but grace into an authentic free and meritorious act of man.[56]

By claiming quantifiable demands for material goods, the workers of the first hour distorted and made impossible what would have been a pure loving relationship, in which human measurements are not allowed. *God gives his Spirit without measure* (Jn 3:34). The harsh words of the Paterfamilias, addressed to one of the disobedient but referring to all of them, thus acquire their full value and meaning: *Friend, take what is yours and go.* In the love relationship, everything that belongs to each of the lovers becomes the possession of the other, including their own persons:

My Beloved belongs to me, and I to him.[57]

But if Love is reduced to being the object of the petty category of quantifiable and measurable material goods, It is destroyed in Its very essence. There is no longer any such thing as a loving self–giving, whose foundation is none other than the generosity and lack of self–interest on the part of the one who loves; it follows then

---

[55] *These talents you gave me, here they are; and others more besides which I have gained for you.*

[56] According to Rev 22:12, the Parousia will entail retribution to each according to his works. It should be noted, however, that such retribution does not necessarily involve a ratio of this particular amount to this other particular amount. In the relationship of the creature with its Creator, an equivalence of exchanges is not conceivable. Man cannot claim before God the possession of any right that has not been previously granted to him: *All is grace*, said the Country Priest of Bernanos at his death.

[57] Song 2:16.

that *what was each one's own remains each one's own*. One can now understand the immense sadness, the stony hardness, and the firmness of the farewell clearly contained in the expression: *Friend, take what is yours and go*. Certainly, it could not be otherwise: *Take what is yours. But now go from my side, inasmuch as there is no longer room for union in the intimacy of love*. It remains true, therefore, that when someone demands what he believes to be his, he is reduced to the nakedness of nothingness.

What is evident in all of this is that with God there is no room for bargaining. What is offered unconditionally and totally cannot be accepted conditionally and partially. In fact, Jesus Christ never accepted any kind of conditions or delays when following Him out of love was the issue (Lk 9: 57–62). It is the challenge of divine totality and human totality. For the totality of infinity is compatible with the totality of finitude; conversely, the whole cannot be corresponding with the part. *Jesus, having loved his own who were in the world, loved them to the end.*[58] Since love to the end only admits a response to the end, even an abundance of good works would not be sufficient if the impetus of the first love is lost (Rev 2:4).[59]

The problem arises with all its gravity when charity grows cold (Mt 24:12), inasmuch as charity is the warp and woof of Christianity. It may happen that Christians stop believing in Love. In fact, Love has already been displaced from the central place it occupied in the Official Catechesis, replaced by other questions, more or less marginal, which seem to be more topical. A proof of what has been

---

[58] Jn 13:1.

[59] One might think that we are dealing with a hypertrophied exaltation of Love that goes beyond the contents of the New Testament. However, the doctrine presented here is nothing more than the strict application of the first and foremost of the Commandments: Thou shalt love the Lord thy God *with all* thy heart, *with all* thy soul, *with all* thy strength, etc.

stated, for example, is a fact difficult to explain: Catholic praxis has ceased to insist on the indissolubility of the conjugal bond and has opened the doors instead to the most varied causes of nullity invoked by anyone who wishes to dissolve his or her marriage.[60] It seems normal that, if we do not believe in Love as a totality, perennity is no longer accepted as one of Its notes. It is now possible to believe that Love can fade away or disappear, since that charity which, according to Saint Paul, *never passes away* (1 Cor 13:8) has been marked for oblivion.

In the parable of the *Laborers Sent to the Vineyard* we can guess the concern of the Paterfamilias, extremely busy with His various outings, in search of workers to carry out the labor. Nevertheless, the task to be done is more abundant than the men available: *The harvest is plentiful, and the laborers are few...* Even at the eleventh hour, despite the fact that the end of the day is near, the Paterfamilias is still looking for laborers: *Do you not say that there are still four months to harvest? Well, I say to you: lift up your eyes and see the fields already golden for the harvest.*[61] Which seems to indicate that there must be a lot of urgent work to be done, since He does not seem to care about how late in the day it is. But the extraordinary thing about the case is the fact that, despite the proximity of the end of the day, He still found men available. They were quietly in the square, sitting on their hands, with apparently no activity attracting their attention. Hence the rebuke of the Paterfamilias, as important to the context of the parable as the answer received: *Why do you stand there idle all day?* To which they answered: *Because no one has hired us.* And He sent them also into His vineyard.

---

[60] Of course, there is no talk of divorce since the indissolubility of the marriage bond is of Divine Law; however, it is always possible to change the name of things.
[61] Jn 4:35.

Once again and as always, the words of the parable narrate, in a brief and simple way, ordinary and trivial events of daily life. Like the one we are now contemplating, for example. Let us pay attention, however. Because under the apparent inanity of the futile story, there are always hidden profound teachings; for this and no other is the object of the parables.

And here something surprising seems to be happening. Despite the abundance of work to be done, and despite the hours that have already passed during the day, there are still people who seem not to have found any tasks to perform. And —what is even more extraordinary— no one has called them to give them a task to do. *Why do you stand there idle all day?* The harvest is certainly plentiful; but the workers —the real workers— are few. And I speak of the true workers because available people certainly abound. According to the parable, there is a multitude of idlers who have spent the day, sitting on their hands, simply because no one has hired them. And now we can ask the relevant question: What if someone had called them? Would they have responded affirmatively? According to the parable the answer is clearly affirmative, since these workers of the eleventh hour agreed to the request of the Paterfamilias without the slightest objection.

The Church is undergoing the greatest crisis in her history with regard to priestly vocations and, in general, to consecrated life. There are no priests, and the People of God are disoriented and confused, like sheep without a shepherd. The Seminaries are empty, the Novitiates deserted, both sighing, overcome by the nostalgic memory of times gone by. The solutions–of–the–moment (permanent deacons, activist nuns, committed laymen, etc.) are increasingly proving to be insufficient and inoperative. It is useless, on the other hand, for propaganda to try to disguise the crisis or to cloak it with triumphalism...

And yet, there is *an enormous multitude of people who are idle* and could therefore work; as the parable expressly recognizes: *Why do you stand there idle all day long?* We already know the answer; therefore, perhaps it would be worthwhile first to ask for the meaning of the question; and still more for the reason that has led to it. The Church lamented, in the times before the Second Vatican Council, that she had lost, according to her, the working class. Now, although she does not do so, she could also lament —and perhaps with greater reason— the loss of youth. But all in all, and in spite of all the circumstances, *the youth is still there.*

Because it is true. The youth immersed in sex, drugs, alcohol, rock music, pubs, and discos; the youth of empty souls and lost hopes and ideals is a horrible reality. It is not true that the youth is with the Pope. And no one with common sense is going to be fooled by the rigged, ostentatious shows of the great concentrations of boys and girls who appear to display enthusiasm for religiosity, when in reality they are only trying to forget, through hustle and bustle and organized tourism, the inanity of their destroyed lives.

Say what you will, it is an appalling reality. It pales, however, *before the even greater reality that young people are strong and have overcome the Evil One* (1 Jn 2:14). It is also certain that the Apostle John was addressing the young people of his time —indeed of all times— in a convinced and hopeful manner. But was the youth of the first century worse or better than the youth of today? In my opinion, the question does not make much sense: that youth, like today's, was and is simply youth. It is quite possible to equate the concepts of empty and hopeless lives with that of simply idle lives. After all, they mean the same thing: emptiness and nothingness.

But they have nothing to do, no horizons to glimpse, no lofty ideals to nourish their spirits and satisfy their hearts. They are simply idle —they themselves say so— *because no one has hired them.* How could anyone think that the Charter of the United Nations, or the Declaration of Human Rights, or the Constitution of the United States would be able to seduce their spirit? Are old people convinced that young people are old too? If no one, or almost no one, is willing to believe in many of the ideals offered to the youth, why are they offered to them as if they were valid? This approach is similar to what happens with food that is about to expire, which the large food markets give away to charities. As for children, certain methods and procedures used by ecclesiastical experts in children's pedagogy (such as publishing propaganda leaflets, with stickers and pictures of athletes, to *recruit* vocations) are insulting; apparently, they are convinced that children are incapable of thinking or of using common sense. They try to project their own inability to see into the minds of children, ignoring the astonishing words that the Apostle John dedicated to the little ones: *I am writing to you, little children, because you have come to know the Father.*[62] In which it is no longer, therefore, a matter of having defeated the Evil One, but nothing less and nothing more than the incredible wonder of having access to the very face of God (Mt 18:10). So where then is the childish inability to gain knowledge of the supernatural, as well as of Jesus and His ways?

The virtual workers of the eleventh hour —who in this case, since they were young people, could also be considered as of the first hour— would also generously accept the call to go to work in the vineyard... provided it was an authentic call to work in the vineyard. That is, when the prospects offered to them were sufficiently

---

[62] 1 Jn 2:14.

high; when the task they were offered was not watered down with comforts, as if it were a wide and easy path and not a road as harsh and risky as it truly is; when they could be convinced that it is no longer a matter of compromising with the world and the things of the world, but of falling madly in love with Jesus Christ and living His destiny; when they were taught that the priest of Jesus Christ is not a collaborator of some NGO, but someone who immolates his life for men out of love for them and for Jesus Christ; and when they were told openly, without complexes of any kind, that their mission, as such a priest, is not to implant on this Earth the pretended Kingdom of Man, but to work for the longed–for–and–expected Kingdom of God (which is only in it its beginning, and nothing more than its beginning). In short, we can therefore be sure that, as long as it is men who try to hire the idle, for merely human purposes and tasks, it is more than probable that the possible laborers will not be willing to abandon their attitude of continuing to wait. It will be necessary for the Paterfamilias Himself to propose to them the task of going to work in His Vineyard. I mean to His Vineyard, and not to another place, nor to another different job. There will no longer be any idlers, nor will the sheep of the People of God feel helpless. And in the end, both those who arrived first and those who came later, will receive something more than the previously adjusted denarius: *a hundredfold, and then eternal life.*[63]

---

[63] Mt 19:29.

VOCATION OF SAINT MATTHEW

(THE DANCE OF THE DAMNED)

MEDITATION

(Mt 9: 9–13)

And when Jesus passed on from hence, he saw a man sitting in the custom house named Matthew; and he saith to him: Follow me. And he rose up and followed him. And it came to pass as he was sitting at meat in the house, behold many publicans and sinners came, and sat down with Jesus and his disciples. And the Pharisees seeing it, said to his disciples: Why doth your master eat with publicans and sinners? But Jesus hearing it, said: They that are in health need not a physician, but they that are ill. Go then and learn what this meaneth, I will have mercy and not sacrifice. For I am not come to call the just, but sinners.

Matthew, or Levi, was a publican (tax collector), and considered therefore, without further ado, as a member of the caste of the *damned*. Nobody has ever liked to pay taxes, as anyone acquainted with human nature knows. For the Jews, however, things were much more serious, to the point that the term publican was synonymous with sinner, especially for the more cultured class. The fact that the Chosen People had to pay taxes to hated Rome was considered an opprobrious sign of their forced submission. Some even thought that, as inevitable as the situation was, paying taxes was still criminal or sinful (Mt 22:17).[1]

As usual, the sacred concepts of Freedom and Nationalism were at stake, both interwoven in a well–known and harmonious conjunction. Actually, another of the numerous curiosities offered to the student of human nature. With respect to Freedom, for example, although everyone talks about it and even brandishes it as a flag, and despite the fact that it is one of the many decisive issues clearly explained in Sacred Scripture —given its fundamental importance—, *nobody agrees about its meaning, nor does anyone refer to it in a sense accepted by all.* Which is not the worst. In the strange and sometimes paradoxical way human beings behave, it is even not uncommon to see Freedom invoked and used as an instrument of oppression and tyranny.

Incredible as it may seem, what God understands as Freedom —and, therefore, its opposites Slavery and Oppression— *is totally different from what the world thinks and uses.*[2] On the other hand, there has never been so much talk about Freedom and Human Rights as in modern times, and, at the same time, they have never been

---

[1] The other synoptics point out the fact very clearly: Mk 12:14; Luke 20:22, which proves that this issue was decisive and extremely important for the Jews; not so much for the money to be paid, but for what it meant in submission to the Romans.

[2] The Christian concept of Freedom appears clearly in various texts. Cf. Jn 8: 32–34.36; 2 Cor 3:17; Gal 4:31; 5:13; 2 Pet 2:19.

Vocation of Saint Matthew

so trampled and violated as they are now. The means of mass manipulation have been so much perfected that the average citizen (the man on the street) has few possibilities, and even less desire, to think for himself: the truth and the knowledge of what really happens are for him only what the politician in charge dictates and what is broadcasted on television or by other mass media.

The manipulation of concepts such as Freedom and Homeland, carried out especially in current times, has led to the total subversion and falsification of their meaning, which, in turn, has led to the exacerbation of nationalism, ethnic groups, and racism.

However, as is easily seen in the Bible itself, these are not excrescences of our time. Jesus Christ, for His part, showed a complete indifference with respect to nationalism: *Render therefore to Caesar the things that are Caesar's and to God, the things that are God's.*[3] It is true, though, that Jesus Christ sometimes seems to lean in the opposite direction, apparently admitting a certain policy of preference towards those of *His own house*.[4] But it soon becomes clear, if the numerous texts are examined together,[5] that it is merely a preference of turn, without any consequence.[6]

The position of Jesus Christ on alleged nationalism is sufficiently clear: He did not care at all about the damned condition of Levi, the future Apostle and Evangelist Saint Matthew, notwithstanding

---

[3] Mt 22:21 and parallels texts. Where is, therefore, the problem? The seriousness of these questions consists in attributing absolute character to what is only relative. Or what is worse: manipulate concepts in favor of ideological, political, or social interests; almost always hidden and unavowable.

[4] Cf., for instance, Mt 10: 5–6; Mk 7:27; Acts 13:46, among others.

[5] The Pauline texts on the subject are abundant. Cf. Romans 1:16; in some, the Apostle is extremely explicitly universalist: *I owe myself to the Greeks and the barbarians; the wise and the ignorant* (Rom 1:14; cf. Col 3:11).

[6] Mt 28:19. The text of Mk 7:27 expressly says it so.

the attitude of the do-gooders of His time who were scandalized by this situation, as the Gospel amply proves.

At a closer look, there is no other way of confronting this issue. The so–called nationalisms are always basically racist. For racism is nothing but an adherence to a particularistic vision of realities that are in themselves universal; deeper still, such tenets materialize in rabid and even Manichaean selfishness: *We, in addition to being different, are the good ones; the others, on the other hand, are the bad guys.* The hatred of the Pharisees against the publicans lay in something deeper than an alleged understanding of these people with regard to the Romans. It fed on an egotistical, and of course particularistic, vision of a reality that was rather *on the absolutely opposite side of Christianity.* Opposite, not merely strange to Christianity. The Master explained it in a clear and blunt way: *the publicans and the harlots shall go into the kingdom of God before you.*[7]

Chapter 4 of the Gospel according to Saint John tells us an episode that sheds abundant light on the subject. For starters, we must understand that this problem is not just a modern one, it has only become more acute now. Everyone knows the enmity then between Jews and Samaritans. Both were an integral part of the same Chosen People; which was not an obstacle for both communities to consider each other as strangers, and even as exclusive possessors, each of them, of the only correct key to solve the problem. The dialogue between Jesus Christ and the Samaritan woman settles the issue once and for all, expressly outlining a universalist vision of Christianity that today, unfortunately, seems to have been forgotten again: *Woman, believe me, that the hour cometh, when you shall neither on this mountain, nor in Jerusalem, adore the Father. You*

---

[7]Mt 21:31.

adore that which you know not: we adore that which we know; for salvation comes from the Jews.[8] With or without intention, it is evident that the Samaritans were attempting to circumscribe the religion of the one true God to a territorial sphere, which today we would even brand as nationalistic; and also quite limited, which is what usually happens. Which makes us understand how shortened, particularistic, mediocre, and remote the human vision of reality is, compared to the broad and deep vision of the reality of things that is God's own.

Salvation comes from the Jews, of course. But if it comes from them it is precisely because it does not remain in them; it radiates from there, like a luminous and incandescent focus, to men of all places and of all times.[9] Hence the famous and well-known text of Saint Paul, in which the Apostle echoes the words and intentions of the Master: *There is neither Jew nor Greek: there is neither bond nor free: there is "neither male nor female." For you are all one in Christ Jesus.*[10]

Needless to say, the text between commas ("neither male or female") is exclusively mine. But underlined or not, it is revealed text; and it also leads us directly to some of the burning problems of our time, such as the much-vaunted issues of *machismo* and *feminism*, for example. If we allude to them here it is because they seem to be intimately connected with the exacerbated racisms and nationalisms of our time.

Perhaps it is convenient for us to start with the warning that we are not going to even allude to here the ridiculous accusation of

---

[8] Jn 4: 21–22.

[9] Note well that the text does not say that salvation is for the Jews. Such an aberrant interpretation would be against each and every page of the New Testament.

[10] Gal 3:28. Cf. Gal 5:6; Acts 15: 8–9.

a *chauvinist character* attributed to Saint Paul. He would not like either to be nominated for the First–Class Stupidity medal, so justly deserved and obtained by some sectors of the exegetical theology of our time.[11]

What is clear in Saint Paul's text is the evidence that, from the Christian point of view, *the machismo–feminism dichotomy cannot even be considered*; nor can they be studied as distinct or independent problems, typical of human nature. For Christianity, neither machismo nor feminism exist, only men and women: both with equal dignity, although with different and complementary functions and missions. Of course, the New Testament contemplates in a special way each and every one of the miseries of human nature: lust, greed, pride, etc. The set of everything that is proper to a fallen nature which, although repaired by grace, has nonetheless not been entirely freed from concupiscence.

But machismo and feminism, to the extent that they really exist, are not primarily the fruit of the unfortunate concupiscence that preys on the human being. *They are rather the result of a deliberate and malicious will*, whose object is none other than the destruction of the human person; and more specifically of the family (above all the Christian family) as support and foundation of Society.

I have deliberately said "to the extent that such phenomena actually exist" because the so–called machismo concretely, rather than

---

[11]I had the opportunity to meet some *expert* nuns according to whom the Bible was not sexist, of course. Obviously. But it was very clear, according to them, that Saint Paul was. Christian charity forbids us, in this specific case, to make any kind of comment on the subject. I will limit myself to pointing out that it is not uncommon that the *expert* in ecclesial matters (clergyman or layman) becomes a danger to normal citizens; but when it comes to nuns who have perhaps obtained —or have attributed that title to themselves— the status of a scholar, then there is no other way out but to pray the Litanies of the Saints, adding fervently at the end a new imprecation: *ab expertis libera nos, Domine.*

a tangible reality, is an instrument wielded as a weapon precisely by the Feminist Movements. In a corrupted Society such as ours —and this is always the case with any Society in the process of collapse and disintegration— what really exists as a global phenomenon is the Matriarchy.[12] As much as it sounds heretical and worthy of the stake, the truth is that *machismo* in modern society is more ghostly than real. Skeptics on the subject could carry out a survey covering as many married men as possible.

The Society in which we live has become accustomed to considering living a lie as a normal situation. Which also logically implies *the will to never thoroughly investigate the true causes of social events*. Let us take as an example a highly topical case. Everyone is aware of the undeniable fact of the alarming increase in domestic violence in which almost always, or always, the husband is guilty. Or at least that is what is taken for granted. Faced with such a worrying situation, all kinds of possible solutions have been arbitrated, among which is, as expected, a greater profusion of legal measures and repression, although with meager, or barely perceptible, results.

We do recognize as good the duty to punish the guilty spouse and the need to implement the appropriate measures, both to penalize crime and to prevent it. But the most extraordinary and striking crux of the problem is not that. Given that domestic violence (and its worrying increase in modern times) is a social fact, *the least that could have been tried, according to the dictates of the simplest Logic, which are also those of common sense, is to investigate the causes that have produced it*. No sociologist would be willing to maintain that social phenomena or facts appear at random; in reality, there is

---

[12] To be precise, rather than the superiority or greater influence of the authority of the mother, we should actually speak of that referring to women; or merely to the wife.

always a cause that produces them.[13] Perhaps, therefore, a serious investigation in this regard would not have been a trivial enterprise.

Which endeavor probably would have brought to light surprising results. *Probably* for the reason that today, to further complicate things, we also fall short of serious and honest investigators. Perhaps then it would have been found out that the main culprit of this social scourge is precisely *feminism*. Taking into account the dangers that generalizations entail and trying to avoid them as much as possible so as not to incur falsehoods, it is clear that it would not hurt to try to clarify the reasons why so many husbands (desperate in most cases) have ended up in such sorry situations. Of course, I am neither trying here to justify these crimes nor advocating that they should go unpunished. I simply believe that, when it comes to punishing people (and even more so when serious penalties can be imposed), the attitude of not investigating the causes and all the circumstances that have occurred and that have given rise to the punishable act is also criminal. It is possible that cases were found —again we want to avoid generalizations— of husbands reaching the limits of what human patience is capable of withstanding. And let us insist again that we cannot justify what is not justifiable. But ever since the dawn of Law —or from when the Rule of Law— the existence of extenuating and even diriment circumstances have been taken into account for the application of a Justice worthy of its name. And what no one can deny is that the Feminist Movement has exacerbated feelings to unjustifiable degrees. Similar to what happened with the famous *promotion of the laity* —whose results in the Church are yet to be determined— there has also been a *promo-*

---

[13]Both facts: that chance is a word that has little meaning and that there is no effect without a cause are truisms known since time immemorial. It is not easy to explain the ease with which they are forgotten.

tion of women which insisted, even ad nauseam, that the female sex needed to fulfill itself. Consequently, it was necessary that women equalize their rights and functions to those of men; a refrain which was arbitrarily established as something categorical. True, we must admit the unfortunate and isolated incidents that have occurred in the past (and will always occur); but it is not less true that until now the problem of an alleged inequality of rights between the sexes had not appeared; at least as a social phenomenon worthy of the name. The age–old topic of male authority over women has always been true in most cases (and legitimate, according to the Bible), but fairly analyzed, it never had alarming consequences. The truth is different. When the woman, in the exercise of the qualities and virtues proper to her sex, has been truly feminine, she has also always obtained from the man what she has wanted, longed for, or desired.[14] The diversity of functions is in no way inequality of rights, nor does it in itself imply discrimination against women. From the Christian point of view things have always been quite clear. For the Apostle, for example, *neither is the man without the woman, nor the woman without the man, in the Lord*;[15] where shortly before he had also said that *the woman is the glory of the man.*[16]

I have said before that, deep down, the philosophy of the Feminist Movement feeds on a design, as intelligent as it is perverse, whose objective is none other than to manipulate women more and more. In this way, they intend the destruction of the Family as an institution, for which purpose they do not hesitate to carry out an authentic attack against the very foundation of Society. From a

---

[14]The biblical episode of the Wedding at Cana (Jn 2: 1–11) is very instructive in this regard.
[15]1 Cor 11:11.
[16]1 Cor 11:7.

more superficial point of view —although no less true— Feminism feeds, as always happens in these ideologies, on a partial, flat, blunt, and extremely short vision of reality. At which point we arrive at the meeting place of all racism, nationalism, and the enormous set of *isms* in which the *good* describe the others as strange, evil or, in general, as *damned*. The self-righteous Jews, who wrapped publicans and sinners in an identical package properly labeled as *damned*, would have agreed with Karl Marx in condemning the bourgeois class as guilty of all the misfortunes of humanity.

Unfortunately, spiritual myopia is more widespread and more commonplace than it seems. With the aggravating circumstance that this disease, which limits and hinders vision, brings on a source of corruption that influences the whole: *If thy eye be evil thy whole body shall be darksome*, said the Lord.[17] This malady also affects the ecclesiastical world, as many examples demonstrate. I am going to limit myself to one which is current and important despise been silenced and placed in the back burner. I am referring to the problem of what has been called *diocesan spirit*, referring now to diocesan secular priests.

The Conciliar Decree *Presbyterorum Ordinis* spoke clearly about the convenience for secular priests —more commonly known as diocesan priests—, in order to be able to help each other and make their ministry more efficient, to be grouped in Associations approved by the Church: *One should hold also in high regard and eagerly promote those associations which, having been recognized by competent ecclesiastical authority, encourage priestly holiness in the ministry by the use of an appropriate and duly approved rule of life and by fraternal*

---

[17] *Si autem oculus tuus nequam fuerit, totum corpus tuum tenebrosum erit* (Mt 6:23).

aid, intending thus to do service to the whole order of priests.[18] The prescription of the Conciliar Decree is contained within Section 8 of Chapter II, which deals precisely with the union and fraternal cooperation among the presbyters, as well as their intimate union with their own Bishop, and the authentic Presbytery that results from that effort. Which makes it implausible that there could be, in the mind of the Council, the slightest suspicion that such a spirit of association could interfere in the development of an authentic diocesan spirit.

So far things couldn't be clearer. Except that then they stumble, unfortunately, upon the reality of life. The Progressive and Neo-modernist Movements, which seem to be the ones that mark the course in Theology and in the Pastoral Ministry of the current Church, have adopted, with respect to the last Council, a singular and strange attitude. On the one hand, they use it as a throwing weapon against those who dare to oppose any ideological tenet of such Movements. The unlucky daredevils who go so far are immediately branded as pre–conciliar, anti–conciliar, Tridentine,[19] conservative, disobedient to the teachings of the Magisterium, nostalgic, fundamentalist, and a multitude of titles and medals whose prolixity makes the abundance of decorations of any official of the Army of a third world country look ridiculous. On the other hand, they

---

[18]*Magni quoque habendæ sunt et diligenter promovendæ associationes quæ, statutis a competenti ecclesiastica auctoritate recognitis, per aptam et convenienter approbatam vitae ordinationem et per iuvamem fraternum, sanctitatem sacerdotum in exercitio ministerii fovent, et sic toti Ordini Presbyterorum servire intendunt* (Vatican Council II, Decree *Presbyterorum Ordinis*, II,8).

[19]It is useless to try to find logic or common sense in all these and many other common disqualifications. It is a *locus theologicus* where everything is admitted in order to nullify the opponents: contradictions, manipulation and falsification of data (historical and non–historical), misrepresentation of Conciliar Documents, etc.

have no qualms about using the Council for their own convenience. Which means that, when the Council contains prescriptions or provisions that do not adapt to their particular ideology, such texts are ignored or hidden, and even, if necessary, manipulated and falsified. Which is exactly what happens with this topic. If some unfortunate secular priests, thinking perhaps of strengthening their vocation and diocesan spirit and of helping each other, wish to associate —which as we have seen is in the mind of the Council, and always counting on the Bishop—, they are automatically pilloried as *damned* priests and *anti–diocesan*.

This is, in a nutshell, the strange issue of the vaunted *anti-diocesan attitude*. A rare monstrosity about whose exact nature it is dangerous and useless to inquire. It would be an idle inquisition because, to answer it, one would first have to know what *being diocesan* exactly is.

Of course, the Council Documents, and more specifically the Decree *Presbyterorum Ordinis* sufficiently explain what *being diocesan* means. Unfortunately, we see that the documents do not correspond to reality. Here too, as in so many places, the problems are cascading.

In what form and to what extent will any group of diocesan priests who wish to associate —with the blessing of their Bishop and without losing sight of fraternal love for the other priests, his brothers— become an obstacle to *diocesan spirit*? Strange question, whose very formulation is already almost a crime insofar as it directly affects the mythical world of topics which do not require any explanation. This is what usually happens with all pillorying: all it takes is to be pilloried in any subject area, no need for specifications or explanations.

The concept of priestly diocesan spirit is delineated with sufficient clarity in the *Presbyterorum Ordinis* and has always been lived in peace and tranquility; better or worse, but without problems or tangled speculations. In modern times, however, certain modifications have interfered with that spirit and, to that extent, have become a problem, no matter how painful it is to admit it.

In the first place, we must concede that *diocesan spirit* does not make any sense if it is severed from the Bishop. Priests, according to the very constitution of the Church and the will of her Divine Founder, are nothing without the Bishop. But it happens that the role and functions of the Bishop have become somewhat blurred after Vatican II. Whether you want to recognize it or not, and no matter how much is said to the contrary, it is true that Episcopal Conferences have in fact reduced the autonomy and freedom of action of Bishops in their own dioceses,[20] with logical consequences. Because the loss of the Head's prominence inevitably leads to a cer-

---

[20]In this case, the commonly accepted principle that *union is strength* is invalid. First, because it seems that the will of the Founder of the Church, with respect to her constitution, revolves around the idea that the territorial unit (or the territorial cell, later united to the others of the group) is the *diocese* (or what the primitive Church knew by the name of particular Churches), and not the *nation* (which, being a political entity above all, has an unstable, relative, and protean consistency). Second, because the Episcopal Conferences have been shown in practice to be easy prey for Ideological Pressure Groups, and the most obvious consequence has been to unite the Bishops, true, but in a *submissive and docile acquiescence to the directives of such Groups*. As usual in these cases, I will be branded as exaggerated, and from there upwards (or downwards, depending on how you want to consider it). But an honest and serene examination of the problem, unprejudiced and loving the truth, probably will demonstrate that I am at least partly right. Obviously, those who reject these affirmations can always resort to the resource of drawing up a list, as complete as possible, of Bishops who dare to act outside the guidelines of the Episcopal Conferences; although it is very possible that it will not be an easy task for them.

tain negative repercussion on the Organism as a whole, diocesan in this case, and ends up in its disintegration. A fact that ordinarily goes unnoticed, but is no less real for that: *My sheep are lost for lack of a shepherd*;[21] or also: *Wound the shepherd and let the flock scatter.*[22] And although the application of similar texts to the problem may seem exaggerated or unreasonable to some, and perhaps rightly so, reality forces us to recognize that those texts do exist.

Almost all Bishops belong to one, or several, of the innumerable Commissions and Sub–commissions that structure the Episcopal Conferences. The need for continuous travel, in order to be present at the numerous meetings and deliberations of such Organisms, results in a frequent absence of the Bishops from their respective dioceses. It is becoming more and more difficult for priests to receive personal help from their Bishop —their Father and Pastor— and entrust to him problems that only he could help solve. On the other hand, the crisis of faith that currently affects the Church, and the environment of naturalism that permeates and floods it, have also contributed to the fact that the figure of the Bishop, as Father and Pastor, has been gradually changing into that of Bishop Executive, or Bishop *Businessman.* Given the multitude of occupations to which the Bishop must attend, priests are forced, if they wish to see their Pastor, to go through the bureaucratic procedures of requesting interviews (for dates that are sometimes disproportionately far off), laborious negotiations with male and female secretaries, Chiefs of Staff, those in charge of the corresponding Miscellaneous Affairs..., in order to deal with them on issues that, perhaps due to their delicacy or importance, only the Bishop would have need to know about. Even though it may seem like a joke, the Bishop has to spend so

---

[21] Ezek 34:5.
[22] Zech 13:7.

much time on issues of a *social* nature that he no longer has the time to deal with those of a *religious* nature.

All of which could not fail to have a negative impact on the spirit of priestly brotherhood, as much proclaimed in the Council Documents as it is lacking in real consistency. In the frequent and numerous meetings that modern Diocesan Curiae organize for priests, a Canonical Hour is usually prayed in common *as a testimony of fraternity and unity among diocesan priests*. And after that, as the popular adage goes, *if I have ever seen you, I can't remember*. But if fraternal charity and diocesan spirit are reduced to that, as reality seems to show, can anyone explain the type or category of diocesan spirit or unity of the Presbytery against which the unfortunates who, following the directives of the Council and intending to associate to help each other, both in the tasks that affect their ministry and in those that concern their personal spirituality, are attempting to go? It seems evident that, if the concept of diocesan spirit is more evanescent than consistent, the alleged attack that some *daring people* launch against it is more phantasmagoric than real. And yet they are treated as anti–diocesan and are simply incorporated into the group of the *damned*; without the need for the accusers to present any evidence or the possibility for the accused to appeal. Once again, unfortunately, the concept of publican is synonymous with the concept of sinner; and hence they always appear in tandem and as associates.

Lack of vision, or narrow–mindedness as some may call it, is a scourge that affects not only the individual who suffers from it but also always has a negative and regrettable impact on others. The struggle of Jesus Christ against persons with this vice is reflected in almost every page of the Gospel. Not infrequently the defect afflicts the individual from his birth, like the eunuchs that the Lord spoke about (there are also eunuchs of the mind). And it is already known that the lack or paucity of intelligence is the only disease whose symptoms are perceived by others and never by the patient who suffers from it (although in reality it is others who usually suffer its consequences). Other times, however, this disease has its origin in a selfish and closed heart; and hence the determination of many who suffer it to not admit anything, whatever, which does not fit into the narrow world that they have built for their particular use: if they do not understand something, then that something is wrong; if they do not like this or that, or if they do not think that something is right, then that something is bad or wrong; if it has not been possible for them to achieve something, it is unthinkable that someone else could have accomplished it: *Woe to you, scribes and* Pharisees, hypocrites, *who close the Kingdom of Heaven to men! Because neither you enter nor let those who try to pass enter!*[23] Neither enter nor let enter, neither do nor let do, seem to be, in effect, the mottos of many who are often those who act according to the well–known *law of the funnel*: placing the wide part of the utensil towards themselves and pointing the narrow part towards others. They are usually the same ones who turn a trifle into a mountain, and then treat the mountains as if they were trifles: they strain out a gnat and swallow a camel (Mt 23:24).

An American Bishop once reproached me on the subject of *altar girls*. The fact of not having established them in our parishes scandalized and alarmed (pastorally, of course) this good man. But the worst of all this is the conviction that, once the minutiae is admitted and set in motion, the world is going to turn differently. There are those who are convinced, for example, that the problems of today's Christianity are going to be solved, automatically, at the

---

[23] Mt 23:13.

very moment that lay Eucharistic Ministers of the parish outnumber the simple faithful; when the girls are the altar servers in the celebration of the Eucharist; at the moment in which women go up to the presbytery to read the corresponding liturgical texts; etc.[24]

Although the statement may sound like a joke, perhaps it is appropriate to say that Jesus Christ had a broad and deep vision of reality. That is why He called Matthew and then included him in the group of the Twelve, *not caring at all about the fact that the future Apostle was a publican.* It is clear that Jesus Christ, as the Pharisees themselves recognized, had no respect of persons (Mt 22:16).[25]

Let us be very careful, however, not to distort perspectives. It would be false to deduce from this fact the idea that the Master

---

[24] On the opposite side are those —deserving of respect, of course— who, concerned about the new ideologies that run in the current Church (and which, according to them, are alien to and even contrary to *quod traditum est*), advocate a series of measures that are more nostalgic than effective. Reestablishing the Mass of the Tridentine Rite and the Missal of Saint Pius V back into force does not seem particularly feasible or very effective. Much less feasible seems the idea of creating an Autonomous Prelature for those Catholics who wish to avail themselves of the Liturgy and the conditions prior to Vatican II. What the Church really needs is a profound reform *in Capite et in Membris*, according to an expression that circulated freely in antiquity but which would not be allowed now. In any case, there is no glimpse on the horizon of any intention, on the part of anyone, to carry out such a reform.

[25] When we arrived in the United States, as a small group of priests who wanted to exercise their ministry in that country, we were already warned that we would never be appointed pastor of a parish, given our Hispanic status. The unfortunate and sad thing about the matter is the fact that, for most of the North American clergy and Hierarchy, the word *Hispanic* has a pejorative meaning that denotes a certain discrimination. Although it is painful for me to say it, it is a worrying reality that in the Country of Democracy, Champion of Human Rights, there are symptoms of racism. Since the United States of America has always been for me —and continues to be— a very dear Nation in which I have found my best friends, my sorrow at this situation is even greater.

did not attach much importance to the choice of the men closest to Him (the future columns of the Church), and that He proceeded in this delicate matter somewhat like a gambler. The truth is just the opposite, as evidenced by the fact, for example, that He spent a whole night in prayer on the eve of the election of the Twelve.[26] So it is not surprising that He chose, to be one of them, a true Israelite in whom there was no shadow of deceit (Jn 1:47). As for Matthew (Levi) specifically, of course Christ did not mind his publican status; *but He did take into account the generosity and greatness of this man's heart,* who did not put conditions nor resort to delaying tactics when called by the Lord. He left the table of the telonium without further ado, forever forgetting his profitable office as publican, and generously (like Zacchaeus, also a publican)[27] invited many to participate in the food to which he treated the Master to celebrate their meeting, etc.

If we start from the basis that the vocation to the priestly ministry comes expressly and directly from God (Heb 5:4), we must assume that those, and only those, who possess a nature capable of honestly fulfilling sacred functions will be elected among men. The exercise of the priesthood is not a joke and admits no doubt as to the capacity for sacrifice, the greatness of heart, and the aptitude for heroic effort that are necessary in the candidate for the ministry. As much as it is true that grace heals and elevates nature, it does not, however, modify its basic qualities, since everything seems to indicate that God does not like unnecessary miracles; so that pretending otherwise would be making a mockery of God and the sacrament of

---

[26] Cf. Lk 6: 12–13.

[27] For Zacchaeus' magnanimous behavior, see the account of the event in Luke 19: 1–10, especially v. 8.

Holy Orders.²⁸ Grace grants the candidate the *supernatural* gifts and charisms that he needs for the exercise of the priesthood, although it does not provide him with the *natural* qualities on which she herself must be based. It is impossible to think that God is going to demand the fulfillment of some functions, not easy in this case, without counting on the necessary gifts, both natural and supernatural. The former are linked, by definition, to nature; while the latter are granted directly by grace.

The vocation to the priesthood, even though it comes directly and expressly from God,²⁹ does not at all rule out necessary preparation for such a sublime office. The serious provisions that the Council of Trent established on the subject are well known; so that, for several centuries, the *Council Seminaries*, also called *Tridentines*, despite their many defects and deficiencies, functioned fulfilling their mission. Generations of priests were formed in them, about whom it would not be fair to doubt their possessing a high degree of faith and piety capable of feeding the whole of the Christian People in a quite acceptable way which couldn't be perfect. If we are honest in recognizing the reality, we will have to accept that the great mass of the Flock of Christ, although there were always just and sinners, lived by faith. Their all having perfect piety would have been the result of a fantasy: that all the priests were saints. A dream that has never come true outside of the unknown Kingdom of Utopia. In those days, however, saints were scarce, as precious stones have always been scarce, and hence the high price and high esteem that have always accompanied them. Nothing more was nec-

---

²⁸Here it is worth bringing up, even in an analogical sense, the old adage according to which *quod natura non dat, Salmantica non praestat*.

²⁹The determination, clear and without any doubt, about the authenticity of such a vocation, corresponds exclusively to the Church, specifically to the person of the corresponding Bishop.

essary, which, by the way, seemed to be God's plans. Heroes would cease to be heroes, no longer serving as a model and incentive for others, at the very moment that all men were proclaimed heroes. It is for this very reason that no one would ever have thought of bumping into saints around any corner; just as no one would wish that diamonds could be harvested, like carrots or tomatoes. For in what way would diamonds be useful then? Once they ceased to be rare and scarce, hence useless to fuel human pride and conceit, no one would know of any practical use for them. As for carrots or tomatoes, at least they are good to be eaten.

With the arrival of modern times, the deficiencies of the old seminaries became more evident and the need for their reform became more urgent. With the new and splendid Spring that the Second Vatican Council, even before it was celebrated, promised for the Church, the long–awaited reform seemed like a done deal. To question the reality of its arrival would have meant falling into the sin of defeatism, pessimism, skepticism, and some other *isms*; because everyone then took for granted that the *new* is always synonymous with the *best*. Decidedly, there is only to recognize that human nature is difficult to understand.

However, and quite contrary to what everyone expected, the long-awaited improvements never arrived; on the contrary, the ensued disaster was of such magnitude that it threatened to do away with everything that existed. Indeed, no matter how much it is admitted that History is the Master of life, it should never be forgotten that it always ends up keeping great and inexplicable surprises for us.

So, instead of the long–awaited Spring, a Winter appeared, perhaps harsher and icier than anything known before. The cold winds of Neo–modernism blew strongly everywhere, and adaptation to the modern world was confused by many with assimilation of the worldly (or mundane) spirit. With regard to the training of priests, it was no longer considered necessary to retain supernatural piety and fervor, no matter how possible it was to have adapted them to the circumstances of the modern world. Why does human psychosis frequently interpret *adaptation* as *destruction*? The Ancients had serious misgivings about innovations: *Nihil innovetur, nisi quod traditum est*, they used to say. It is clear, however, that an intelligent adaptation, which would take care to preserve all the good of the old, would not only be admissible but even necessary: *It is necessary to do these things, but without omitting those*,[30] said Jesus Christ. Of course, He was referring to those who paid the tithe of anise and cumin and forgot about justice, mercy, and fidelity; but it is almost certain that, with regard to our case, He would have thought the same. He probably would have taught us that adaptation was just as important as *not quenching the Spirit* (1 Thess 5:19). It is well known that Saint Paul used to speak always echoing the doctrines of his Master and Lord (there is no known disagreement between one and the other). Likewise, it is also true that Jesus Christ considered, as equally integral parts of the treasure of a good teacher, both old and new things: *nova et vetera* (Mt 13:52). Provided, of course, that both were worthwhile: the former, of being preserved; the latter, of being introduced.

The currents of thought that circulated in the Church were convinced of the urgency of showing the world, as if it were the most important thing at that moment, that the priest *was not different at all from the rest of men*. This gave rise to the appearance of

---

[30] Mt 23:23.

the strange specimen of the *priest–testimony*[31] genus, which encompassed, in turn, another multitude of increasingly diversified species and subspecies, namely, the worker priest, who could appear as a plumber, electrician, bricklayer..., or, in general, any trade that would put aside the fulfillment of properly priestly functions.[32]

Unfortunately, times came when prayer was no longer considered necessary for the task of choosing candidates for the priesthood; and the same goes for other supernatural means. Everything also pointed to the fact that it was no longer necessary to attribute importance to Saint Paul's serious warning to his disciple Timothy: *Impose not hands lightly upon any man, neither be partaker of other men's sins.*[33]

But the promised Springtime, long waited for after the Council, nevertheless appeared in the form of a harsh Winter —without anyone having satisfactorily explained how or why—, sweeping away Seminaries and Novitiates; the Christian People soon found themselves without Shepherds and without religious. The only explanation that high officials of the Vatican Curia have given so far, at least to my knowledge, is that the disaster happened *post hoc, non propter hoc*. The *hoc* was, of course, the Council. The precision of the date —the *post*— was not necessary at all since the fact was patent for everyone to see. However, the causes —the *propter*—, which would

---

[31] The fact that everyone was aware, always and everywhere, that the priest was called to be a living witness of Jesus Christ was forgotten.

[32] The statement that the priest should not show himself different from other men is false. If the text of Heb 5:1, in which it is said that the priest has been *taken from among men*, has any meaning, it is precisely that, for that very reason, he has to be different from them. Otherwise, the words of Jesus Christ would also be empty of meaning: *They are not of the world, just as I am not of the* world (Jn 17:14). It is possible that what the faithful as a whole most desire is precisely that the priests be different from the others.

[33] 1 Tim 5:22.

have been the most interesting to know, were left unexplained and therefore open to free speculation.[34]

As for causes, I think it is fair to say that it is impossible to attribute them to a misguided pastoral policy, or to the mere lack of application of the provisions of Vatican II. Such explanations, in addition to being insufficient, do not escape the evident fact that they are trying to hide the reality. Everything seems to point, however, to a spectacular crisis of faith within the Church: in *Capite et in Membris*. But above all *in Capite*, by which I mean, of course, the Hierarchy in general, no matter how painful it is to admit it. Pope Paul VI already acknowledged before his death that he had been wrong in many of his decisions, and even that —these were his words— *the smoke of Satan had entered into the Church.*

Be that as it may, the obvious fact is that, as has been said before, the Seminaries and Novitiates were left empty and many of them —the majority— closed. In order to remedy this evil, the times that followed the Second Vatican Council saw the implementation of a Youth Ministry..., whose failure has been even more spectacular. The first mistake that was made with the application of this new Pastoral, in my opinion, was to present it, not as a necessary change of course —which would have been the honest and intelligent thing

---

[34] According to the *Irish Independent* news, only eight candidates will be ordained in 2004 at the only Seminary left in Ireland for twenty–six dioceses (cited by *The Catholic World Report* July 2004). The Post–Conciliar Springtime continues to bear fruit; or perhaps it would be better to say that it continues without giving any. This is the present condition of *Catholic Ireland*, whose former power to send so many priests to foreign countries, especially to the United States of America, is known to all. As a term of comparison, perhaps it is worth remembering that, when I was a student at the Seminary of Murcia (a diocese that was far from being one of the most important in Spain), around the middle of the last century, we had six hundred seminarians. By the same token, *The Catholic World Report* also informs that this year sixty parishes will be closed in the Archdiocese of Boston.

to do—, but with triumphalist airs without any real foundation. It was no longer a matter of remedying a serious situation (whose existence was not recognized), but of elevating the Youth to top places never reached until now, according to what was proclaimed. Meetings and even Youth Councils multiplied, with massive acts that could not avoid their air of spectacles. *Youth with the Pope,* and slogans like *Totus Tuus* and the like, became popular and traveled the world, despite their lack of veracity or an ambiguity that no one bothered to explain. On the other hand, the action programs that were proposed to young people were impregnated with purely human ideology, into which any allusion to the supernatural was missing.[35]

It was around this time that the strange Vocational Recruitment Campaigns arose. Unfortunately, they were very far from the practice of spending the night in prayer prior to choosing the candidates. The figure of the new seminarian appeared in the brochures and propaganda posters, guitar in hand and *rire jaune* (a traditional French expression that comes to mean something like a rabbit smile, or a forced laugh), but this time accompanied by girls with similarly happy faces. As if wanting to imply that life passed happily in the Seminaries, in which everything contributed to having a good time. It is my firm opinion that this was what broke the camel's back and what the young people of the time found excessive, to the point that it caused them to desert massively, as if they were fleeing an epidemic. Indeed, it is decidedly necessary to recognize that the sense of perception of the ridiculous, and the rejection of what is too easy, is more frequently found in the young than in older people.

---

[35] The so-called *identity crisis of the Priesthood* in addition to the *Promotion of the Laity*, which progressive theologians tried to spread everywhere, also contributed a lot to the phenomenon of general desertion.

I have before me a notice dated Vienna, July 13, 2004,[36] referring to an advertising campaign for the recruitment of vocations in the Austrian Archdiocese. There are posters containing slogans, of which the news highlights some such as the following: *Whoever wants to open the hearts of men becomes a surgeon or a priest... Whoever wants to bring light to the world must become an electrician or a priest... Whoever wants to strengthen people must become an aerobics instructor or a priest...* And others like these. It is to be expected that, after such encouraging statements, young Austrians will rush *en masse* to apply for admission to the Seminaries; unless they consider such slogans to be an insult to their intelligence and generosity.

On the other hand, as much as one wants to resort to good will, it is difficult to believe that the opening of Seminaries to homosexuals (as has been done in some places, mainly in North America) responds to a feeling of anguish before the pressing need for priests. Unless you want to assume in those responsible a degree of ingenuity bordering on blindness or mental abnormality. The results are easy to see. Indeed, it would be impossible to think that they could have been different. Is it necessary, therefore, to look for reasons? If some are found, perhaps they are the same ones that have prompted the modern world, more anti–Christian than merely pagan, to consider the legality (and even the dignity) of things such as homosexuality or the dissolution of marriage. However, everything leads one to think of a hidden plan to destroy the Catholic priesthood.

The problem is that modern Pastoral activity, insofar as it can still be called that, has abandoned the contents of the New Testament.

What is clear, in the narration that we are commenting on, is that Jesus Christ, ignoring the stigma of *damned* attributed to them,

---

[36]See *Libertad Digital*, Internet, July 14.

interacts with publicans and like people, staying with them. Although with a well–defined intention, which is to look for them and heal them: *They that are in health need not a physician, but they that are ill... For I am not come to call the just, but sinners.* The words of the context clearly point to the fact that the Teacher is not interested in what would be a mere change of social conditioning. His objectives have nothing to do with purposes or modes of conduct that do not go beyond the purely natural. What he really seeks, on the contrary, is a radical change in the human heart, capable of being the origin and source, in turn, of *simple* or pure feelings (Mt 6:22) that lead to and materialize in the characteristic behavior of the *new man* (Eph 4:24). Or put another way: an interior change, animated and moved by grace, with supernatural aims or objectives. As He Himself says to the well–meaning murmurers, with an evident tone of reproach: *Mercy I want, and not sacrifices* (rituals). The Christian, indeed, is not merely a being who —as would now be said— has committed himself to the marginalized, nor is he a champion of social justice; but someone who has been grafted into Christ and who lives, from that moment, the very life of the Lord (Jn 6:57; Rom 8: 9–10). Christianity is a doctrine that leads to existence in Christ; it must be born in the heart of man and from there —from an interior transformation into Him— permeate all his being. Doctrine that definitively puts an end to merely external rituals, which never change the human being or modify his behavior as an *old man* (Rom 6:6).[37]

The imperative addressed to Matthew is very clear and specific: *Follow me!* The object of the invitation —concise and final, on

---

[37]Words cannot be more forceful: Woe to you scribes and Pharisees, hypocrites; because you tithe mint, and anise, and cumin, and have left the weightier things of the law; justice, and mercy, and faith (Mt 23:23).

the other hand— is the following of the Master. Nothing more, and nothing less, than following the Master, with all which that entails.[38]

As can be seen, we are still far from the idea of comparing the *perfect* following of the Master —*Sacerdos est alter Christus!*— with ideas such as becoming an aerobics instructor or a surgeon. If the existence of any Christian, and in a more special way that of the priest, is to consist of a true *Christification*, to what extent is it convenient that modern Pastoral activity proposes to youth, as an ideal to be realized, the slogan *be yourself*?

It is true that a correct connotation can be found for that expression, if perhaps it is examined with a sufficient dose of good will. It would then mean something like *I know how you should be yourself*. Or something similar perhaps. But it is necessary to recognize that, as simply stated, it is an ambiguous idea, and therefore dangerous.[39] According to the spirit of the New Testament, in order to be oneself it is necessary to stop being oneself: *he that shall lose his life for me, shall find it*;[40] *As the living Father hath sent me, and I live by the Father; so he that eateth me, the same also shall live by me.*[41] Of course, oneself does not stop being oneself,

---

[38] We could quote here a multitude of extremely eloquent texts that open previously unsuspected supernatural horizons. For example, Mt 10: 38–39; Lk 9:23; 14:27; 2 Cor 4:10; Gal 6:14; etc. They all refer to the same thing, namely: sharing the existence of the Master and above all His death on the cross. Whoever decides to accept such an invitation must know that the Son of Man had nowhere to lay His head (Lk 9:58) and that he must be willing to drink from the same cup (Mk 10:38).

[39] People tend to take things as they sound, just like that, which is perfectly natural. Unless they are clearly and openly obvious metaphors, such as the expressions *if thy eye scandalize thee...* or *if thy hand, or thy foot scandalize thee...* or other similar ones. But the slogan *be yourself* is by no means a metaphor.

[40] Mt 10:39.

[41] Jn 6:57.

to the point that it would be absurd to suppose otherwise.[42] But it is evident that the slogan *be yourself* connotes an idea of permanence in oneself, of self–contemplation or narcissism if you will, of self–affirmation and fulfillment in and by the same subject; or, in a nutshell, of self–sufficiency. However, for the New Testament —which is the Revelation of Perfect Love and of the purpose for which man was created, which is none other than Love— the consummation of man only takes place through the *exiting/taking leave of himself to surrender to the other*. And the only gaze that leads man to self–knowledge is the contemplation *of the other*, since only through the *thou* is he capable of knowing his own *I*. Made by Love and for Love, the human being is the lover who only becomes such through the reciprocal contemplation that takes place between him and the loved one:

> *When thou didst look on me,*
> *Thine eyes imprinted upon me thy grace;*
> *For this cause didst thou love me greatly*
> *Whereby mine eyes deserved to adore*
> *That which they saw in thee.*[43]

---

[42] In the well–known text of Saint Paul of Gal 2:20, where the Apostle says that: *Vivo autem iam non ego, vivit vero in me Christus*, two things can be clearly observed. In the first place, the affirmation that he lives the very life of Christ (he has made the Master's existence his own); second, that he, Paul, is still himself. A careful analysis of the phrase shows it clearly: if, on the one hand, Christ lives in him, it is precisely in him that He lives; consider also the strong expression at the beginning: *Vivo autem*, in the first person indicative. Both affirmations, in which the different personalities and the life of each of them in the other are alluded to, must be understood in an equally strong sense and provide yet another example of the paradox which surrounds so many mysteries of the Christian supernatural world. Within the Trinity, the *I* of the Father contemplates Himself in the *I* of the Son, although both are the same thing (but not the same Person). In reality, the *I* of the Son is not an entelechy: *As the living Father hath sent me, and I live by the Father* (Jn 6:57). Needless to say, when dealing with created beings, analogy must be reckoned with.

[43] Saint John of the Cross, *Spiritual Canticle*.

The Christian's mission is to bear witness to Jesus. This applies in a special way to the priest, since he, more than anyone else, is called to be *alter Christus*. Hence, now is the time to formulate the question: How can he pretend to be a testimony of Christ unless he stops looking at himself in order to contemplate, instead, the Master and imbue himself with His life and with His death? Indeed, because according to the Apostle: *Always bearing about in our body the mortification of Jesus, that the life also of Jesus may be made manifest in our bodies. For we who live are always delivered unto death for Jesus' sake; that the life also of Jesus may be made manifest in our mortal flesh.*[44] From which it follows that the testimony is for all times and for all places: *Always bearing about...* Which means being delivered to death, for and with Jesus, *continually*. And above all, it also follows, that what others will try, and will want to see in us —the only thing that interests them and what they really need— is that *the life of Jesus be made manifest in our mortal flesh*. Strong expression —that of mortal flesh—, which comes to show that the testimony must be as literally visible as it is clearly patent.

And this is how the proposal to become an aerobics instructor is still far away. Surely Matthew the publican, if he had followed the ideal of being himself, would never have left the telonium or become an Apostle. And hence, as long as the Catholic Ministry for Youth continues to be gripped by the fear of proposing the ideal of Christification —which, it must not be forgotten, also includes that of the crucifixion— it will continue to be as inoperative as it is useless.

The Apostle Saint Paul, who never had been the victim of complexes or vain desires to please the world, spoke clearly and openly: *But we preach Christ crucified, unto the Jews indeed a stumbling*

---

[44] 2 Cor 4: 10–11.

block, and unto the Gentiles foolishness: But unto them that are called, both Jews and Greeks, Christ the power of God, and the wisdom of God. For the foolishness of God is wiser than men; and the weakness of God is stronger than men.*[45]* Where it is clearly stated that Christian preaching must seem *madness*, both to Jew or Gentile, to believer or non–believer, to insider or outsider. So much so that, only to the extent that it appears so, *it is authentic Christian preaching*. Without forgetting something that is also contained in the text and that could go unnoticed: only this type of preaching (apparent madness and weakness) carries with it, by paradox again, strength and wisdom: *Wiser than men... stronger than men...*

The scandal produced by Jesus, allowing Himself to be invited to eat by Matthew and mixing with the other publicans and *sinners*, has already been rolling through history for more than twenty centuries. While at the same time everything seems to indicate that the Church of the End Times has also been trying for too long to flee from scandal, on the one hand, and to ingratiate herself with the world, on the other. It seems that she has forgotten that Jesus said of His own that *they are not of the world; as I also am not of the world.*[46]

The modern Pastoral Laboratory seems to have forgotten that the desire to please, in and of itself, using, for example, flattery to others, is not only entirely useless, but is only capable of provoking —in those to whom it is directed— a feeling of self–sufficiency, or rather of false joy bordering on stupidity.[47] Authentic pleasure, or true joy, are never the consequence of self–contemplation —what and

---

[45] 1 Cor 1: 23–25.

[46] Jn 17:14.

[47] Such manipulations are usually known in ordinary language as *brownnosing*. The Merrian–Webster Dictionary defines it as to ingratiate oneself with; curry favor with. It is always, however, insincere and uninterested.

how many are the graces that an intelligent person can contemplate in himself?—, but the fruit of going outside to perceive a beauty *that is always there, beyond and outside the seer*. If perhaps we want to please others...; or better yet, if we want to lead them along the path of Authentic Joy, it is necessary to induce them to come out of themselves. Only in this way will they be able to perceive beauty and, consequently, to know and savor the taste of Perfect Joy, something promised to be achieved fully in our Homeland, but also as first fruits in our current earthly pilgrimage:

> *Scattering a thousand graces,*
> *He passed through these groves in haste,*
> *And looking upon them as he went,*
> *Left them, by his glance alone,*
> *Clothed in beauty.*
>
> ....
>
> *Let us rejoice, Beloved,*
> *And let us go to see ourselves in Thy beauty,*
> *To the mountain or the hill*
> *Where flows the pure water;*
> *Let us enter farther into the thicket.*[48]

As it always happens in Love, the lover's outing *towards the other*, the loved person, is mutual; and the same can be said of the consequent contemplation.[49] The Bridegroom is also ecstatic at the beauty of the wife:

---

[48] Saint John of the Cross, *Spiritual Canticle*. Note that the Saint–poet speaks in this last stanza of a reciprocal joy as a consequence and condition of the contemplation of beauty.

[49] The lover is both lover and beloved; and the beloved is both beloved and lover. Each is a *thou* for the other.

> *How beautiful you are, my beloved,*
> *how beautiful you are!*
> *Your eyes are doves.*[50]
>
> *How beautiful you are, my beloved,*
> *How beautiful you are!*
> *Your eyes are doves, behind your veil.*[51]

The joy, or the happiness, or the contentment, or where the culmination of oneself is perceived and savored, are only consequence and result of the contemplation of the beautiful.[52] Such contemplation, however, is only possible by each one exiting himself, in order to place himself in a position to direct his *gaze outwards*.[53] And this is how, once again, we are far from aerobic monitoring and even farther from *being yourself*.

Perhaps the most impressive thing about this narration, and surely the most important, is the fact that the Master, not only does not have a problem mixing with the *damned*, but even treats them with familiarity..., and even becomes as one of them: *The healthy do not need a doctor, but the sick... I have not come to seek the righteous, but sinners*. But claiming that He became one of them is not a hyperbole. When we study the conduct of the Lord, as narrated in the Gospel, we are often overwhelmed by the tendency to not value situations sufficiently, and therefore to consider them superficially. It becomes difficult for our limited understanding to accept that things are as they are; or that the truth is as hard and

---

[50] Song 1:15.

[51] Song 4:1.

[52] Or the perception of goodness. Although, as is well known, perceiving goodness and contemplating beauty are equivalent and the same thing.

[53] The so-called *lack of vision*, often blamed on people as a natural defect, is more the consequence of excessive selfishness than the result of poor intelligence.

Vocation of Saint Matthew

deep as it may sometimes seem. Even the opposite often happens: we do not want to, or cannot, understand what seems excessively sublime; since the wings of our hearts and our minds are not so capable of undertaking such steep ascents: *For my thoughts are not your thoughts: nor your ways my ways, saith the Lord.*[54] However, the most grandiose, in this specific case, is that Jesus, the good Master, considers an honor making Himself equally *cursed with the damned*. As the Apostle says in his *Letter to the Galatians,* echoing and quoting *Deuteronomy*: Christ has redeemed us from the curse of the Law, making Himself a curse for us, as it is written: *Christ hath redeemed us from the curse of the law, being made a curse for us: for it is written: Cursed is every one that hangeth on a tree.*[55]

Now, if His purpose, according to His own words, was precisely to heal the sick and call sinners (even looking for any place where they can be found, like the good shepherd searches for his lost sheep), then it is that He has come to meet us. And *particularly with me.*

And, again, the paradoxes of Christian existence. Difficult, and even impossible to understand, for those who do not open their hearts to the truth simply and humbly: *I praise you, O Father, Lord of heaven and earth, because thou hast hid these things from the wise and prudent, and hast revealed them to the little ones.*[56] Because, although the fact of knowing that I am a sinner could be a cause of deep sadness for me..., such sadness would be relative, however: bittersweet perhaps, and even somewhat joyous, since I am aware that this is precisely why He has come for me. It is even possible that, once found after a risky and difficult search, and as happened with the lost sheep, He will lovingly place me on His shoulders to

---

[54] Is 55:8.
[55] Gal 3:13, quoting Deut 21:23.
[56] Mt 11:25.

return me to the fold. Perhaps the Apostle intended to allude to something of this when he said, with an expression as profound as it is disconcerting and sublime, that *as for me, I will only glory in my weaknesses*.[57] Hence the hopeful and consoling plea:

> *If ere from thy side I flew,*
> *Search for me again, my friend, come look for me.*
> *And when you find me anew,*
> *Take me to the path, I plea,*
> *There where you first met with me and I with thee.*

But if my sins are for me a cause for tears, although softened by hope, my *damned* condition, on the contrary, has never saddened me in any way, or at least has never caused me excessive concern. Especially after having verified that the Master had no problem in interacting with this class of people; and even, as in the case of Matthew, in calling them to the apostolate. Because during almost all my long priestly life, in effect, I have been singled out, marked, and classified with the label of *damned*.

I still do not know in depth the reasons that may have led so many people to agree to assign such a qualificative to me. Nor have I been able, after so many years, to draw safe conclusions about whether to be sad, happy, or perhaps adopt a posture of indifference in this regard. The truth is that I do not think that my personal feelings matter too much, and therefore it is not worthy for me to take it into account.

From the data that has come down to me, however, for so many years, everything seems to indicate (although I would not dare to take it for certain) that what is alleged against me is my refusal to

---

[57] 2 Cor 12:5.

change. This will not be difficult to understand, provided that it is possible to reach an agreement about the nature of such a change. Because, what kind of change are we dealing here with? What exactly is it that I have not wanted to accept?

First of all, I consider it my duty to affirm here, solemnly and before God Who will judge me, that it is true that there are things about which I have not changed since my priestly ordination.

The first one is my love and fidelity towards the Church. In her I was born, by the grace of God, to supernatural life, and in her I grew and matured in that form of existence. With my gaze always fixed on divine mercy, which is what keeps me in the hope of dying also in what is for me the One and True Church. And I categorically affirm exactly the same with regard to my fidelity and obedience to my Shepherds, as well as to the teachings of the legitimate Magisterium.

I affirm before God that I do not remember a single case in which I have disobeyed my own Bishop, or the other Prelates to whom I have also been subjected for various pastoral reasons in various places. Nor have I ever carried out, not even in the slightest, any work or task without previously having the knowledge and approval of my hierarchical superiors.[58]

For this reason, I summon here whoever so desires, in a manner as solemn as affectionate, to point out a single case of disobedience on my part to the Hierarchy, or one in which I have deviated from the injunctions of the Magisterium.

Despite this, it is evident that I am in any case a declared and confessed *damned*. And it is that human nature —weak, but not

---

[58]Even when the mandates or suggestions went entirely beyond the realm of episcopal jurisdiction, I never objected to them in the slightest. As it happened when my Bishop told me of his desire to send me to South America to stay there for five years, which I indeed did.

always as bad as it may sometimes seem—, as everyone knows, is a fickle and capricious entity, little addicted to logic, and often more inclined to prejudice than to a serene examination of things. Taking this into account, as it should be, it is easy to conclude that there are no serious reasons for anger. As for the term *damned*, it responds to a globalized concept —using a fashionable word— in which anyone can include, indiscriminately, qualifications such as pre–conciliar, fundamentalist, conservative, old-fashioned, enemy of the Post–conciliar Springtime Renewal, and as many etceteras as you want. All are and will continue to be well taken by me, since I am convinced that each one of them will have some kind of misunderstanding at its basis. Actually, I neither want to believe in anyone's ill will, nor do I feel offended by anyone.

To somehow understand my case —if I am allowed to explain myself, at least to myself— I would have to do a bit of history. It all started, or so it seems to me, around the year 1958, coinciding with the death of Pope Pius XII. The words of his successor, Pope John XXIII, according to which *it was necessary to open the windows of the Vatican*, marked the beginning of the Great Change. It had to live that moment in history that divided two different worlds, which included in themselves two forms of the Church's existence that were also different. So much so that one might have been tempted to believe, in view of the torrent of events soon to take place, that the change had paved the way for the emergence of a new Church, different from the old one. Pure temptation, of course, since it is well known *by faith* that the Church is indefectible, in such a way that her perennialism is assured until the end of time.

I am aware that many adamantly deny that there has been such a change. Or else they openly acknowledge it —which is the case of the majority—, but in order to assign it a triumphalist and profoundly positive character. I confess, as regards the latter, that I would have liked to share such points of view, as optimistic as they are apparently hopeful; after all, just as it is true that one feels happier breathing the air of an optimistic world, it is also true, on the contrary, that it is painful to feel the anguish of living in a Society which seems to be walking blindly to its destruction.

Unfortunately, things do not always go as one would have wished. And if one's eyes are open to reality, animated by an honest and sincere intention of seeking and recognizing the truth, then there is no other way but to perceive things as they are.

In the desperate struggle to live faithfully to the Church, as well as to the principles on which I had been formed, I could hardly free myself from the feeling that many things *were now very different, and not precisely for the better.* In such a struggle I continue, after so many years, hoping from God's goodness for the grace to persevere in fidelity to the Church until my death. The task, however, is as difficult as the struggle is painful. The price to pay for standing firm, without giving in when it comes to principles that are known to be immutable, but at the same time remaining loyal and submissive to the legitimate Hierarchy?[59] Too high, of course: accepting the condition of being *damned* and suffer, day after day, the agony of having to contemplate a World that was Christian and that now ceases to be so. The disappearance of a People made up of sheep that, although at one time they belonged to Christ, have now abandoned the sheepfold confused, bewildered in a broken and destroyed flock, towards unknown directions and each one on their own. At the same time, one has to suffer the heralds of the *Springtime of the Church* proclaiming from the roof tops the triumphant moment, never known until now according to them, of the Bride of Christ.

---

[59] Needless to say, such submission and such loyalty are also part of the principles.

On top of it, there is not the slightest trace of a shadow of a Good Shepherd going to appear on the horizon, or anywhere, marching again in search of the lost sheep; although rather than speaking of the lost sheep, everything seems to indicate that the time has come to speak more properly of the loss of the entire flock.

Of course, I am aware of the invectives that I am going to deserve for expressing myself in this way... However, who said that bearing witness to the truth is ever a pleasant thing? Jesus Christ already alluded to this before Pilate, in the crucial moments of His Passion; and I do not think that Jesus' statement about truth was merely circumstantial.[60]

During the years that have passed from the Great Shift, as I personally call it, to the present times, much has happened in the Church. For instance, quite a few changes, often very important, and sometimes even in matters that were always considered fundamental or immutable. For many —perhaps the majority— such changes have meant steps forward, and for this reason they have always been quick to qualify those shifts as being of an eminently positive nature. Others, on the contrary, among whom I count myself, do not see it that way at all; rather we have considered them as the cause of the tremendous disaster that God, in His mysterious designs, has allowed to loom over His Church.

We have even spent many hours, and not a few years, reflecting on the problem. Always convinced that, in the tremendous effort to find a convincing answer, we had not yet fought to the point of bloodshed (Heb 12:4). Perhaps that is why we never managed to find the longed–for explanation; or perhaps simply because the loving designs of God must, by nature, escape our understanding,

---

[60]Saint Paul referred to this testimony by saying that Jesus had testified before the Roman Procurator His *bonam confessionem* (*Neo–vulgate*, 1 Tim 6:13).

and it cannot be otherwise. Be that as it may, we have been forced to abandon the answer, even without knowing it, within the framework of faith and trust in God. Quite sure, however, that the answer exists and that *God*, as they say, *is on it*.

Too many important things have undergone profoundly radical change. The indissolubility of the bond contracted in the sacrament of marriage, for example, was established by Divine Law and considered as such for twenty centuries, without the slightest hesitation or exception.[61] Now, however, divorce is widely practiced within the Church as something perfectly natural and convenient. Of course, it is not called by that name —such a thing would not be possible, given that Divine Law and more than twenty centuries of ecclesial practice are involved—, but rather it is merely an official declaration of the *inexistence or nullity of the bond*. There was no valid bond at the time of the celebration of the marriage, and therefore the sacrament cannot be considered to have existed. Seen in this way, it seems that everything runs along the paths of legitimacy and normality. The problem arises at the very moment when someone begins to reflect: Is it enough to change the name of an institution —in this case divorce— to keep it out of sight, despite the fact that, in any case, its essence and its existence remain intact? This is what the profane world has done with things like abortion, for example,

---

[61] The few and extraordinary cases contemplated, as an exception, by Revelation and by Canon Law do not suppose an argument against it. They actually refer to the so-called Pauline and Petrine Privileges, and to the situation of a *ratum sed non consummatum* marriage in cases that are reserved solely and exclusively to the Roman Pontiff. Taking into account their extraordinary exceptionality, they almost never meant something disqualifying the divine mandate of indissolubility.

which is now known as *termination of pregnancy* (examples could be multiplied and are well known).[62]

Another of the changes which occurred, which has plunged me into deep perplexity, refers to Ecumenism. But understand well that I speak of things that cause me perplexity, and not that they seem good or bad to me. *Doctores habet Ecclesia.* Since I have not been called to judge, neither is it my place to do so. I limit myself to exercising the right, inherent to any human being, to express my suffering at the contemplation of things that I do not understand and that appear to be promising misfortunes. Besides, there are no reasons for alarm: my feelings of confusion are tempered by trust and faith in God..., and in His Church. Having clarified this point, it is painful for me to recognize that what it always was, for those of us who were born and have lived in it for many years, the *Catholic Church* is now officially known, quite often, as the *Church of Christ*. Of course, it is the same thing, and both denominations are equally correct and legitimate. Therefore, there would be no reason to be alarmed... if it weren't for the fact that everything seems to indicate

---

[62] Among the abundant cases that I know of —more unfortunate than unlucky— is this one of an annulment granted to these spouses who had been married for more than twenty years and had many children. The husband later marries civilly, only to divorce shortly after and cohabit with who is now called another sentimental partner. I ask myself the following question: How is it possible that the corresponding Diocesan Curia considers itself to have sufficient authority (legal, moral, or whatever) to declare —officially!— that there was no marriage, despite the fact that more than twenty years have elapsed, and involving children? Has the investigation file been extensive enough, as well as efficient, as to ascertain the non-existence of the bond, in hindsight and after so much time has passed? And even if the time had been much shorter, is it not to be admired the incredible capacity for retrospective vision of such Diocesan Curiae? Unfortunately, I know of many similar cases, more than enough to regret that they contributed to the destruction of the Family in such an unfortunate way.

(the official and unofficial Documents and Speeches of High Hierarchs of the Church[63] always point in that direction) that the issue is related to the demands of modern ecumenism. Which seems to tend to recognize the *legitimacy and sufficiency of any Church, including non–Christian and even pagan "religions,"* in order to reach salvation. One thing is to say that the theological motto —recognized as valid in the Church for so many centuries— according to which *outside the Church there is no salvation*, although true, is of such profound and mysterious content that its exercise and mode of application only to God are known. And it is quite another to see the Catholic Church equated on an equal footing with other Christian Churches, with *foreign* religions, and even with esoteric and entirely pagan cults.

It is never advisable to judge intentions, even less so here. For my part, I have no hesitation in considering them good. But, apart from that, two delicate matters converge on this issue that *no one can honestly deny*. The first of these has to do with the fact that ecumenism has undergone a radical turn with respect to the orientations emanating from the Magisterium up to the Second Vatican Council. The new guidelines, I insist on it, are drastic and profound, and have nothing to do with nuances or questions of mere detail. Given the depth and radical nature of the change, it is undeniable that there is an apparent incompatibility between two different Magisterium operating at different historical moments. True, it is unnecessary to expressly recognize that there is only one legitimate Magisterium in the Church; but given the danger of confusion, it does not seem dishonorable either to humbly seek reassuring and comforting ex-

---

[63]Either with the character of private persons, or —more frequently— without ceasing to put at stake the institutional responsibility of their Senior Officials.

planations. Which would surely come, as reasonable prudence from sound Theology and the legitimate Magisterium seems to advise.[64]

The second delicate and important question refers to the fact that, even considering the new ecumenical orientations to be legitimate and opportune —apparently so contrary to those coming from the Magisterium up to the Second Vatican Council—, such a change of course has produced profound disorientation, and no small confusion, in the faithful as a whole.[65] Not a few people have placed all religions in a situation of parity, and even more have ended in a state of skepticism and even loss of faith. Evidently, their attitude cannot be justified, but this does not nullify how serious and alarming the situation is.

Another field of Pastoral activity and ecclesial life that has undergone a change, a rather radical one I would say and not merely profound, is that referring to the cult of the Saints. It is not a trivial matter, as some might think. For centuries on end, the simple and ordinary People of God paid fervent worship to men and women who, having heroically practiced the Christian virtues, were surely very close to God. Hence, they were also considered as intercessors and powerful allies, as advocates before the High One in the solution

---

[64]Explanations that could refer, it is to be assumed, both to the change in the policy of tactics and to the demands of the so–called *Dialogues*.

[65]Perhaps an important clarification should be noted here. The change in ecumenist policy is not based on, nor does it acquire its legitimacy from, guidelines emanating from provisions of Vatican II (which would have been contained in Documents or texts of a greater or lesser coercive nature). *Having emerged rather after the Council*, often following mere instructions from the Vatican Congregations or from their respective officials in charge (frequently expressed as mere statements to the Press), its value and legal scope are quite doubtful, in the best case. Not to mention its debatable opportunity. To put it more clearly: what many question are not in any way provisions or Magisterial declarations, but certain frameworks or machinations of Vatican policies.

of difficulties and needs, and even as bridges and shortcuts on the difficult path that leads to God. The Church proposed them to the Christian People as models, or as further proof that holiness —the perfect practice of Christian virtues— is not something inaccessible as long as God's grace and human generosity are involved. Logically, and as always happens with things that are too precious and even more so if they are proposed as models, saints were not abundant; certainly, it was not common to find them easily around any corner. The value of a diamond depends on its rarity, and almost solely on it, since its main use seems to be to satisfy human vanity. It is evident, however, that if precious stones abounded in number like tomatoes —to give a rather vulgar but true example— their value would drop rapidly to the ground and would almost disappear. For human nature behaves no differently.

In the times which, by the will of God, we have been given to live, the Church has carried out beatifications and canonizations in numbers far greater than at any previous time in its history. Pope John Paul II, during the long years of his pontificate, has beatified and canonized Servants of God in numbers far exceeding those canonized by all the Popes who have governed the Church for twenty centuries before him. As is logical, and as we have said above, it is not up to us to make judgments about any pastoral policy that the Hierarchical Church, at a given historical moment, may find appropriate.

However, we still have the right, which certainly corresponds to us as children of God, to express a concern that, on the one hand, respectfully submits to the dictates of a Hierarchy as the only one with the power to decide, on the other hand, feels overwhelmed by the possible consequences of an action that we consider —wrongly or not— the result of disastrous approaches. Nothing drives us other than the simple desire to provide a minimal contribution — perhaps of no value, and insignificant in any case— that may be able to contribute to the improvement of certain aspects of Pastoral activity.

It is easy to understand, both from simple common sense and from everyday experience, that if everyone is a hero, no one is a hero; or at least that nobody will recognize anyone as such. If it is perhaps objected that it is not everyone but almost everyone, the conclusion remains the same. The popular masses, like individuals, have their own peculiar psychology, which is simply based on the way human nature acts. If the number of saints were to become so abundant —and pardon the hyperbole— that there were many people who knew or treated a brother–in–law, a possible relative, or perhaps an upstairs neighbor who had been canonized..., it is quite likely that the idea of sainthood suffered a serious deterioration in the mentality of the people.

The Church has always presented the saints as intercessors before God for the Christian people, but also as gigantic heroes to imitate and look at with admiration. After all, people throughout the ages *have needed to admire and follow their heroes*. Human beings, and in a special way young people, require the incentive of the heroic, of the sublime and wonderful, so that it is proposed to them as an ideal. Humanity has always been guided by leaders; of one color or another, but leaders. Those of us who have dedicated our lives to Youth Ministry, for example, know the strength that the ideal, *almost* always seemingly unattainable, of holiness has at all times represented for young people. For what requires little effort, or costs little, inevitably will not be highly valued.

During his long Pontificate, Pope John Paul II made many trips, as everyone knows. In almost all of them, for pastoral reasons considered by him as opportune, he has celebrated innumerable beatification and canonization ceremonies. It is evident of course that, as Supreme Pastor of the Universal Church, he was in possession of the right to do so. The problem arises when other circumstances appear, apparently also worth considering or maybe not. At any rate, I do not believe that I am acting at all dishonestly when bringing them, with sincere respect, to the consideration of whoever proceeds.

It has been a centuries–old doctrine upheld by the Church that both beatifications and canonizations should be carried out with two well–defined purposes: to present to the Christian People the case of heroic virtues to imitate and admire, and that of supplying them with some intercessors to whom they can turn lovingly and trustingly. The saints were men (or women) like the others, and hence the importance of their testimony; but, due to the intensity of their love for God and their heroism in living the Christian existence, they made it clear that holiness was an ideal *as sublime and lofty as possible.* They also meant, at the same time, something like a wonderful mirror in which the greatness and magnificence of God were reflected, Who was the One Who made such things possible with His grace.

Lately, however, it has been difficult to avoid the idea that the elevation to the altars has been motivated by other reasons. I am referring to political or conjunctural reasons, which have almost always prevailed over those that I have just pointed out. The Pope made a trip to a certain country, often never or rarely visited by the High Hierarchs of the Church, and in which, on the other hand, either Catholicism was not valued in much esteem, or it was even the object of some form of persecution. A very appropriate situation to consider the convenience of elevating a son or daughter of the country to the altars. Unfortunately, and as we have said above, the true candidates for a well-deserved exaltation to that degree have never been abundant. Hence, sometimes, although the need to proclaim the presence of authentic virtues has been borne in mind, nevertheless their corresponding degree of heroism has seemed so doubtful as to require careful examination to perceive it.

It is quite possible that I am wrong in my statements, or, at least, that I let myself be carried away by such an excess of imagination that I ended up exaggerating. But there is also no doubt that, for example, throughout the history of humanity, there can be counted thousands upon thousands of women who have preferred to risk their lives rather than endanger that of their unborn child. The mentality of the simple People, even though it has always considered such behaviors as worthy of all praise, had never counted them among the number of those deserving of the sublime distinction of holiness. After all, it is what any woman who truly felt like a mother *would do*. This case has no more value than that of being an example of the many that could be brought up.

In reality, there are still compelling reasons to be considered, apparently at least more serious ones. Everything seems to indicate, from what one can see and reaches the public knowledge —again we walk along paths of probability—, that the Beatification and Canonization Processes have suffered a deterioration —manifested in their apparent loss of seriousness— in their juridical procedure and development. This result would seem a logical consequence that should have been considered if there was a prior determination to considerably increase the number of blessed venerated by the Church as such. It is easy to imagine that my knowledge of the case, as regards the Process of Beatification of Pope John XXIII, is limited to what is known through the media. Which, however, have published details as apparently and extraordinarily innocuous as they are indeed truly interesting. It would be worth examining some of them, as a paradigm and historical curiosity. It has been said, for example, that the Devil's Advocate[66] in the Process of Beatification of Pope John XXIII, adduced, as an objection to the possible sanctity of the Servant of God, the fact that the Pontiff did not dislike accepting a glass of champagne on big festivities. Something interesting, indeed, but without a doubt a fact that, if true, lacks seriousness. The life of Pope John XXIII was too intense and abundant in episodes of historical importance for the entire Church. Therefore, using such trifles as arguments —for or against—, while leaving aside the possibility of talking about serious things, seems to be an insult to the People of God, holders, after all, of the right to know the truth in matters of such transcendence. Let us be real, is there anyone in their right mind who dislikes a glass of champagne...? If the Juridical World and the Law, also within the Church, have reached such low levels then dangerous winds are blowing. Seriousness, truth, authenticity, sincerity, and honesty were always attributes inherent by nature to Justice and Law.

The Beatification and Canonization Processes were always well-known for their seriousness, scrupulosity, and probity. The Ecclesiastical Jurisprudence, as regards at least these matters, enjoyed a reputation of being more demanding than the Civil Jurisprudence. The alleged miracles, attributed to the Servants of God, were carefully examined by various Commissions, often made up of non-Catholic scientists, which took great care not to happily dictate the miraculous nature of a cure, for example. It was a fairly common practice that the Church let a good number of years elapse before proceeding to open a process of this kind; perhaps thinking that it is never bad to give way to a wide space for reflection, on

---

[66]Equivalent to the prosecutor in a criminal civil court.

the other hand always useful and convenient to learn more about the truth. Today, however, although it is reasonable to assume that such precautions —dictated by centuries-old wisdom— have not been disregarded, it is sometimes difficult for the simple faithful to avoid the impression that this is not always the case.[67]

There are reasons to think that, if we do not act with sufficient caution, we may witness the extinction, once and for all, of the devotion and worship always paid by the Christian People to the Saints.[68]

It is true that many things have changed. We numbered six hundred candidates to the priesthood in the *Tridentine* Seminary where I pursued my priestly studies during my youth. In the modern

---

[67]In the Process of Beatification of Pope John XXIII, there was talk of an apparition of the Pope to a nun whom the Servant of God had cured of an irreversible illness; perhaps cancer, it was hinted. Anyway, if we follow the information disclosed by the *media*, the pertinent Medical Commission ruled immediately after the definitive cure of the patient.

It is necessary to think, logically, that the Court had sufficient reasons to accept the miraculous nature of the cure and the authenticity of the testimonies. And yet, perhaps it is not dishonest to recall (with no intention of establishing any more relationship between one thing and the other than that of a mere change in policy or practical action) that, at least until now, a Commission of experts in Medicine had never rushed to declare a cure of cancer definitive. As for the apparition, and without doubting this one or others worthy of consideration, I personally have always been cautious when it comes to the testimonies of nuns who claimed any kind of supernatural visions, as the experience of a long ministerial life has taught me to do.

[68]In modern Spain there has recently been a fostering of *enthusiastic and crazy* local devotions to certain invocations of the Virgin Mary, popular pilgrimages to sanctuaries, and even the use of local forms of worship of saints that are quite reminiscent of pagan festivals. Everyone knows, however, that they are rather an interested racket of a folkloric nature, animated by Mayors of towns and Authorities of the Autonomous Regions, with the sole purpose of securing votes for the following elections.

Seminary that now replaces my old one, although I am not quite sure of the number, it seems that the candidates are no more than two or three dozen.

Many things have changed, indeed. And not always for the better. During my years of preparation for the priesthood, I was educated in an atmosphere of intense piety. Not everything was perfect then, as you can imagine. But in one way or another, with exemplary sincerity, those in charge of our formation strove to put into practice the traditional and constant doctrine of the Church. They instilled in us, for example, the pious practice of frequent confession, as the Magisterium had always taught so clearly. At present, on the contrary, I am aware of some Seminary where its Spiritual Director indoctrinates the aspirants in a very different sense: a single annual confession is enough, according to him, to fulfill the Sacrament of Penance. Faced with things like this, one cannot help but feel overwhelmed. For my part, I try to receive the Sacrament at least once a week approximately; but more often when I think it is necessary. And yet, I do not stop feeling a respectful fear for my salvation: *Initium sapientiæ timor Domini*.[69] Truly, it is amazing how liberated from concupiscence people feel today: as if original sin had never existed. Although it can also happen that the conviction that everything is admissible is latent here..., for those who do not believe at all in the existence of original sin. Consequently, let no one come now with the pretense of telling us that things have not changed, or that if they have, it has been to provide us with the gift of a flourishing Ecclesial Springtime.

It is possible, perhaps, that the most interesting thing about the evangelical narration that concerns us is the fact, almost surprising for many, that Jesus appears in it having the pleasure of alternat-

---

[69] Ps 111:10.

ing amicably with publicans and other sinners. I mean, with the *damned*.

As far as we are concerned, we have endeavored not to give up principles that were instilled in us as immutable. On the other hand, from the moment of our baptism, our life of faith has always held the unshakable belief in the indefectibility and immutability of the Church. None of us would have admitted that the Bride of Christ was, in any way, a reed moved by the wind (Mt 11:7). And at the same time also, within that same order of things, we have always professed as fundamental the principle of fidelity to the Hierarchy. The well-known fact that two apparently different things are equally important, does not mean that they are always easily reconcilable. Which has been exactly which, willy-nilly, we have been forced to experience in our own flesh.

The effort on our part to maintain these two fidelities at the same time, which in reality are one and the same, is what has caused us to be termed, by some who have not understood us, as *damned*. And that is how we have become, without intending or wanting it, the *bad guys* in the movie. Fortunately, that has not made us commit the mistake of considering ourselves as if we were the *good guys*, the misunderstood victims. Nor has God allowed us to fall into the stupidity of believing ourselves to be better than others: should that have been the case, we would have automatically passed from the group of the *damned* (publicans and other sinners around us) to that of the *bad-mouthed* or the goody-goody (Pharisees and others law enforcers).

Hence, faced with this strange and undesirable possibility, we are prepared to admit that, as far as we are concerned, we find ourselves at home in the group of the *damned*. Although we know that there will always be those who feel surprised by such a strange determination. There is no cause for alarm, however. In reality, everything is better understood when one also realizes that those who point their fingers at us, to classify us as unwanted, are surely acting in good faith; for one even supposes that they even do it thinking that they render a service to God (Jn 16:2).

In addition, we are fully satisfied with the situation in which we find ourselves. Right or wrong, we believe that because of it we are in some way the object of the sympathies of Jesus Christ. First of all because, according to His own words and as we have already verified in this narration, He had come to look for sinners and to heal the sick. Therefore, exactly for us. We came to think that it was worth being the lost sheep, if perhaps it was the Good Shepherd Who, leaving the rest in the fold, came looking for us and carried us lovingly on His shoulders. And that is not all, because there are also other reasons for joy. Here is one of them that is very important, for example, if we stick to what the Master had already said: *Blessed are ye when they shall revile you, and persecute you, and speak all that is evil against you, untruly, for my sake.*[70] The fact that those who act like this, to our disfavor, have not thought of using lies as an instrument, does not seem to matter too much. After all, they act in good faith... and so do we. On the other hand, all this happens to us, as Jesus Himself points out at the end of the text referring to Himself, *because of Him*; which leads us to the peace of mind that the text is not subject to any distortion.

If perhaps —it must be said— there is any reason that could be an occasion for sadness for us, it is the fact, difficult to understand on the other hand, that those who ordinarily do not understand us are not precisely strangers, *but our own brothers* (Mt 10:21; Mk 13:12;

---

[70]Mt 5:11; cf. 24:9.

Lk 21:16).[71] However, considerations capable of dispelling the bitterness immediately arise here as well: especially if one thinks that the condition of being *damned* is not only desirable, but even necessary to be able to intervene, as an active part, in the important business that is at stake here: one's own salvation..., and that of many others; the achievement of Perfect Joy for oneself, first of all, and then also for so many, a number that we cannot appreciate and that only God knows.

If someone is surprised by what I have just said, perhaps it is due to the mere fact that he has not reflected enough on what Christian existence consists of.

It is possible that we have not realized that the leading figures, both in Christian existence and in the entire History of Christianity, *were always graced with the consideration of the damned.*[72] This is precisely what happened, for example, with Saint Francis of Assisi. An extraordinary figure whom his own biographers, far from always treating him with sufficient historical rigor, have rather presented him as a singular man with an even more singular saintly fame; a near—fabulous miracle worker of spectacular virtues such as his poverty; a man of overwhelming and easy triumphs with massive conversions; an unhindered winner; a character pampered by the Church; a teacher admired and revered by his many followers; and perhaps much more. And, of course, we can take it for granted that many of these things, or perhaps most of them, are absolutely true. But what is undoubtedly true is that the core of the sanctity of the *Poverello* of Assisi does not reside in them. *The Saints were not such*

---

[71] Cf. also Mt 10:36, citing Mi 7:6.

[72] We have said outstanding figures. But let no one be fooled by that. Actually, the condition of being reviled and mocked is an indispensable attribute, to a greater or lesser degree, for anyone who wishes to live a true Christian existence (2 Tim 3:12).

thanks to the spectacular nature of their miracles, much less because they seemed to satisfy perhaps the expectations —supernatural or natural— of the men of their time; but because they shared in an eminent degree the Life and, even more so and above all, in the Death of the Lord.

Poems and *The Little Flowers* aside, the great truth about this is that the Saint's life was not easy. The Church herself, in addition to pampering and blessing his person, took good care to appoint Cardinals Protector for the Order he founded, who were in reality nothing but Moderators and practically Inquisitors, whose mission, as can be assumed, was none other than to channel the apparent excess of idealism of the Saint. Mother and Teacher the Church, as always. On the other hand, despite the growing number of his followers, not many understood either the spirit or the intentions of the Saint. The *Chapter of the Mats* meant his failure and the demonstration that the claims of the Seraphim of Assisi, regarding the reading and putting the Gospel into practice, were not followed by anyone. After many comings and goings, and despite the hopes of the Saint, in the end it was the Moderates, with Fray Elías at the head, who prevailed against the Founder. Saint Francis ended his life surrounded by the few disciples who remained faithful to him, naked on the hard ground as the best expression of the Poverty in which he had lived. Although the most tragic of his existence has to do with the stigmas imprinted on his body. Which, far from signifying a mere sacred and glorious symbol, actually consisted of deep and tremendous wounds, with the rivets of the nails included. They caused the Saint such physical pain and suffering, in addition to the consequent spiritual and moral anguish, that we can safely say that they made him share the Passion of Christ as few men have done in history.

However, the *damned* condition is even more palpable, if possible, in the person of Saint John of the Cross. Persecuted, imprisoned, and flogged by the friars of his own Order, the figure of the Holy Poet of Fontiveros is, in this sense, a clear symbol of the struggle between two different conceptions of Christianity. Or, if you also prefer, of the opposition of the two tendencies that fight for primacy in the human being: that of the light, or that which looks upwards, and that of the low man, which points towards the demands of concupiscence. What his brothers of the *Mitigated* Rule detested was the Saint's intention to maintain the integrity of the principles contained in the *Original* or Primitive Rule. In short, what took place there was nothing but another new confrontation between the Radicalism of the Gospel and the relaxation of the Half–measures. The radicalism of total Love against the lukewarmness of the mediocre. The New against *Quod traditum est*. What is unfathomable by the human mind and heart against what fits well within the narrow limits of man's reason.[73] As if the Evangelical Truth, always pure and well–endowed with defined edges, had something to do with the mixtures and compromises intended by those who, blind–minded and short–hearted, wish to convince themselves that they live the Gospel; but without ever deciding to definitively set aside worldly criteria and views: *For what participation hath justice with injustice? Or what fellowship hath light with darkness?*[74]

Everything apparently indicates that the terms of holiness and *damned* seem convertible. At least never the first without the sec-

---

[73] Gnosis is much older than Christianity. It is possible that it existed already since Ancient Times, perhaps since man lost his first condition of elevated nature. And always about the same issue: trying to smooth out the greatness of God's thoughts, in order to put them on a par with the minuscule entity of the human mind.

[74] 2 Cor 6: 14–15.

ond.[75] Fidelity to noble and elevated principles —whether in the world of the supernatural, or even in the realm of the purely natural— has never been well regarded by the World: *For I think that God,* said the Apostle, *hath set forth us apostles, the last, as it were men appointed to death....*[76] Someone pointed out that the same can be said about men as that which is said about Countries: happy are those who have no history. Perhaps it would be interesting to attach to that saying a new one, which is, however, as old as the life of Man on Earth: happy those who, having lost their sanity due to their determination to maintain the integrity of love, the world considers crazy. After all, the madness of God is wiser than men; and stronger than them is the weakness of on High (1 Cor 1:25).

---

[75] The historical case of Saint Robert Bellarmine is unique and extremely curious. The neo–modernists of the times after the Second Vatican Council, angrily considering, with retrospective vision, the work of the Jesuit Bishop, have seen fit to grant him the character and the condition of *damned* many years after his canonization. His main audacity consisted in considering the hierarchical constitution of the Church as Divine Law.

[76] 1 Cor 4:9.

THE RICH YOUNG MAN

(THE CHALLENGE OF THE EAGLES)

MEDITATION

(Mt 19:16 ff.; Mk 10:17 ff.; Lk 18:18 ff.)[1]

A questo invito vegnon molto radi:
o gente umana, per volar sù nata,
perché a poco vento così cadi?[2]

And when he was gone forth into the way, a certain man running up and kneeling before him, asked him: Good Master, what shall I do that I may receive life everlasting? And Jesus said to him:

---

[1] The text that we are going to comment on is a concorded narration which includes the complementary details provided by each one of the three synoptics.

[2] "A scanty few are they, who, when they hear such tidings, hasten. O, ye race of men! Though born to soar, why suffer ye a wind so slight to baffle ye?" (Dante, *Divine Comedy* Pg. XII, 87–90).

Why callest thou me good? None is good but one, that is God. Thou knowest the commandments. He (the young man) said to him: Which? And Jesus answered: Thou shalt do no murder, Thou shalt not commit adultery, Thou shalt not steal, Thou shalt not bear false witness. Honour thy father and thy mother: and, Thou shalt love thy neighbor as thyself. But he answering, said to him: Master, all these things I have observed from my youth.

And Jesus looking on him, loved him, and said to him: One thing is wanting unto thee: go, sell whatsoever thou hast, and give to the poor, and thou shalt have treasure in heaven; and come, follow me. And when the young man had heard this word, he went away sad: for he had great possessions.

Over the centuries, the innumerable commentators who have paid attention to this episode have found in it, or have at least had the opportunity to do so, an ambivalent meaning. Bittersweet perhaps, as we would surely say in today's language. Which seems logical since the narration lends itself to offering two (somehow) different conclusions. However, both sides of the episode, at first glance at least, seem contradictory: the invitation to a heroism capable of undertaking the most sublime of adventures, on the one hand; and the negative answer, fruit of petty cowardice, on the other. In spite of which, at a closer examination, the contradiction is more circumstantial than essential. What actually underlies the narration, as the most important element, is the greatness of Love and of divine designs, offered as a gift to man. That this issue is an occasion to make clear, in this case by contrast, the frequent pusillanimity of the human being does not manage to blur the excellence of the situation.

What is certain, however, is that we are facing the core of what has been the History of humanity, as it has occurred from its origins to the present day.

But the History of humanity has already passed through its own Center. A Culminating Point which, while dividing it into two parts, gives meaning to both: I refer to the coming of Christ, from which all things have necessarily been pigeonholed in the *before* or *after*. Without a doubt, an issue too important to be forgotten at any time. Since then, the eternal truth has been made manifest; namely: the Christocentric essence of the whole of creation.[3] Hence, this narration is eminently Christocentric, since it is also part of the Gospel. By which I mean that what prevails in it, bestowing upon it all its strength and meaning, is the figure of Christ as well as the magnitude of the call to the great adventure of Holiness: *One thing is wanting unto thee: If thou wilt be perfect, go, sell whatsoever thou hast..., and come, follow me.* The young man's reaction, however petty it may seem (indeed it is), and although it is a paradigm of a very common attitude among humans, can be considered here as purely conjunctural, without further significance. What counts in this evangelical episode, bathing with its blinding light the perception of anything else, is *the call to follow Him that the Master directs to those who have the heart to do so.* Or put another way, it is the call of Perfect Love to those who are capable of (understanding what it is) loving. In short, we are faced with the call to choose between two different possibilities: the one that leads to Perfect Joy, made

---

[3]This has nothing to do with the trifles and crazy daydreams contained in the theories of Teilhard de Chardin. It is hard to believe that such pantheistic vagueness, as empty of theological content as it is overloaded with cheap fantasy-fiction, has been able to deceive so many naive (and others less naive). Here we move, on the contrary, within the Pauline doctrine on this issue, contained above all in the *Letter to the Ephesians* and in the *Letter to the Colossians.*

accessible to those who respond affirmatively to the call..., or the one that ends by leaving forever, immersed in Sadness, those who decide to ignore such an invitation.

However, at least for this moment, the History of Joy is going to leave the History of Sadness submerged in the shadow of oblivion. For, although both are included within the scope of the narrative, the young man's refusal (with his consequent sadness) contrasts in such a way with what the received invitation implies and involves that the former becomes irrelevant. In fact, not even the name of the character has been preserved by history. Although it is true that a soft wind, materialized in this case in the so-called *riches*, can make weak human nature waver, and even fall down, what can that mean when compared with the extraordinary event to which it has been called, to fly up to the heights?

According to the narrative, the young man *ran* to where Jesus was, before Whose feet he fell to his knees. An unprejudiced mind will consider it normal for a young man to rush, even race, in order to reach the Master as soon as possible. Trying to achieve such a goal, one wonders if any other way of reaching it would be reasonable. And even more so when it comes to a young man, to whom the pertinent ideas of strength and victory are logically associated (1 Jn 2: 13–14). On the other hand, it is evident that the possibility of reaching the prize vanishes if one gives up the race (1 Cor 9:24)[4].And the need for rushing becomes even more evident when one is running, not without a definite purpose or at random —*quasi in incertum*: 1 Cor 9:26; cf. Phil 2:16; Gal 2:2—, but, as in the present case, to get to where Jesus is. In effect, it seems to the Bride of the *Song* that there is no other way to follow the Bridegroom but running: she feels so urgently driven by the force of love.

---

[4]Conf. Phil 3: 12–13.

Is it possible to think of a different way for the lover to go to where the loved one is? Hence, the enamored Bridegroom, protagonist of the sacred Poem, who wants nothing more than to sit next to and in the shadow of her Bridegroom (Song 2:3), turns to Him impatiently. For this is how lovers are driven to run, each to meet the other:

> *Draw me: we will run after thee!*
> *The king hath brought me into his storerooms.*[5]

For Love, in effect, only understands anxieties and haste.[6]

> *As the apple tree among the trees of the woods,*
> *So is my beloved among the sons.*
> *I sat down under his shadow, whom I desired...*[7]

As far as the search for the loved one is concerned, Love is not willing to admit even the idea of possible mistakes or deviations from the path, which could cause delays in the long-awaited meeting:

> *Shew me, O thou whom my soul loveth,*
> *Where thou feedest, where thou liest in the midday,*
> *Lest I begin to wander*
> *after the flocks of thy companions.*[8]

---

[5] Song 1:4.

[6] Usually, I write the word Love with a capital letter, not only when I refer to Substantial or Infinite Love, but also when it seems appropriate to highlight the idea of the entity and depth of the *love relationship* (disregarding here the fact that Love is always a relationship, which, as such, takes place between two); whether it refers to divine–human love, or even to simple human love. It is not necessary to clarify that we do not use the word *relationship* here in the precise sense used in the Trinitarian Mystery; unless we want to help ourselves with analogy.

[7] Song 2:3.

[8] Song 1:7.

The first stanza of the *Spiritual Canticle*, by Saint John of the Cross, begins with a painful cry of impatience, quite characteristic, on the other hand, of a love that suffers from the nostalgia caused by absence:

> *Whither hast thou hidden thyself,*
> *And hast left me, O Beloved, to my sighing?*
> *Thou didst flee like the hart,*
> *Having wounded me:*
> *I went out after thee, calling, and thou wert gone.*

The Bride of the *Song* also sighs impatiently in the absence of the Beloved:

> *I adjure you, O daughters of Jerusalem,*
> *If you find my Beloved,*
> *That you tell him that I languish with love.*[9]

And anxiety is added to impatience, for the two are always together and inseparable when it comes to Love. Saint John of the Cross, in his poem *Dark Night*, tells us about the anxiety that fed his soul with gentle ardor:

> *On a dark night,*
> *Kindled in love with yearnings,*
> *Oh, happy chance!*
> *I went forth without being observed,*
> *My house being now at rest.*

---

[9]Song 5:8.

The fact that it is a young man who swiftly approaches and asks the Lord about the way to attain eternal life, may not be occasional. Given the character of the episode, it seems normal that it is a teenager who is interested in inquiring about the best course to take for his existence. After all, it is young men who *have their whole life ahead of them*. And just as it is natural for old men to look more frequently towards the past, it seems logical that it is the young person who directs his eyes and his thoughts towards the future. Let us remember that the essential theme of this narration points towards the *beginning* of an adventure that assumes Perfect Love as its basis; as well as the necessary means to carry it out. It also often happens that, when it comes to matters in which Love is involved, it seems more in accordance with that virtue to attribute it to the young rather than the elderly. Later we will add important explanations that clarify this point and put things in their place. But now we are interested in underlining the fact that the protagonist of this narrative is a young man who seems to pursue a didactic purpose, rather concrete in this case, since all Scripture has no other purpose than to teach (2 Tim 3:16). The central character is also appropriately suited to the ideas that we have proposed to develop in this commentary, as we will see.

It is well-known that Love has no age and that It does not admit any before or after. It existed *before* Time appeared, when the inexorable march of the duration of everything created had *not yet* begun. Hence, it cannot be said that Love is the heritage of young people, as a too superficial vision of things might think, nor of anyone in particular for that matter. In reality, Love justifies Itself, it is governed by its own rules, and it does not need to seek a foundation in anything that is external to It. Love *loves because It loves*, because It wants to, and when It wants to: *The Spirit breatheth where he will; and thou hearest his voice, but thou knowest not whence he cometh, and whither he goeth.*[10] That is why it would be vain to claim that human Love is more adequately shown in the young than in the elderly. But rather the opposite happens. From the moment that Love is present in human existence, everything is ready for it to increase in intensity (Rom 5:5). And so it does until reaching a fullness known only to God, according to the measures determined by Him and freely decided for each human being (Eph 4:7). In this way, to mature in Love is to mature *in Christ*.[11] The Christian's existence is destined to reach the fullness of his consummation with Christ and in Christ..., although that consummation is only reached at the end of his earthly itinerancy. In this way, Christian death is not simply the last and definitive act by which man carries out his consummation in Love (for which he was created, existed, and lived), but it also supposes for him *the last opportunity to achieve it, since no other will be granted*. According to which, it could be said that the Love of the young man lives and feeds on hopes; looking towards a future which is to arrive and, consequently, always projected forward. While that of the old man, on the contrary, sinks its roots in realities already achieved, at the same time that he looks back; although not with nostalgia for things already lost, but with the joy of hopes that once were and are now present (Rom 8:24).

---

[10] Jn 3:8.

[11] An expression difficult to explain. It points towards the assimilation of the life of Christ in order to make it one's own, namely: to feel like Him, think like Him, and live like Him. All this until reaching a communion of lives that only Love is capable of achieving, and whose depth will only be fully understood in Eternal Life.

Everything happens so that *Charity never falleth away: whether prophecies shall be made void, or tongues shall cease, or knowledge shall be destroyed.*[12] *Now there remain faith, hope, and charity, these three: but the greatest of these is charity.*[13] Both forms of Love in Christian existence —that of the young person and that of the man who has consummated his earthly existence— although they are equivalent, therefore, to a beginning and an end of the path, they are always actualized *in the present*. Like faith and hope, which only become a true reality at the very moment that charity becomes present with them. Both forms or stages of Love in human life are ordered towards their fullness: from a consummation *in fieri*, which, because it is not yet, looks towards the goal, to a reality *in facto esse* that is already beginning to savor the Joy of the path traveled.

In this way, Love, in the Christian who is about to complete his journey, gives rise to a condition of serenity and calm; if it is possible to consider as calm and repose the possession, finally achieved, of the Beloved. Which takes place at the end of an itinerancy that has been forced to overcome all kinds of obstacles: suffering caused by sharing the life and existence of the Master, to which must be added the nostalgia produced by His absence and delay, and all sealed with a fidelity paid even with blood (2 Tim 4:7). We thus find ourselves before a final stage, in which all restlessness has finally led to a state of serenity and rest. It is the moment in which existence is already closer to the *already* than to the *not yet*:

---

[12] 1 Cor 13:8.
[13] 1 Cor 13:13.

> *I remained, lost in oblivion;*
> *My face I reclined on the Beloved.*
> *All ceased and I abandoned myself,*
> *Leaving my cares forgotten among the lilies.*[14]

The dialectic of *already* and *not yet*, a characteristic of Love as It is shared by man during his period of trial, acquires particular importance when considering the two forms of existence that we have been talking about: that of the Christian who is already at the end of the Path —closer to the *already*—, and that of the one who begins to travel the path that will lead him to the House of the Father —fully immersed in the *not yet*.

In this regard, Tolkien's Epic offers us two prototypical figures whose use can be beneficial, as a common thread, in our whole narrative. Both Bilbo and Frodo have had the same experience, and their encounter with the Ring of Power has forced them both to make a choice that has marked their lives forever. Such an encounter has not been by any means casual; neither is the option for or against

---

[14] Saint John of the Cross, *Dark Night*. We stumble again upon the insufficiencies of human language. To speak of rest, in a situation in which Love is perfect for having reached its consummation, seems incongruous. However, the expression contains in this case only part of the truth, and not the most important. Since Love consists in an overabundance of life, it supposes the most perfect Act that can be imagined in terms of intensity of existence, which goes for both Lovers. Mystical Theology has always made it clear, with respect to contemplative prayer, that it can only occur in the context of a situation of complete passivity on the part of the creature. However, if one takes into account the notes of reciprocity and bilaterality always present in Love —without forgetting either the moment of *intense and most abundant life* that floods the human being in contemplative prayer (Jn 10:10)—, it is difficult to accept (at least without numerous nuances) such passivity. Another thing is the presence of grace, of absolute necessity, on the part of the creature, and of total gratuitousness on the part of God.

Love, which every man who comes to this world must ineluctably decide to take.[15]

As far as our case is concerned, Bilbo has already completed his Journey with the Ring. For a long time, after having found it, he was its Bearer and Custodian. And it does not matter now that the responsibility for his finding (which to Bilbo appeared to be entirely casual) is to be attributed to the will of the Mysterious Object. The encounter with his Destiny is always unexpected for man. How could he imagine that he had been freely created by Love and for Love? Nor could Frodo ever have thought that he would be the next Ringbearer. Indeed, the End to which the human being has been destined exceeds any previous possibility of imagination, understanding, or desire, on the part of the creature. That man meets Love at a well–determined moment of his existence is only due to the fact that *Love loved him first* (1 Jn 4:19). Although what is truly decisive here is the alternative before which Bilbo now finds himself: either he definitively detaches himself from the Ring..., or else he keeps it indefinitely in his possession. Which is by no means an easy decision. Since the Ring has taken such a strong hold on his mind and heart, and it is almost part of his nature now. Getting rid of the Ring means for Bilbo tearing his being apart, even though

---

[15]In Tolkien's epic, it is the Ring itself that decides such an encounter, with a view to carrying out its purposes. As for the human being, created to love and to be loved, it is Love that induces him to make a choice, waiting for a response in which Love is accepted or rejected in complete freedom. What is really important here is not the non–existent alleged parallelism between the Ring of Power and Love, but the existence of a superhuman Destiny before which man has to choose, in an inescapable way: created by and for Love (as a free being, therefore), man cannot escape the option of opening or closing himself to Love's requests.

he understands that he *must* do it.[16] By deciding against the Ring, however, he has led his decision in favor of the Light (the Ring, as well as an option in its favor, is an instrument of Evil, for it belongs to the Dark Lord, or Lord of Darkness), which is tantamount to saying that he has taken sides in favor of the Good.[17]

As for Frodo, he too is faced with the need to decide the course of his existence for or against the designs of the Ring. His agreeing to embark on a long and dangerous journey through the unknown, which will culminate in the destruction of the Ring of Power, means nothing but his determination in favor of Love. The circumstance that the Ring feels identified with Frodo's decision adds, however, a new element of mystery to the situation. Although everything is better understood, in a certain way, when one realizes that the possibility of using the Bearer to achieve its own ends fits into the Ring's designs; which are none other than to return to the hands of its Owner, the Dark Lord. It is difficult for Evil to imagine that someone would decide to choose in favor of Good; even so outright as to shut out any possibility of corruption.

A possibility which, despite everything, is very real. And yet it is the only thing capable of endowing the undertaken task with the character of Adventure, even of sublime Adventure. The reality

---

[16]The option in favor of Light or Darkness is sharp and inflexible, as it is the decisive alternative in which there is no other way out than to choose in favor of Love..., or its opposite, Unlove. Ultimately, what is at stake here for man is the possibility of accepting, or rejecting, with full and free will, the ineffable Love that is offered to him. And since Love and Unlove are opposite sides of the same coin, the rejection of the first is what allows the second to acquire strength and hardness similar to those of the first: *Because love is strong as death...*, although it is no less true that *jealousy is as hard as hell* (Sg 8:6).

[17]In the New Testament, and especially in Saint John, the repeated Light/Darkness dichotomy is parallel and equivalent to the existing opposition between Good and Evil.

of the danger is precisely what forcefully and definitively outstrips the risks that wait on the road of the Adventure. This is how the human being remains open to the possibility of experiencing pain and anguish in all its forms, including death. And for the Christian specifically, that is what imprints on his Adventure the character of a real participation in the existence, in the sufferings, and, of course, in the death of his Lord.

No one has ever seriously said that man's itinerancy during his earthly existence runs along an easy path. *The life of man upon earth is a warfare.*[18] As for the Christian, the Lord spoke clearly enough about the steep and narrow path. That is why both Bilbo's Adventure and Frodo's Adventure are imbued with a profoundly human insight It is no coincidence that Bilbo, despite his determination, feels hesitant and resists parting with the Ring; he even at one point tries desperately to get it back. Even Frodo himself, at the climax of his Adventure, feels powerless to destroy it.

It becomes clear, then, that the encounter of man with Love — some would say with his Destiny— implies a series of factors that cannot be ignored: the forcefulness of its acute realism, the intensity and decisive strength of the invitation that is offered, and the logical and inexpressible anxiety which accompanies a consequent expected response. All of which come with the call that Love directs to the human beings that inhabit the World. And yet we must never forget that they are real human beings, in their present state of fallen and repaired nature. The summons to Adventure, with the offer made by Love, is quite clear. The answer will be rejection or perhaps acceptance. But, in the latter case, *the realization of the Odyssey*

---

[18] Job 7:1. Itinerancy only takes place during man's sojourn in the present eon. Once he has arrived at the Homeland, definitively reaching his own End, walking no longer makes any sense: *But hope that is seen, is not hope. For what a man seeth, why doth he hope for?* (Rom 8:24).

will have to take place through an extraordinary series of vicissitudes, many of which will also often be extraordinary.

We see it clearly in the events that followed the vocation of the first followers of the Master. They generously gave up their trades, definitively abandoned the fishing nets, the tax office, other occupations, as well as their families..., to become true fishers of men. Or so it was at least at the beginning of the Adventure, because soon the difficulties began. Saint Peter, for example, who did not quite understand the mission that the Master had to carry out, felt his faith and trust in Him waver on several occasions, even going so far as to publicly deny their mutual relationship at the decisive moments of the Passion. While already Head of the Church, he was admonished by Saint Paul. And it even seems that in Rome he tried to save himself from Nero's persecution, if tradition is to be believed. As for the other Apostles, things were not always easy or praiseworthy either: like Peter, they also failed to fully understand their Master, they contended about who would occupy the most important positions in the future Kingdom, and even allowed their ridiculous feelings and fears lead them to run away at the moment of the Passion. Each one of them resisted believing those who seriously affirmed that Jesus had risen, and several of them even became convinced at some point that everything had ended: *Nos autem sperabamus...*, said the disciples on the road to Emmaus.[19]

It would be unfair to think that all these actions should be considered as the result of human misery and a consequence, ultimately, of guilt and sin. Human defectibility is attributable to the weakness of nature, although not always mediated by imputability. The human will is fragile and quite often in need of energy, but for that reason it should not always be blamed. Peter, for example, had al-

---

[19] Lk 24:21.

ready been warned by the Master; with a warning, however, that, at least in this case, seemed to be animated by affection rather than by the desire to recriminate him: *Amen, amen I say to thee, when thou wast younger, thou didst gird thyself, and didst walk where thou wouldst. But when thou shalt be old, thou shalt stretch forth thy hands, and another shall gird thee, and lead thee whither thou wouldst not. And this he said, signifying by what death he should glorify God.*[20] And Jesus Christ Himself, Who *was never Yes–and–No; his nature is all Yes...*,[21] also experiences those moments so peculiar —and at the same time so sublime— that so characterize human nature (Mt 26:39). Pain and suffering, which once entered the world as punishment and continue to be a source of fear for man, have now been transformed and given the possibility of *becoming even glorious.*

In the present stage, *if things were not so, the Great Adventure would never be possible for man; and there would be no point in calling him to it, because the Cross would not exist either. In this way, God used human weakness to display His own strength: His very own; and later, or at the same time if you wish, He made it also, as a generous extension, that of man.*

In our narration today we find ourselves before a clear invitation to undertake the *Great Adventure*. An expression that we use here intentionally in order to avoid using the word *vocation*. We refer, of course, to the call to holiness, or to the following of Christ in totality. Although it is well known that the term vocation, whose meaning appeared loaded with seductive meaning, both attractive and challenging, for the youth until the middle of the twentieth

---

[20] Jn 21: 18–19.
[21] 2 Cor 1:19.

century, lacks any standing in the post–Christian society in which we live.

In any case, we will try to show that the elements that appear in this narration, as it always happens with the Revealed Word, are likely to lead us to conclusions as interesting as they are illuminating.

First of all, it should be noted that it is, as we already know, a call from perfect Love, addressed to any human being and which is waiting for a consequent response. However, the fact that the subject to whom the invitation is addressed in this case is precisely a young man cannot be considered, according to what we have said before, as merely coincidental. After all, it is an invitation to embark on the Great Adventure. Which, by definition, seems to be from the beginning a risky, long, and difficult one, promising unpredictable events. It seems logical, therefore, that it be proposed to someone who has the energy of youth and who, precisely for this reason, *sees his life moving forward and ready to begin.* The arduous and challenging, *about to be undertaken, and which also predicts an indefinite duration,* is undoubtedly for young people.

Surely there will be someone who wants to recall here that the *universal call to holiness* is addressed to all men, as follows from the obvious meaning of the expression. Which is entirely true. However, the harsh reality clearly proclaims that not everyone answers that call. Rather the opposite happens, since it is only listened to by a minority who, on the other hand, are increasingly reduced. So, I would almost go so far as to say that universality as such only finds a place here in the world of ideas: when someone echoes it, it becomes, by the very act of acceptance, *a particular and eminently personal call.* It is true that God has offered His Love to *all men* (1 Tim 2:4) through Jesus Christ; although it is also true that *many are called, but few are chosen.*[22] For the rest, we are talking about the invitation to perfect Love while waiting for a generous and resounding response. But the call, or the whisper of Love, is something delicately personal, demure, and effusively intimate, as it is addressed to the loved one and only to her and excluding all others and everything else. It is always this way with Love.

> *Shew me, O thou whom my soul loveth,*
> *Where thou feedest, where thou liest in the midday,*
> *Lest I begin to wander*
> *After the flocks of thy companions.*[23]

On the other hand, the Gospel mentions a situation similar to the one we are commenting on. The two most relevant facts of our narration are also underlined there. On the one hand, the invitation is addressed to young people; on the other hand, the warning about the riskiness of the undertaking is not forgotten either: *Can you drink the chalice that I drink?* Jesus' rebuke to the brothers James and John (Mk 10:38) and its context leave no room for doubt that this is a truly risky undertaking. And so it is, in effect, because the expression *drink the chalice* speaks for itself, as we will see immediately.

Both situations share other similar characteristics which can go unnoticed despite their importance. Jesus Christ, for example, when he confronts both the Rich Young Man and the sons of Zebedee, addresses them *directly and decisively.* He speaks to James and John in an almost recriminatory tone: to sit on my right and on my left in my Kingdom...? You don't know what you ask for! *Can*

---

[22] Mt 22:14.
[23] Song 1:7.

you drink the cup that I drink...? On the other hand, this and no other is the normal way for the Master to behave when it comes to candidates to follow Him: *Consider that the foxes have holes, and the birds of the air nests; but the Son of man... to bury your father? Let the dead bury their dead. To take leave of your family? No man putting his hand to the plough, and looking back...* Since the pleas are so reasonable, Jesus' answers cannot be more forceful and expeditious.

With regard to the Rich Young Man of our narrative, Jesus Christ immediately addresses the issue directly. Of course, now it is not about *being good* anymore, not even of attaining eternal life; at least not in the way the young man had imagined it: *Why callest thou me good...? You still lack one thing... If you want to be perfect...* Evidently the boy questioned Jesus Christ about what mattered most to him, what we would call his own interests: his eternal salvation. But as much as the theme is granted all the transcendence and importance that it truly has, it is nevertheless clear that the young man *had not yet come out of himself* and that, therefore, he had not understood much about *the only important thing.*[24] Hence the radical nature of the proposal that is addressed so lovingly —and also so defiantly— to him: You are still missing one thing. *One thing is wanting unto thee: go, sell whatsoever thou hast, and give to the poor; and come, follow me.* What is proposed here is nothing less than an invitation to renounce one's own life, which is the same as saying to *lose it completely.* Without forgetting that the various evangelical texts that speak of losing one's life (even

---

[24]The fact that the possibility of getting rid of his riches had not crossed his mind, as the text goes on to say, shows that he had not understood too much about Love. The sharp and radical invitation addressed to him by Jesus Christ deals, instead, with putting things in their place and directing them to the true path.

if it is for love) must be interpreted in a radical and profound sense. And so, for example, the very expression of losing one's life must be understood *in all the plurality of its connotations and meanings.*

We are already very far from any superficial aspect, however minimal, that could be attributed to the proposal we are dealing with. We are talking seriously. When it comes to following His Person —and even more so when, as in this case, it is about following in totality—, Jesus Christ does not hide the painful aspects involved or circumstances that could further exacerbate the difficulty of the situation: *If they persecuted me, they will also persecute you;*[25] and even more poignantly and radically: *Behold, I am sending you out as sheep in the midst of wolves.*[26]

It is evident that the modern, happy, and smiling Vocation Ministries understand little about the task that they have to carry out. First of all, because they have not taken charge of the psychology and way of being of the Youth. This, in turn, has prevented them from realizing the nature of the procedures followed by the Master. Although we will insist on this later.[27]

The Rich Young Man narrative of the Gospel contains an important depth of meaning that often escapes traditional interpretations. Of course, that is what always happens with the Word of God, capable of transcending at all times the narrowness of the human mentality and the passage of time and the diversity of places (Lk

---

[25] Jn 15:20.

[26] Mt 10:16.

[27] To be more precise, it should be said here that the fact that modern Vocational Pastorals have not been developed properly is not due to having misunderstood youth psychology and, therefore, to not having assimilated the pastoral procedures practiced by the Master. The order to follow in this case is rather the opposite: because they have not understood Jesus Christ, they have not been able to understand the Youth either.

21:33; Heb 4:12). As for the issue at hand, it has been the standard, for centuries, of the call that Jesus makes to someone to follow Him; of the Master's attitude towards the young; of the possible selfish reactions to that invitation motivated by attachment to the things of this world, etc. However, *the event is capable of being interpreted in even deeper layers of thought.* This is not to say that we are dealing here with a mystery too difficult to penetrate. In reality, the texts are clear enough, or at least it seems so, to allow the drawing as a whole picture of the theme. In short, a *puzzle* which does not appear to be too complicated; albeit disturbing.

What is at stake here is a challenge whose depth is beyond all measure and beyond all possibility of understanding, both by the human mind and the human heart alone.[28] *Because what Jesus Christ proposes to the Rich Young Man is actually an amazing and daunting challenge.* And the same could be said of His direct challenge to the sons of Zebedee by the question He puts to them. The invitation addressed to a simple human being, weak by nature, to share the appalling tragedy of the destiny of Jesus Christ, *is an unfathomable mystery as tremendous as it is fascinating.* Calling it an impressive challenge, or an overwhelming challenge, is but another demonstration of the insufficiency of human language.

If we admit that the central theme (really the only one) of the episode is none other than the challenge of following of Jesus Christ with a total commitment, what we have just said is quite expressive. It is worth clarifying, however, that what is at stake here is not the universal call to holiness, but the vocation to follow Christ in order to share His life in its entirety. More specifically, it is a vocation

---

[28]Everything is clear when the texts are read with enough humility as to allow the light of faith to do its work. Actually, this is the correct placement of the pieces of the puzzle which we have talked about before.

to the religious or priestly life.[29] But there is more to this topic. Hence the convenience of bringing up details and nuances which, despite their importance, could go unnoticed. It is worth insisting, with respect to what follows, that here we are going to keep mainly to the topic of the priestly vocation.

The role to be played in the world by the priest has never been an easy task. As minister and witness of Jesus Christ, continuator and doer of His work, the destiny of the priest cannot ever be other than those of his Master. And that is not all. It is not enough to admit that the priest is a minister, witness, or continuator of the mission of Jesus Christ...Nor is it enough to recognize that he acts *in persona Christi* (unless it is made clear that his intimate nature lies in the factual reality of being *alter Christus*). If a faithful, by virtue of being a Christian, accepts to live the existence of the grain of wheat that dies in the earth to bear fruit (Jn 12:24), no one like the priest is called to carry out in himself that destiny.

However, towards the middle of the last century (the times of the Second Vatican Council and those that immediately followed), the growing paganism unleashed in society, with the consequent secularizing and anti–Christian spirit that spread everywhere, made riskier

---

[29]The so–called *religious life* in classical language is characterized, as is well known, by the practice of the three evangelical *counsels*, always considered by the doctrine as different from the evangelical *precepts*. Without dwelling too much on terminology here, nor on the classical theme, it is worth remembering that our issue does not point so much to the general call to holiness as to the vocation to total following. Of course, the latter presupposes the former. But the invitation to holiness is for everyone; and we have already said above that human maturity —not to mention maturity in Christ— is more typical of the end of life than of its beginning. It seems normal, however, that when it comes to *undertake* an adventure, as in the present case, the project is proposed to those who are in the *not yet* —that is, to the youngest— rather than to those who are closer to the *already*. Later we will expand more on this important topic.

the acceptance of the challenge required for priestly existence. Perhaps for this reason, the arrival of the *Springtime of the Church* after the Council, promised and long awaited with a great outpouring of optimism, coincided with the appearance of two events of enormous implication in our case.[30] I am referring to the *Promotion of the Laity* and the everywhere–heralded *Crisis of Priestly Identity*.

For mysterious reasons that are not the case at hand (and which we have discussed at length and in detail elsewhere), theologians and people belonging to the clerical world decided that laymen should be *promoted*.[31] And even worse, since things did not stop at that. The fact was that the much–heralded promotion seemed to have come at the cost of the recognition and dignity of the ministerial priesthood. But we have already said that it is not for this place to talk about the subject: let us just remember that the *equalization* or recognition of the rights of the laity, until now *oppressed*, was carried out according to the typical Marxist socializing style: not through the procedure of climbing up by those below; but through the most expeditious and easy way of bringing down those above.

In short, and to summarize the problem: the clerical establishment, which despite so many vicissitudes of history had been enjoying, at least in recent times, a certain status of prestige, came to be confined to a situation of oblivion, if not of vexation and contempt

---

[30] The phenomenon is much more complex, and it is not possible to understand it in its entirety by merely analyzing these two symptoms. Although there is no doubt that both were the ones that most clearly influenced the appearance of the crisis. Here it would be necessary to refer also to the influence of Protestant theology, for which, as is known, the ministerial priesthood is absorbed within the common priesthood of all the faithful.

[31] The curious thing is that the laity had never been aware, until this moment in history, of the state of misery and prostration in which they found themselves, according to the opinion of the innovators.

(even by prominent elements of the Church herself). It was then that the Great Desertion of thousands of priests and religious took place while, at the same time, ideas were given sway that questioned the role and usefulness of the priesthood.

In short, and to summarize the problem: the clerical establishment, which despite so many vicissitudes of history had been enjoying, at least in recent times, some prestigious *status,* came to be confined to a situation of oblivion, when not of vexation and being despised (even by prominent elements within the Church herself). It was then that the Great Desertion of thousands of priests and religious took place, while, at the same time, the role and usefulness of the priesthood was questioned.

The result of the described situation (of which we have made here but a very brief summary) was that the difficulty of the challenge increased exponentially. Where could young men capable of accepting the call to the priesthood now be found? Who would be willing to be part of a class whose usefulness had been questioned, at best, and whose surviving members were in disarray?

If we are to confront the problem in all its realism, without concealing its seriousness and severity, the following should be added in relation to the current moment: *The situation during this first decade of the twenty–first century continues to be the same or even more serious. Not only are there no signs of a favorable change in the more–or–less near future, but rather signs of worsening appear everywhere.* Which leads us to draw some important conclusions.

Although before exposing them we must clarify that we start from a real base. By which we mean that here we dispense with propaganda statistics and demagogic proclamations. The vocation to the priesthood today is far from appearing as a sublime and risky adventure. Quite the contrary. Or better yet, because it may seem riskier than sublime, being willing to undertake it today supposes nothing less than consenting to being part of a despised, humiliated, and persecuted state: *harassed as useless, obsolete, and impossible to come together with the drive and dynamism of the new times.* Something that today's young people will have to take into account.

And yet, this is what gives our episode its importance and depth. Since the Master was not unaware of the timeless circumstances which surround the priestly vocation,[32] the invitation addressed to the young man contains a profound challenge (valid for all times) impossible to imagine. The words then acquire a meaning which we could describe, without hyperbole, as terrifying: *Go, and sell what you have, give it to the poor, and then come and follow me.*[33]

The Bible (which contains the perennial actuality of the Word of God) has been written, in different and distant times, by human authors of different character and styles and for very different circumstances. This explains the variety and diversity of the so–called literary genres. The whole set, however, is concerned with the salvation of man; and all the books that make it up recognize the Holy Ghost as the main Author and sole Person responsible for their au-

---

[32] What the affirmative response to the vocation implies, along with the open willingness to embrace all its consequences, adapts itself to all places and moments in history. Each factor determines the mode, manner, and character of the difficulties of the enterprise, which will always be as important, difficult, and painful, as well as impossible to overcome if the help of grace did not intervene.

[33] Other well–known, similar texts could be added here: *Can you drink the chalice that I have to drink?... Let the dead bury the dead... Say goodbye to the family? The one who puts his hand to the plow, and looks back...* Which, on the one hand, confirm the meaning of the words addressed to the Rich Young Man; on the other, though, delve into the deep and *tremendous* scope of the invitation (which practically coincides with the text we are commenting). What is being proposed here is too risky an adventure: the most challenging and difficult one that human beings have ever known or imagined.

thenticity and inerrancy. The common thread is always the same: the story of divine Love offered to man and the expectation of an affirmative response in reciprocity. An easy trail to follow through the complex fabric of a variety of styles that sometimes involve a strange and curious heterogeneity.

The blunt and challenging invitation of Jesus to the Rich Young Man (like others of the same style contained in the Gospel), is a requirement to take part in an authentic tournament of Love: Do you dare to follow Me and share My existence? And, again, the insufficiency of human language, for what is meant here is something deeper and more complex than mere *sharing*. This word implies the idea of two beings following parallel or similar destinies leading to the same end, *but which are always two destinies that in turn lead to two lives that are also different*. What is at stake in this case is a more complex, mysterious, and of course, loftier reality, which could be described, in a vain attempt at simplifying things, as *living the same existence or the same life* by two who love each other. It would be like a communion of lives, capable of making both of them one heart and one soul. But, since we are referring to the mysterious reality of Love, we are in danger of misunderstanding the terms and confusing metaphors with realities.

Communion of lives, therefore, with one heart and one soul. But beware, because we have already said that the language of Love tends to interpret metaphors literally, with the consequent risk of giving rise to naive confusions that have nothing to do with the reality spoken about.

It is important to insist here that there are two *different persons*, namely, the respective singularity of the *I* and the *thou* of those who love each other; which is, with regard to divine–human love, and even merely human love, an analogical derivation of what in Trinitarian Theology is called the *opposition* of the Three Persons. The communion or *assimilation* of lives, and the total *differentiation* of persons are the two necessary elements, as complementary as they are (apparently) contradictory, which make possible the most mysterious and sublime of all realities of the Universe: Love. It is not difficult to realize that the first of the two terms —the *assimilation* of lives— requires an explanation (which does not promise to be simple) about the sense in which it is to be understood; as for the second —the *differentiation* of persons—, it is enough to stick to its strict meaning. Hence, the essence of human love, and even more so that of divine–human love, is but a projection or (analogical) participation in the Trinitarian Mystery.

We have already said that the communion or assimilation of lives is a reality that is difficult, if not impossible, to explain, for we are facing here the unfathomable Mystery of Love. The fact that the creature has been called, by free design, to participate in the ineffable reality of Divine Life does not detract from the character of mystery in that participation. Actually, we move here within the realm of a deep and inexpressible truth: the human being has been granted to participate in the greatest of mysteries, that of Divine Life.

But let us examine the Pauline text of Galatians 2:20: *Vivo autem iam non ego, vivit vero in me Christus*. The two terms of the first hemistich seem to compose a perfect aporia: *I live*; however, *it is no longer I who lives*, since it is Christ Who lives in me. According to these words, does the apostle Paul live his own life or has he lost it entirely to give way in himself to the life of Christ? In what sense are the Master's words to be interpreted: *Qui autem perdiderit animam suam propter me et evangelium, salvam eam faciet?*[34] Obviously, whatever interpretation is to be given to the Pauline text, the two terms with which the verse begins, apparently contradictory, *must be taken in a strong sense*; *both of course*. By this I mean that the affirmation that *it is I who lives* must be understood in as real and proper a sense as the statement *it is Christ Who lives in me*. If the first statement is stressed (taken in its strict literal sense), any semblance of pantheism is dispelled. It remains to explain the meaning of the second (the living of Christ in the apostle), which is what the core of the mystery points to and what should be addressed primarily. Another

---

[34]Mk 8:35.

expression of Jesus Christ makes us face the same problem: *Qui manducat meam carnem et bibit meum sanguinem, in me manet, et ego in illo.*[35] How is the expression *abides in me and I in him* to be understood?

It is worth insisting that, first of all, we must put aside the fantasies of false mystics and false theologies. To speak of the identification of the soul with God, or of the loss of one's own self in the divine essence, etc., is beyond absurd and aberrant. In the first place, they are an attempt against the very concept of Love by eliminating the differentiation of persons (*opposition*, although the term must be understood in an analogical sense when the creature is involved). Needless to say, with respect to creatures, it would be inappropriate to speak of differentiation between persons as a *relation of opposition*. The recourse to the concept of analogy should be used here with caution since we are dealing with a theological term —the relation of opposition— with exclusive application to the Trinitarian Life. However, when it comes to the love relationship (whether one speaks of divine–human, or merely human, love), there is no doubt that there is a certain *opposition* of the *I* and the *thou*; precisely what is necessary to establish the relationship of reciprocity and bilaterality that is essential in Love: that which makes the two who love each other contemplate each other in an ecstasy of admiration, that they relate to each other with loving compliments and caresses, and that each one of them, in short, *comes out* of himself to *give himself* to the other. In any case, it should be borne in mind that it is the Lord Himself Who establishes a relationship of similarity between the identification of His life with that of the Father, on the one hand, and the life of the disciples with His own, on the other (Jn 14: 20). Admitting any possibility of composition in God or with God, or that of the creature turning into God, is as deplorable as the attempt to destroy the very concept of Love: without plurality and real distinction of persons there is no Love. But God, however, is Love (1 Jn 4:8). And what would really be ineffable about the fact that I stopped being myself to lose myself in God? How could I love Him if I didn't see Him as other than myself? How would I be able to love Him if I stopped being me? How

---

[35] *He that eateth my flesh, and drinketh my blood, abideth in me, and I in him* (Jn 6:56).

could I yearn to give Him everything I have, and even myself, if I didn't see Him as an *Other, Who is not myself*? And how could I be happy without the perfect vision (which supposes also the perfect admission) that God is; while I am nothing but the contingency of a being who has left nothingness behind by decision of Pure and Infinite Love, which has taken Him out of it, so that *I* can be the *other* for Him and so that He can be the *Other* for me? Why shouldn't I rejoice, with total happiness, that Being is Being and that creatures are creatures (which is the same as saying that things are as they are and that they are what they are)? And why, and for what possible reason, would I want the aberration and nonsense that Christ was for me a bizarre *Omega Point* when He can be a Person *whom we have seen with our eyes, whom we have looked upon, and our hands have handled* (1 Jn 1:1)? I admit with sincerity and humility that I completely ignore how and in what way a strange *Omega Point* could wrest my heart since no one has explained to me *what* it is, and which I cannot even imagine. Contrarywise, I am certainly willing to give my love to Someone who has shown me His in such a way, and Whom I can feel, touch, kiss, and hug; Whom I can call *Thou* and Whom I can hear, in turn, pronounce my own name (Jn 10:3) and call me to His side.

Pantheism and false mysticism directly attack the concept of Love. If the soul loses itself in God, or identifies itself with Him, it can no longer have Him in front of it as *Other*, before Whose contemplation it will be enthralled and by Whose sweet voice it will be seduced. If the creature identifies herself with God, she is no longer herself: she ceases to be an *I* in front of a *thou*; whence Love becomes impossible, and one cannot even speak of It in any way. And why or to what end would the creature want to become God? If such an aberrant absurdity were feasible, it would be necessary to conclude that the creature *could no longer possess God, nor make Him her own*. The possibility of the greatest and most unimaginable of all blessedness would have disappeared: that of being one for the other. Losing oneself or becoming God, when the creature can make Him hers —He for her, she for Him— without ceasing to be herself and without losing sight of the infinitely Lovable Lover, as *Other*, and therefore infinitely Loved? If they are no longer different, there are no longer *mutual* compliments, *mutual* caresses, or *mutual* glances of love.

The Rich Young Man

Because narcissism —or solipsism— is the furthest thing imaginable from Love. Because it is precisely through this mutual reciprocity, or bilaterality, that the light which illuminates, in some way, the path that leads to the Mystery is turned on.

Precisely because such bilaterality belongs to the very essence of Love, God places Himself at the height (He lowers Himself to the level) of His creature in order to give way to the possibility of Love: The disciple is not above his master, nor the servant above his lord. It is enough for the disciple to "become like his teacher and the servant like his lord."[36] Hence, the compliments and caresses of love are mutual, and it is not even conceivable that things could be otherwise:

> *How beautiful you are, my beloved,*
> *How beautiful you are!*
> *Your eyes are doves...*
>
> ....
>
> *How beautiful you are, my love, and how you delight me!*
> *Our bed is the greensward.*[37]
>
> ....
>
> *Come then, my beloved, my lovely one, come.*
> *Show me your face, let me hear your voice...*[38]

That is why Jesus rebukes Peter, at the Last Supper, when the apostle refuses to let the Master wash his feet: *If I do not wash you, you will have no part with me.*[39] But what Peter might have interpreted as an extreme act of humility actually contained a fullness of meaning that went far beyond all that. It was about complying with one of the formalities

---

[36] Mt 10: 24–25.
[37] Song 1: 15–16.
[38] Song 2: 13–14.
[39] Jn 13:8.

that constitute the essence of Love; even though the disciple was not then in a position to understand it: *What I do, you do not understand now; you will understand later.*[40]

The identification or communion of lives between the Lovers can be better understood, as far as the light that is granted us reaches and without the danger of daydreams, by delving deeper into the doctrine on the essence of Love. Perhaps we can thus achieve a better and more correct knowledge of the (mysterious) realities that are contained here. We have already wondered above about the possible meaning of expressions such as *living for the other* or *remaining in the other*, which only Love can make true and give meaning.

Love, as is known, supposes *leaving* oneself to *give oneself* to the other. Again, and as always, the deficiencies of human language. It is interesting to realize the peculiarity that these two expressions contain: while the first of them —*leaving*— is metaphorical, the second instead —*giving oneself*— must be taken in a strictly literal sense. It should not be forgotten, however, that metaphor always points to a *reality* that is either difficult, impossible, or less beautiful if expressed in any other way. The statement that Love is essentially Donation is absolutely correct.[41] Accordingly, it is true that each of the Lovers comes to belong entirely to the other. Regarding the mutual belonging of the spouses in Christian marriage, it can easily be understood that it is no more than the shadow or figure of the mutual and real belonging of Christ and His Church (the parallelism is established by Saint Paul himself in Ephesians 5: 22–33).We find, again, human love showing itself against the background of the divine–human and the purely divine love; nevertheless, the reciprocal belonging is real in all of them.

We are not making mere elucubrations; we are talking about authentic, although ineffable, realities, which are beautifully and boldly confirmed by the *Song of Songs*. His words exude poetic sense —it is a Sacred Poem— while pointing to the ineffable realities of Love:

---

[40] Jn 13:7.

[41] *Donation* is one of the most characteristic expressions used to designate the Person of the Holy Spirit.

> *My beloved is mine and I am his.*[42]
>
> ....
>
> *I belong to my beloved, and my beloved to me.*[43]
>
> ....
>
> *I belong to my beloved,*
> *And his desire is for me.*[44]

The possession of the Lover by the Beloved, and of the Beloved by the Lover, has to do with their mutual immanence (whatever immanence within Love means, and whose mystery we will not be able to exhaustively unveil), which is shown by the very words of the Master: *All the things that the Father has are mine.*[45] Which can be interpreted in two ways: everything that the Father possesses has been given to me, and now therefore belongs to me; or rather, everything that the Father possesses is mine, since it was I myself who have given it to Him. In reality, both meanings are reduced to one, in such a way that bilaterality and reciprocity appear again here; which are perfect when, as in this case, the issue at hand is substantial Love Who, by being so, makes the two the same thing (Jn 14: 10–11; 10:30). Hence, the apparent paradox of Love (two different Lovers and both one and the same thing) becomes an *apparently perfect paradox* in Uncreated Love, insofar as the Lovers are *really* different and at the same time only One.[46] In created love, the differentiation of persons does not give rise to an identification of natures; which, as we have said before, apart from the absurdity of the idea, would not make any sense. And hence we must examine in it, as far as possible, the way in which the immanence of those who love each other is to be understood, and the

---

[42] Song 2:16.

[43] Song 6:3.

[44] Song 7:11.

[45] Jn 16:15.

[46] In uncreated Love, the distinction refers to the Persons, whereas the identification is in Nature.

possible relationship between it and the perfect possession of one by the other.

If in divine–human love everything that belongs to the Beloved belongs to the creature He loves, such a thing can only mean that the intellectual and affective life of Jesus, His thoughts and affections, become the thoughts and affections of the enamored disciple. Which means that the disciple has made his Master's life *his own*: he thinks like Him, loves like Him, and acts like Him. This in no way invalidates or destroys his own spiritual life. If the understanding and the heart of the Master (His way of understanding, His way of loving, and His way of acting) were not now his (the disciple's), that is, if they were not possessed *by him*, it would happen that *he would no longer enjoy the life of Jesus, now made his*; and what is even more unimaginable, it would also happen that he (the disciple) would no longer be he either, nor could he therefore say that he had made the Life of the Beloved his own. In short: if there is no *I* and *thou* in the operation of Love, there can be no such Love and there are not even two who love each other. In order for me to be able to rejoice in the Love of my Beloved (joy which is ineffable), *I* must necessarily be the one who rejoices, and *He* must also necessarily be the object of the joy.[47]

But there is still more. Because appropriating the life of the beloved person is to manifest it or show it in the life of the lover. People *see* the

---

[47] According to the memories I have of my adolescence, when I finally made up my mind to give my unconditional consent to Jesus, in order to continue in the priestly vocation to which He invited me, there are things that are quite clear for me. Because what really seduced me, and the only thing that encouraged me to undertake the adventure, was the idea of *being like Jesus*. Or put another way, *to reproduce His life in my life*. Which is the same as saying that I was driven, even without understanding it, by the mysterious and inexplicable dynamism of Love: the desire, not just to be next to the loved person, but *to be like him*; well understood that being like him is not being him. If I had identified myself (become one) with that person, I would never have been able to enjoy that person, when my joy was born precisely from the deep desire that he be precisely he. I felt in love with Jesus and could not understand my own existence without Him, and without Him being Him. Why would I have wanted to exist without Him? And how could I have enjoyed Him without me being me?

Person of the Master in the life of the enamored disciple, for he is someone who thinks like Him, loves like Him, acts like Him, and lives like Him. It is precisely what the doctrine of the testimony of Jesus Christ has always tried to say, but now it has become a reality. The Master, Who was the perfect *Faithful Witness* (Rev 1:5; 1 Tim 6:13), is the One Who could say of Himself: *I and the Father are one.*[48] The enamored disciple cannot say that he is one with his Master; but he can claim that he is *like* his Master (Mt 10:25). But if the disciple would not show in his own life that of his Master Jesus, there could be neither the glory of testimony nor the testimony of glory. That is, the glory of Jesus Christ would not be shown resplendent in the weakness of His creature, nor the glory of the disciple, capable of displaying and bearing upon himself the glory proper to his Master. The greatness of the great saints consisted precisely in that: that they appeared as images of Jesus and resplendent testimonies of the Life of the Master. Hence the profound and mysterious reality of the expression referring to the priest when he is said to be *alter Christus*. Hence the strength of his ministry and his mysterious *power* before the Devil and before the World.

But if we admit that everything that the Gospel Message implies is contained *in nuce* in this challenge, and if we agree that the New Testament is nothing but the complete fulfillment and perfection of the Old (Mt 5:17), it becomes possible to conclude that the mutual request for love, contained in the *Song of Songs*, reflects a situation that coincides with this challenge. And even more, because the challenge contained in the *Song of Songs* has no other purpose, like in any authentic challenge and therefore also in the one addressed to the Rich Young Man, than to become *a true declaration of war and consequent battle*. If we want to put it another way, we could insist that, when we talk about the game (or battle) of divine–human Love, we are far from juggling words, or using mere literary metaphors.

---

[48] Jn 10:30.

And once again it must be admitted that here too the challenge is mutual.

> *He has taken me to his cellar,*
> *And his banner over me is love.*[49]

The Sacred Poem, under the layer of sweet and mutual compliments, arranged in an order that seems to ignore chronological or even logical requirements, actually contains a true and *hard* love story: started and developed, but which has not yet reached its final consummation...[50]

It is necessary to recognize that if a young man today, called by the Lord to live a priestly vocation, agrees to such an invitation, he faces a greater and graver risk than he can imagine.[51] The disrepute in which the priesthood is plunged today (and I am not referring so much to priests in general as to the very concept of priesthood), even within the Church herself, is quite deep. Additionally, the future's perspectives in this regard are not uncertain but more alarming and discouraging. If the priestly vocation has always been the greatest challenge that a young man could face,

---

[49] Song 2:4.

[50] The apparent unconcern for any chronological order in *The Song of Songs* (countless arguments to this effect have been elaborated over the centuries) does not seem to be without explanation. Who will be able to fix the exact chronology of a love story? What if it is also, as in this case, a divine–human love? On the other hand, there is no way to establish a possible relationship of Love with time. Love, true Love, comes from beyond Time and points beyond Time. In divine–human love, although one of the lovers —the one who lives within History— listens to the loving invitation at a certain historical moment, the call as such is *metahistorical*: both in its initial origin and in its pointed to end.

[51] What we are going to say is also valid for anyone —whether man or woman— who feels ready to give himself to Jesus Christ through a consecrated life. The current serious crisis affects all forms of consecrated life within the Church, and not only the ministerial priesthood.

as Jesus Christ Himself clearly warned: *Behold, I am sending you out as sheep in the midst of wolves*, now it involves an even greater degree of risk. Everything seems to corroborate the reality of the scarcity —actually, we should speak of non–existence— of priestly vocations, notwithstanding triumphalist statistics whose deceitful and self–interested character everyone knows.

And yet this situation is not enough to satisfactorily explain the problem. The truth is that not even the increasing paganization of society, nor the greater ferocity and extension of anti–Christian and anti–Catholic campaigns, provide sufficient cause to justify this scarcity. It is a fact, on the other hand, that the existence of risk, even to a high degree, is common in many activities of profane life. In society there are elite Special Corps, specifically prepared for specific tasks and missions (Army Forces and Special Intelligence or Espionage Groups, etc.), for which there is never a shortage of candidates. It does not seem that risk alone is a factor capable of dissuading Youth from undertaking a difficult task, and even less so when it promises dangerous imponderables.[52]

Everything seems to indicate, therefore, that there is something more here. Indeed, there is, in my opinion, a gigantic and well–

---

[52] I remember my teenage years, as full of naivete and lack of experience as they were full of dreams. At that time, both my closest friends and I were convinced that the priests of the environment in which we lived *did very little to Christianize the People*. Poor us. Those were kind and humble priests, surely very unprepared and rather poor in spirit, but full of faith and pious men. There is no doubt that they did more than enough to keep the flame of people's faith burning. What would have we thought of the current situation? So, ready as we were to repair Christianity at any cost, as if it were a new Portiuncula, we took hold of our shield, our lance, and our Mambrino helmet, and quixotically plunged ourselves into the adventure... What I mean by this it is that the *disastrous* clerical situation of that time, at least that is what it seemed to us, far from being an obstacle, became rather an incentive in our lives.

organized campaign to destroy the Catholic priesthood at any price until its total disappearance.

Various factors, of different nature apparently, have collaborated to achieve the desired effect. To the phenomena that we have mentioned above, referring to the promotion of the laity and the priestly identity crisis, we should add others which, being seemingly innocuous and even advantageous, have had a bearing on our problem. We will try to list some briefly and without going into too much detail.

The permanent diaconate has been instituted (or restored if you will) with the evident purpose of trying to solve needs, sometimes urgent, in certain regions at least. But perhaps a better solution could have been found; for example, an authentic reform of the Seminaries and, in general, of the formation of the clergy; although we must admit that, given the new doctrines spread by the innovators from the first moments that followed the Second Vatican Council, this solution would have been difficult to carry out. However, a good solution is not always the best; and sometimes it is not even that good.[53] The enormous proliferation and abuse of ordinations of permanent deacons, in numbers and cases often unnecessary, has had the effect of blurring the sense of the need for priests. Some go a step further in interpreting the facts, even going so far as to say that, since the majority of such deacons are married men, such an unnecessary overabundance of ministers actually pursues a second, albeit unavowed, objective: that of preparing the mentality of the faithful so that, given the evident need, they would admit the convenience that all, or almost all, of these ministers receive priestly ordination. This would deal a death blow to priestly celibacy, so abhorred by so many new-wave theologians and ecclesiastics. An institution —that of celibacy— that has been for so many centuries the shining crown of the Catholic priesthood and that will have

---

[53]Substitutes are always useful, since they somehow solve needs, whether urgent or not, when the original products are missing or scarce. But sometimes it happens that the originals are completely displaced by the substitutes, which can make people no longer feel the need for the former, and even to forget them. Pork *pâté*, for example, has led to the oblivion of authentic *foie gras* or, at least, to consider it as something people can dispense with. And the same can be said about artificial or synthetic caviar and other products whose list would be too long to enumerate.

led so many souls to Heaven (both of the Shepherds and of the sheep led by them, who received the testimony). This loss due to the Reformation makes one suspect, as one more among many things allowed by God, that He is *not in agreement* with such a restructuring Movement. After all, God has many ways to inflict punishment.

As far as Seminaries are concerned, there are two extremely important facts that amply demonstrate the existence of a campaign to prevent, at whatever cost, the formation of new and good priests. The problem is never discussed, even though it is quite obvious. Here we will limit ourselves to stating the facts briefly.

The first has to do with the new open–door policy of Seminaries towards homosexuals. The new ideas about sexual morality have granted access to the priesthood to individuals clearly abnormal in this regard, more openly in some countries and in a more hidden way in others. There is no need to talk about the ensued disasters; they are too painful and are also sufficiently well known.[54]

The second refers to the personnel in charge of the Seminaries. At the head of which have been placed, too often and in the face of an inexplicable silence on the part of those responsible, men of rather doubtful faith, and of an even more doubtful fidelity to the authentic Magisterium of the Church. The results have not been long in coming here either, although it is to be assumed that they will be more apparent as time goes by.

Of course, we realize that we will be the target of multiple accusations. The mildest of which will be that we generalize too much, that we are painting the darkest possible picture, that we are completely wrong (we are enjoying the *Springtime of the Church*), or even that we lie shamelessly, etc. As for other accusations, it is preferable to ignore them and consider them non–existent. The point here, however, is that mere denial of the facts

---

[54]It would be an affront, both to the intelligence and to the mentality of the simple faithful, to justify such a policy by resorting to speaking of the need to solve the problem of the shortage of priests. Any person of good will, willing to apply even a modicum of common sense, knows well that such procedures are the best way to destroy the Catholic priesthood, which has had the pride, for centuries, to make a deserved ostentation of the sublime virtue of Purity, in addition to the glory of a celibacy lived with joy for a higher Love.

—which are all too obvious— *does not make them disappear;* ultimately, truth will overcome falsehood in the long run.

As for the Female Religious Families,[55] the situation is in a certain way even more serious. The desertion of conventual nuns and the shortage of new candidates in the Novitiates is a phenomenon that is present and which, like everything that happens in the world in which we live, demands an explanation.

The life of prayer has been practically forgotten. The nuns leave the dormitory rather late in the day, mainly because they retire late at night to rest. The reason? There are many communities that consume too many nightly hours watching television, ignoring the contents of the small screen, quite often full of filth and often even sinful.

On the other hand, not a few communities, *because of their poverty*, have to dedicate most of the day to remunerative work in order to survive. What began as a humble artisan occupation (nun's cakes), ends up becoming a true industry requiring many hours of work, equipped with modern machinery, and in need of a complex *marketing* process. Subsistence *aid* has become a lucrative business, capable enough to distract nuns from what should be essential.

Fortunately, however, the Bishop in charge, for his part, tries to fulfill his responsibilities with respect to these chosen souls. To which end, he appoints a *Religious Delegate*, who is usually a good priest who is aware of the problem. In many cases he even gives the nuns a greeting visit, promising them that he will attend them as his many occupations allow him. Actually, the corresponding Bishop cannot do more in most cases: the numerous meetings of the Commissions and Sub–commissions of the Episcopal Conference which he has to attend (he is a full member) and his frequent stays in Rome do not allow for anything else.

It would be appropriate to make some consideration, albeit in passing, regarding the *industrialization* of some (cloistered) convents, and the corresponding new ideas about poverty.

Christian poverty is a dangerous virtue, as it lends itself to mystification, falsification, and misunderstanding. Obviously, that can happen with

---

[55] I include in this global denomination a large number, quite heterogeneous, of Groups of Women of consecrated life.

any virtue, although it is necessary to recognize that this one in particular has peculiarities that make it more suitable for such distortions. The proof that we are not exaggerating can be found in what happened with the *Fraticelli* during the fourteenth and fifteenth century. They ended up being condemned as heretics because of their erroneous ideas about this issue. This is one of the many other cases recorded (and unrecorded) by our History.

Frequent, and worthy of praise, is the case of Religious Families (both men and women) who, animated by the ardent desire of faithfully living the Gospel, begin with very strict demands regarding the virtue of Poverty. Their brave and generous dispositions in this regard end up attracting many people (the sincere experience of the evangelical spirit always seduces), and this is precisely where danger lurks. Actually, the issue was already raised as a problem for Saint Francis and the first Franciscans. As the number of followers and the complexity and importance of the activities of such a Religious Family increase, so do the infrastructures, structures, and financial set-up necessary to attend to both the tasks and the people who carry them out. With the necessary increase in goods, and with the greater and essential attention that must be paid to pecuniary operations, the danger that the *Spirit will be quenched* (1 Thess 5:19) increases considerably. Whether you like it or not, the fearsome ghost of incompatibility, already warned by the Lord, between the world of the supernatural and the commodities of this world inevitably appears: *You cannot serve God and riches.*[56] And it must be admitted that the sentence, had it not come from the mouth of Jesus Christ Himself, would have seemed like a curse. More than twenty centuries of Christianity, during which many men and women of good will have tried to reconcile both terms..., and the failure has been total, as if we were dealing with witchcraft. Because in reality everything seems to point to the absolute necessity of goods: how would it be possible, without them, to set up structures, recruit and train new militants, extend apostolic action to other countries, build places of worship and residence, take advantage of the immense multitude of means that modern technology places within man's reach, seize the means of influence, etc., etc.? Everything, absolutely everything, with the intention

---

[56]Lk 16:13.

to do good and spread the Gospel; of course, and without the slightest doubt. And yet, again and again, and always again, the Specter of incompatibility inexorably reappears: *Non potestis Deo servire et mammonae.* And in case something was still missing, it even seems that the Devil is pleased to ironize the situation. At the same time that the fame of the *extreme poverty* of a particular Religious Family is spreading, its influence in society, its possibilities of action, and the means at its disposal are also increasing. More and more each time. The poor nuns and poor friars cease to be, slowly but surely, poor nuns and poor friars. Sometimes even accepting the rush too. And it is still true that the *applauded poverty* ends up becoming anything but poverty.

The situation created is not to be taken as a joke. This is another of the apparent aporias of the Gospel in which, necessarily and uncompromisingly, one must decide for one thing or another: God or riches, take it or leave it. This choice, upon little consideration, has been capable of deciding the success or the failure of any evangelizing action of Christianity for more than twenty centuries.[57]

---

[57]This is how situations arise that would even seem funny were they not a consequence of a very serious matter. I remember the experiences we had with a group of Mother Teresa's nuns in one of our parishes in New Jersey. The community of friendly nuns had settled in a house of considerable size (the number of nuns justified it) near us. Due to the demands of poverty, it was necessary to carry out various refurbishment works of the premises: among other things, eliminating the existing carpet throughout the house and getting rid of the individual telephones located in each room. Peeling off the carpet and the consequent reconditioning of the floor were quite expensive. On the other hand, it was necessary to install a buzzer or bell in each room of the house, in order to notify the nun in question that somebody, on the only phone of the house, was calling her. The installation was not cheap, for in the United States of America there are few professions with low wages. But the misfortunes did not end there, as can well be assumed. Because the poor little nuns did not have a car (demands of poverty), and due to the fact that in North America it is not possible to visit one's neighbor if one does not have a vehicle (because of the distances), our poor priests had to solve the (justified) problem of transporting the nuns to–and–fro by using their own cars despite the limited time available to them for that purpose.

The problem, however, is more delicate than it may seem at first glance and is not to be taken lightly. It has to do, in the first place, with an adequate conception of the virtue of poverty and the means to live it. Which, strange as it may seem, is not an easy thing to achieve, given the prevailing confusion and the lack of clear doctrine on the matter. Well known is the case of an influential Religious Family (this time of men) that also began with ardent desires to fight for Christ and His Church, whose sincerity and honesty cannot be doubted. Such desires were accompanied in turn by the intention of carrying out a peculiar fight in which it would be necessary to trust more —at least initially— in the bravery and personal heroism of its members than in the abundance and quality of the means to be used. The animating spirit of the company was of course militaristic (metaphorically understood), with the more than laudable desire to conquer the world for Christ (remember the founding spirit of Saint Ignatius of Loyola and the term *Company*, adapted from military slang, used by the Saint himself to name his recently founded Work). All correct and full of the best intentions. However, once again, and as usually happens, the Devil was seemingly determined to spoil an enterprise which had started so vigorously. These strong and brave fighters were successfully welcomed —which is quite understandable— and began to receive abundant supplies. These heroic storm troupes became Armored Divisions equipped with the most modern weapons and the most efficient supply equipment. The only thing left was to let time pass and observe the events. But the Devil is pleased to promote successes in order to make the best and most well–intentioned companies fail.

All these Spiritual Families and, in general, all those who wish to follow Christ very closely, should bear in mind what is clearly deduced from the episode of the Rich Young Man in the Gospel. First, *go and sell everything you have and give it to the poor*. When that is done, and only when that is done, *come and follow me*. It seems that, according to what all the teachings of the New Testament agree on, there is no valid Evangelization for Christianity that is not based on that foundation.

The case of the nuns of Mother Teresa, like that of other female Religious Families, is disturbing for any observer of good will. We are not referring now to the good intentions of the Foundress or to the magnificent results of her Work, which cannot be questioned. However, considering things dispassionately, there is a real possibility that serious problems may arise in a more or less near future.

In the first place, the lack of a solid *Corpus* of Doctrine (what is usually called the peculiar Spirituality of a religious Order) can lead to a vacuum and a lack of clear criteria, with the possibility of becoming reasons for serious concern. We have already seen, albeit very superficially, what happens with the implementation of the virtue of Poverty and the problems that it can give rise to. To allude to one, the honest intention of sanctifying oneself *through charity (love) towards the poor* is an ambiguous expression that can cause misunderstandings. No one is sanctified through love for the poor, but *through charity towards the poor for love of Jesus Christ*. It is evident that the confusion, in this as in other things, can be serious and calls for a clear Body of Doctrine.

Secondly, there is the danger, by no means negligible, that once the Foundress has disappeared with her enormous and peculiar personal charisma, the founding spirit cannot be preserved. It must be considered that the formation and spiritual nourishment of the nuns of Mother Teresa (we are talking here about an example loved and known by all) is in the hands of an available particular, in a specific parish or place, and at a specific time. Unfortunately, however, the spirituality of the *available priest* often is lacking in depth. Of course, it will not be easy to find many men with sufficient interior life and who also know the charism of Mother Teresa.

It should be clear that it is not our intention to criticize things that everyone usually recognizes as good. We are only encouraged by the desire, born of good will, to point out obstacles that may hinder the smooth running of Religious Families made up, in our opinion, of heroic men and women who do not deserve to disappear. And it will never be a bad thing to keep in mind that there is a real danger, fed by the confusion of ideas raging through today's Church, constantly lurking, looking for someone to destroy (1 Pet 5:8).

Given these facts, and many others that we do not want to (or cannot) mention here, one cannot be surprised by the great defection of the Youth with respect to the priestly ministry or to the consecrated life in general. Where could a young man with a generous heart, eager to respond to the call of Jesus Christ to follow Him, go in order to obtain a good priestly formation? Perhaps to a youth training center filled with deficient candidates and where the lack of faith is seen as something natural? Perhaps to a Center where those in charge of their formation have no faith, are skeptical of the traditional virtues (including, of course, chastity), and smirk at the teachings of the authentic Magisterium?

Then? What can we say, or what can we do?

For, on the other hand, it is impossible for God to have abandoned His Church, even though it may seem sometimes that He has done so. And since the Lord spoke about prayer being the appropriate means (and perhaps the only one, we say), for the Owner of the harvest to send workers to work in it (Lk 10:2), such a recommendation cannot be ineffective. And it will always be true that hope will not let us down (Rom 5:5). It is true that sometimes it does not seem easy to be able to listen to the voice of the authentic Magisterium, nor to find true foremen who train authentic and hardworking workers to work the harvest. Nor does it seem an easy task to find good training camps to go to for learning... And yet, despite all that, we must remain convinced that there will be some way to avoid the obstacles; which will force us to be vigilant, in order not to miss opportunities that lead us to victory: *Have confidence; I have overcome the world.*[58] A dictum that the Beloved Disciple had understood well: *This is the victory that has overcome the world,*

---

[58] Jn 16:33.

*our faith.*⁵⁹ And who said that the Youth of the world is entirely lost to the Church, or that there are no longer strong and generous hearts capable of picking up the challenging gauntlet thrown down to them? *I will leave me seven thousand men in Israel, whose knees have not been bowed before Baal, and whose lips have not kissed him.*⁶⁰

What we Christians of today must do, faced with the tricks of the System and with regard specifically to the priestly vocation, is to try not to hide or conceal the difficulties of the undertaking. Rather, it is necessary to act in the opposite direction. First of all, because young people do not deserve to be deceived. And then because the Youth, no matter how far removed it may seem from authentic values, will always continue to believe that easy undertakings are for certain boys and girls endowed with the velvety character everyone knows, and who never consider the possibility of facing anything which involves effort or sacrifice.

Accepting the invitation–challenge proposed by Jesus Christ, as can be deduced from the story of the Rich Young Man, means abandoning everything, in order to give it to the poor, and then follow Him. But we must take special care not to fall into misunderstandings or in quick and easy Gospel readings. *Selling everything you have* to donate it, renouncing all the belongings you own, is a more serious thing than it may seem. Giving up your own ideas or your own will, for example, is much more difficult and more decisive than giving up your own material goods.

A young man or woman today who decides to follow Jesus Christ, seriously committing his or her whole life to doing so, would have to be willing to accept a situation high risk in every way. In any

---

⁵⁹ 1 Jn 5:4.
⁶⁰ 1 Kings 19:18.

case, of course, if the decision was serious and involved an authentic following of the *true* Jesus Christ.[61] If so, the adventurer willing to accept the challenge would have to be prepared to maintain:[62] That Jesus Christ is *really* present in the Eucharist (apart from the philological trifles with which the innovators try to confuse the faithful, and using the terms, therefore, in the sense in which they have always been and always are understood). That the Catholic Church is the only true Church founded by Jesus Christ; whence, therefore, it is not true that all religions serve the same purpose. That the dogmatic truths do not change in their meaning according to the diverse and contingent historical circumstances. That Christian marriage between Christians entails an indissoluble bond arranged as such by divine law; from where divorce does not fit even if it is disguised with another name. That the concept and experience of the Catholic priesthood cannot tolerate hesitations or doubts; hence, its sublime greatness cannot be clouded by an artificially created identity crisis. That Thomism has always been the doctrinal system (method and content) preferred and recommended by the Church, both for

---

[61] I mean the Christ of faith, Who is exactly the same historical Christ, as has always been proclaimed by the Church and her Magisterium and accepted as such by the universal faith of all Christian Faithful. Committing oneself to following the *lite* Christ, espoused and preached by the innovative Neo–modernists, would not really entail any risk. In this instance, would it be worthwhile for a person to become the disciple of such an intellectual ghost? And does not this fact perhaps explain the current lack (absence) of vocations?

[62] Since we have started from the premise of a serious following of Jesus Christ, it is evident that no one would be willing to carry it out if they did not firmly believe in what we are going to say next.

the formation of priests and for the explanation of the truths of the faith.[63] Etc.; the list would be too long.

But then, one might ask, where is the so–called risk? The answer is not difficult. In the fact that, whoever firmly maintains such claims *will not find help anywhere and will also be subject to any form of persecution*:[64] he will be termed as pre–conciliar, tridentine, fundamentalist, conservative, Lefebvrian, opposed to the teaching of the Magisterium, etc., etc.

According to which, *can you drink the cup that I shall drink?* Or, if you prefer to say it another way: *Do you know that foxes have caves, and birds of the sky have nests; while the Son of Man, etc...?* Is anyone still willing, after this...? Probably yes. Or maybe not; but then, irritated, the owner of the house said to his servant: "*Go out quickly into the streets and lanes of the city, and bring in hither the poor, and the feeble, and the blind, and the lame.*"[65]

It is a proven fact that if someone stands firm on principles, the whole world rises up against him. Both the outsiders and the insiders; mainly the insiders, which should not be a surprise, especially if one considers that the Lord Himself was in a similar situation. In fact, He was condemned by the religious and civil authorities, both at the same time, starting with the Sanhedrin, which was a political–religious institution. In the religious sphere, it is worth pointing out the absolute coincidence in this regard of the sects of Pharisees and Sadducees, as well as Annas and Caiaphas. As far

---

[63] The Conciliar Decree *Optatam Totius*, for the formation of the clergy, says nothing about Thomism, but uses some vague formula, such as that of *innixi patrimonio philosophico perenniter valido*, and does not even mention the Encyclical *Æterni Patris*.

[64] Even if it is merely the imposition of the law of silence on his person, or he being deprived *de facto* of any position of significance, no matter how minimal, in his own environment.

[65] Lk 14:21.

The Rich Young Man

as the civilian circle is concerned, let us remember that both Herod and Pilate condemned Jesus Christ.

We have already said before, however, that the presence of high risks is not an intimidating factor for brave hearts. Which everyone would be willing to admit. Hence the difficulty of considering it a sufficient reason to explain the lack of priestly vocations. It is, therefore, necessary to take into account another fact. For what is at stake here is the following of Jesus Christ in order to live His own life, share His existence, be by His side, be like Him, and participate in His destiny. All of which means *to be in love with his Person*; for how else could someone follow Him, knowing perfectly well what that following entails, which the next object of our reflection clearly indicates. The young man in question, following the instructions of Jesus Christ, must go first to sell all his possessions, then deliver the profits to the poor, and then, finally, *he must return and follow the Master.*[66]

The data that was missing, and which should be taken into account by the vocational campaigns promoted by the diocesan laboratories of pastoral alchemy, is the need to present the figure of Jesus Christ. In a seductive way because, in this case, there is no

---

[66]Note well the meaning of the text. The donation of one's own goods to the poor is not the ultimate goal to be pursued here, since it is only a necessary means with a view to the decisive end, which is *the following of the Master*. It is enough to pay attention to the literalness of the text to understand it immediately. Which is something that those who proclaim from the rooftops their concern for the poor should not forget; and even less those who claim that such motivation is the only legitimate one that leads to sanctification. Here, in fact, is yet another manifestation of the innovative winds that are currently blowing within the Church: first to man, in order to reach God through him. Or put more technically, anthropocentrism displacing theocentrism. It is a resounding truth, however, no matter how much one tries to distort it, that it is impossible to love man if he first does not love God.

other way to do it. And here, more than anywhere else, it would be necessary to insist on the need to *bear witness to Jesus Christ*.

Perhaps it would not be useless if, in the role played by the bureaucracies of the Diocesan and Supra–diocesan Curia, the figure of the *expert* were eliminated once and for all. Although it would be necessary to start by first eliminating most of said bureaucracy. The excessive technicalities and psychological and sociological methods, in addition to the advanced findings of the modern techniques of commercial or industrial companies, do not seem to fit well with the tasks of Evangelization. A concrete field in which what men endowed with an authentic spirit, animated moreover by the true Spirit, are not capable of doing will be nothing other than *aes sonans aut cymbalum tinniens*. Not to mention here the enormous waste of money, time, and energy carried out by the complex and numerous diocesan bureaucracies. Any Civil Society Company, no matter how small, considers at all times the balance between costs and returns. In the ecclesiastical world, on the other hand (and I am referring above all to the United States, where this phenomenon manifests itself most frequently), it is not an ordinary custom to account for expenses in order to find out if such enormous amounts of money correspond to an equivalent enhancement of the Christian life of the faithful. On the other hand, everything leads one to think that what is at the bottom of such phenomena is nothing more than the influence of Protestant theology: devaluation or annulment of the role of the priestly ministry to equate it with the role to be played by the laity.

As von Balthasar said, *Only that which has form can snatch one up into a state of rapture. Only through form can the lightning–bolt of eternal beauty flash. There is a moment in which the bursting light of the spirit as it makes its appearance completely drenches external form in its rays. From the manner and the measure in which this happens we know whether we are in the presence of "sensual" or of "spiritual" beauty, in the presence of graceful charm or of interior grandeur. But without form, in any event, a person will not be captivated and transported. To be transported, moreover, belongs to the very origin of Christianity. The Apostles were transported by what they saw, heard, and touched; by everything manifested in the form...Both the person who is transported by natural beauty and the one snatched up by the beauty of Christ must appear to the world to be fools, and the world will attempt to explain their state in terms of psychological or even physiological laws (Acts 2:13).*[67]

In the priestly vocation there is no room for thinking about risk; danger is not even considered. What is essential here is the charm and seduction of the Person of Jesus Christ, under Whose *spell*, as von Balthasar would say, the risk is considered worthy of being faced by the one who has received the invitation–challenge to follow. Hence the essential need for witness in vocational proselytism. He who has been *seduced* by Christ to the point of falling in love with His Person has felt a certain *perception*. Without contemplation of Beauty there is neither the attraction nor the desire to possess It: *nihil volitum quin præ cognitum*. Such perception must come through faith, which ordinarily also uses the testimony provided by witnesses: *Let your light shine before men, so that they may see your good works and glorify your Father who is in heaven...*[68] *You will be my witnesses in Jerusalem, in all Judea and Samaria, and to the ends of the earth.*[69]

The words of Jesus Christ addressed to the apostle Thomas could be brought up here: *Because you have seen me, you have believed. Blessed are those who, without seeing, believed.* To understand this, one should remember the distinction, frequently used in theology,

---

[67] Hans Urs Von Balthasar, *The Glory of de Lord. A Theological Aesthetics*, I, San Francisco, pgs. 32–33.

[68] Mt 5:16.

[69] Acts 1:8.

between *credere Christum*, on the one hand, and *credere Christo*, on the other. The second, which goes far beyond mere acquiescence to the truths revealed by the Master, presupposes unlimited trust in His Person, which is not possible without Love,[70] and which implies necessarily the mysterious *perception* that faith alone can provide (perhaps one could speak here of a perception *beyond the senses*). It is not necessary to stress the fact that following Jesus Christ stresses more *credere Christo* as a dynamic element.

It is within these parameters that the priestly vocation is offered. The risks? They are many, indeed. Greater and more numerous than ever. Whoever decides to take the path in order to be *another Christ* knows that he will be despised for even daring to face that risk. Nowadays the priest is nothing, while the layman is viewed with much more respect and esteem. In addition to this, the crazy adventurer knows that he will not be able to become another Christ without being faithful to the Church and to her Magisterium. To complicate things more, it is not always easy, in the current moment of confusion, to guess where the authentic principles and genuine teachings of the Magisterium are. It is sometimes difficult, for example, to find agreement between the teachings of the indefectible Magisterium of the Church, which constitute a single block that cannot change, with the multitude of documents and provisions emanating from official and semi–official Organisms, Congregations, Episcopal Conferences, Diocesan Curias, Conferences of Hierarchs (Bishops, Cardinals, etc.), doctrines of accredited or less accredited theologians, etc. It seems as if, for some, the Magisterium in force until the Second Vatican Council were already outdated and obsolete. And yet, the true disciple who dares to embark on the ad-

---

[70] In some of my books and elsewhere I have many times talked about the difference between the concepts of loving God and being in love with God.

venture knows that there is and will always be only one Church and only one Magisterium..., although he personally will need prayer and a large dose of fidelity to find them. That is why he knows that *he has to be a rebel*, while at the same time he is also aware that *he cannot be rebellious*; that is, he will have to face all kinds of setbacks and vicissitudes while, at the same time, he must maintain, above all, love and fidelity to his Mother the Church. Always keeping in mind, according to what the Apostle said, *I can do all these things in him who strengtheneth me.*[71]

When I was a teenager, in those times when the priest was respected, I would not have been able to feel the slightest attraction to the idea of a priestly vocation. I even let myself get carried away with anger when someone, whether seriously or jokingly, hinted at such a possibility for my future. The same thing that usually happens with any child; in those years I was fascinated with dreams of being a famous lawyer, perhaps a highly recognized doctor, or a military man who would achieve a high degree of human glory in society. The priesthood, on the other hand, represented to me nothing more than the figure of a respectable man who performed a useful and even necessary function but was unable to arouse in my heart the necessary fantasies that could have fed my emotions.

Everything changed for me, however, when the Lord wanted me to realize that being a priest was not the same as *being a cleric*, but was nothing more and nothing less than *being another Christ*. Ironically, for all this would have sounded like a joke to someone who had known me at that time, I felt strangely seduced by the Lord. I still do not know, and probably I will always ignore, which arrangements God had made to achieve such a wonder. But be that as it may, this is how it happened and not otherwise.

---

[71] Phil 4:13.

Which necessarily leads us to a conclusion that admits no exceptions, and which we have been talking about. By this we mean that to feel the call to follow Jesus Christ, and more so to be determined to respond affirmatively, it is necessary to have previously been seduced, or fascinated if you will, by the Person of the Lord. Then, and only then, is it understood that any risk is worth taking. And even more: for the true lover, any danger ceases to seem so:

> *Seeking my loves,*
> *I will go o'er yonder mountains and banks;*
> *I will neither pluck the flowers*
> *Nor fear the wild beasts;*
> *I will pass by the mighty and cross the frontiers.*[72]

Note that the Saint refers here both to the dangers that may arise in the search —*I will not fear the wild beasts*—, as well as to the varied and numerous seductions —*I will neither pluck the flowers*— that the world can offer in order to dissuade a heart in love and full, therefore, of generosity.

It is true that faith is *rerum argumentum non apparentium*.[73] Faith is not, of course, a perception acquired through the bodily or external senses. In spite of which, and since it is not possible to speak of love or infatuation without the mediation of understanding, it is evident that it is necessary to resort here to the existence of a certain knowledge.[74] The Bride of the *Song of Songs,* undoubtedly referring to the knowledge she has of her Bridegroom, prefers to

---

[72] Saint John of the Cross: *Spiritual Canticle.*

[73] Heb 11:1.

[74] Within the Trinity, the Holy Spirit does not proceed only and directly from the Father, but from the Father and from the Idea or Word of the Father, jointly.

speak of the perfumes that emanate from Him or the intoxication that His presence produces (Song 1: 2–4.13–14; 4:16; 6:2). Which does not hinder her, nevertheless, from describing the Bridegroom when she is requested to do so:

> *My love is fresh and ruddy,*
> *To be known among ten thousand.*
> *His head is golden, purest gold,*
> *His locks are palm fronds*
> *And black as the raven.*
> *His eyes are like doves*
> *Beside the water–courses...*[75]

Pure metaphors, of course. But how else could one speak of the Bridegroom? That is why, just as it would be impossible to explain the colors of the rainbow to a man born blind, it is also impossible to talk to him who has never loved or does not know how to love about things such as falling in love with God, or feeling seduced by the Person of Jesus Christ, or welcoming the madness of Love to the point of giving everything for Him: *He that loveth not, knoweth not God: for God is love.*[76]

But what is admirable about this —in reality, only a share of what is infinitely and endlessly admirable— is the fact that, given the characteristics of bilaterality and reciprocity proper to Love, the feelings experienced by the Bride are the same ones that affect the Bridegroom. We must not forget that Love is *nexus duorum* and that it puts both Lovers on the same level: *I will not now call you servants: I have called you friends:* (Jn 15:15). What comes to

---

[75] Song 5: 10–12.
[76] 1 Jn 4:8.

confirm, among many others of the New Testament, a curious and ineffable text of the *Apocalypse*: Behold, I stand at the door, and knock. If any man shall hear my voice, and open to me the door, I will come in to him, and will sup with him, and he with me.[77] And, of course, this other passage of *The Song of Songs*:

> *I belong to my love,*
> *And his desire is for me.*[78]

It would be a difficult thing to explain, in the absence of this feeling of closeness —without the feelings of equality, reciprocity, and mutual possession— the unimaginable realism and relief of the *thou* and the *I* present in the mysterious dialogue of Love. It would be difficult, indeed, to explain here, without the concurrence of these elements, the seduction caused by Jesus which can impel a young soul to give herself to Him, without reserve and forever, in order to follow Him and share His destiny, whatever it may be, because what does that matter in the presence of Love?

The relationship of reciprocity and equality, within the ineffable binomial that Love establishes between those who love each other, reaches extremes that the human mind, by itself, would be unable to reach. In divine–human love, for example, the creature lives in nostalgia, restlessness, yearning, and anxieties of the *not yet*. She has tasted the love of the Bridegroom but still does not have it fully: *We see now through a mirror in a dark manner.*[79] Both extremes of the love phenomenon, so characteristic of the situation of what is still *in via*, appear in *The Song of Songs*. But in such a way —which

---

[77] Rev 3:20.
[78] Song 7:11.
[79] 1 Cor 13:12.

would have seemed incredible— that the relationship of reciprocity is also present there:

> *Your love-making is sweeter than wine...*[80]
>
> ....
>
> *I adjure you, O daughters of Jerusalem,*
> *If you find my beloved,*
> *That you tell him that I languish with love.*[81]

It would be impossible to think that these feelings could equally affect —at least in a similar way— the Bridegroom. God cannot love His creature in the *not yet*. According to the Apostle, there will finally come a time when *I will know as I am known*.[82] Face to face, therefore. However, given the inflexibility of the laws of Love, we are forced to confront the mysterious reality according to which, because that has been His will, *God has wanted to put Himself at the level of His creature*. Obviously, it would be of little use here to ask for the help that the laws of analogy could provide, not the one that ascends from the bottom to the top, and even less so the one that would supposedly descend from the top to the bottom. There is, however, an element of mystery here —another among the many of Love— impossible to explain. At least for now, until we have reached, perhaps, the Term Station that is the definitive Homeland (and we say *perhaps* because all the mysteries of Love will not be revealed to us exhaustively there either). We are with this trying to refer to a strange text of *The Song of Songs* which has passed almost

---

[80] Song 1:2.
[81] Song 5:8.
[82] 1 Cor 13:12.

unnoticed. In it, the Bridegroom addresses the Bride between sighs of love, to tell her:

> *How beautiful art thou, my love,*
> *How beautiful art thou!*
> *Thy eyes are doves' eyes, behind your veil.*[83]

According to which the Bridegroom, in addition to noticing in ecstasy the beauty of the Bride, recognizes that He perceives it *through her veil*. As if He wanted to also say that, as long as the Bride does not fully enjoy the presence of the Bridegroom, namely until He, the Bridegroom, does not live in fullness, in His own heart, the already actual and total joy of the Bride, *for Him, the mutual Love will still be something incomplete and unconsummated*. Of course, this cannot claim to be an explanation; much less satisfy anyone. However, it is enough that the reality of the mystery be such as to wrap even more, if it were possible, in an aura of inexpressible joy the ineffable fact of what mutual Love is. A Love which, although for the creature It is still in the phase of *not yet*, is nevertheless enough, with what she *already* possesses, to fill her with such joy as to make her feel dying of Love:

> *Tell him that I languish with love...*

Within this context, the decision of a young soul to fully follow Jesus Christ would be nothing less than a manifestation of the madness of Perfect Love.

But the Church is, perhaps, facing the greatest crisis in her whole history, which, in reality is but one more consequence of the fact

---

[83] Song 4:1.

that the world has turned away from God. And the values that until now have belonged to the so–called Western civilization, all of them infused by Christianity, seem about to disappear forever. But then, who can save the Church and the world if not the madmen of Love? Would it be possible to find another solution, against the lethal and authentic madness of the world, other than the wonderful and seeming madness of the Love of God? How could one forget that it was the madness of the Cross that has already saved, once and for all, mankind? How could anyone think that such madness will not continue to find an echo and a response also in these stormy times, among so many young souls capable of accepting the proud challenge that Satan, convinced of his victory, is throwing to the face of the world of the early twenty–first century?

Index of Quotations of the New Testament

MATTHEW

5: 3, **147**
   11, **243**
   16, **297**
   17, **281**
6: 22, **218**
   23, **202**
7: 13, **104**
   14, **103, 178**
8: 8, **62**
9: 9–13, **193**
   15, **70, 92, 144**
   37, **173**
   37–38, **172**
   38, **89**
10: 5–6, **195**
    16, **267**
    21, **243**
    22, **103**
    23, **125**
    24–25, **277**
    25, **153, 281**
    36, **112, 244**
    38–39, **219**
    39, **219**
11: 7, **242**
    25, **225**
    25–26, **59**
13: 10–11, **160**
    13–15, **162**
    36, **161**
    52, **213**
17: 25–26, **144**
18: 3, **149**
    7, **136**
    10, **191**
19: 14, **147**
    16, **249**
    21, **168**
    29, **192**
20: 1–16, **157**
    4, **117**
    28, **42, 54, 155**
21: 31, **196**
22: 1–14, **163**
    2–3, **117**
    8, **117**
    14, **265**
    16, **209**
    17, **194**
    21, **195**
23: 13, **208**
    13–39, **136**
    23, **213, 218**
    24, **208**
24: 9, **243**
    12, **170, 187**
    15, **95, 114**
26: 39, **263**
28: 19, **102, 117, 195**

Mark

1: 16–18, **83**
40, **55**
7: 27, **195**
37, **65**
8: 23, **109**
35, **274**
10: 17, **249**
38, **219**, **265**
46–52, **99**
51, **55**
12: 14, **194**
13: 12, **243**
31, **165**

Luke

5: 31, **54**
32, **54**
35, **144**
6: 12–13, **210**
20, **147**
24–26, **136**
40, **153**
9: 23, **219**
57–62, **187**
58, **219**
62, **102**
10: 2, **47**, **79**, **170**, **172**, **291**
13–15, **136**
16, **86**, **118**, **170**
41, **52**
11: 5–13, **163**
42–46, **136**
14: 16–24, **163**
21, **294**
23, **117**
27, **177**, **219**
16: 1–8, **161**
13, **287**
17: 1, **136**
20, **147**
21, **147**
18: 1–8, **163**
18, **249**
19: 1–10, **210**
8, **210**
20: 22, **194**
21: 16, **244**
33, **268**
22: 25–26, **146**
24: 21, **262**

John

1: 4, **102**
5, **162**
11, **120**

35, **81**
35–42, **82**
47, **210**
2: 1–11, **201**
3: 8, **118, 256**
20–21, **162**
29, **92, 144**
30, **83**
34, **186**
4: 6, **101**
21–22, **197**
35, **188**
6: 56, **275**
56–57, **167**
57, **85, 218–220**
64, **35**
8: 32–34, **194**
36, **194**
9: 1, **19**
10: 1, **35**
3, **123, 145, 169, 276**
10, **104, 141, 258**
12–13, **141**
30, **279, 281**
11: 1–44, **51**
28, **123**
12: 24, **21, 269**
47, **54**
13: 1, **144, 165, 187**
7, **61, 278**

8, **154, 277**
13, **143**
14: 3, **170**
6, **100, 145, 178**
10–11, **279**
20, **167**
27, **146**
30, **95**
34, **102**
15: 4, **167**
5, **24, 103**
11, **91**
13, **49, 52**
15, **52, 118, 143, 301**
18–19, **112**
20, **112, 267**
22, **162**
16: 2, **243**
15, **279**
22, **91**
33, **8, 291**
17: 14, **214, 222**
15, **42**
18: 33–37, **143**
36, **146**
37, **143**
20: 21, **86, 170**
23, **86**
21: 18–19, **263**

ACTS OF THE APOSTLES

1: 8, **297**
   11, **102**
2: 13, **297**
3: 6, **123**
13: 46, **195**
15: 8–9, **197**

ROMANS

1: 14, **195**
   16, **195**
4: 18, **6**
5: 5, **256, 291**
6: 3, **97, 177**
   6, **218**
8: 9–10, **218**
   24, **256, 261**
   28, **58**
10: 14, **84**
14: 17, **147**

1 CORINTHIANS

1: 17, **181**
   21–23, **109**
   22–23, **181**
   23–25, **222**
   25, **247**
   26–28, **59**
   26–31, **21**
2: 4–5, **108**
4: 9, **247**
7: _, **165**
   32–35, **164**
9: 24, **110, 252**
   26, **110, 252**
11: 7, **201**
    11, **201**
13: 8, **8, 188, 257**
    12, **302, 303**
    13, **257**
15: 24–27, **148**
16: 22, **136**

2 CORINTHIANS

1: 19, **263**
3: 17, **173, 194**
4: 10, **219**
   10–11, **221**
5: 6, **70**
   21, **21**
6: 14–15, **246**
8: 9, **21, 151**
11: 26, **112**
12: 5, **226**
    9, **58**
    9–10, **179**

Galatians

1: 8, **136**
   10, **109**
2: 2, **252**
   11–14, **10**
   20, **21, 39, 86, 170, 220, 274**
3: 13, **225**
   28, **197**
4: 19, **85**
   31, **194**
5: 6, **197**
   11, **181**
   13, **194**
6: 14, **219**

Ephesians

4: 7, **256**
   15, **85**
   24, **218**
5: 22–33, **278**

Philippians

1: 23, **96**
2: 6–8, **144**
   7, **21**
   9–11, **132**
   16, **252**
3: 12, **90**
   12–13, **252**
   13, **102**
4: 13, **103, 299**

Colossians

1: 18, **142**
   24, **8**
3: 2, **40**
   11, **195**

1 Thessalonians

5: 19, **213, 287**

2 Thessalonians

2: 10–12, **7**

1 Timothy

1: 17, **139**
2: 4, **264**
   15, **180**
3: 1, **115**
5: 22, **214**
6: 13, **230, 281**
   15, **144**

2 Timothy

3: 12, **25, 178, 244**
16, **255**
4: 7, **257**

Hebrews

4: 12, **136, 268**
5: 1, **214**
4, **86, 171, 210**
11: 1, **300**
12: 4, **230**
7, **56**
29, **86**
13: 14, **95**
20, **169**

James

2: 5, **150**

1 Peter

4: 7, **95**
5: 8, **290**

2 Peter

2: 19, **194**
20–22, **102**
3: 16, **161**

1 John

1: 1, **276**
2: 13–14, **252**
14, **190, 191**
4: 8, **275, 301**
19, **151, 259**
5: 4, **8, 292**

Revelation

1: 5, **281**
2: 4, **187**
17, **170**
3: 15–16, **110**
20, **167, 302**
14: 1–4, **164**
17: 14, **139**
19: 15–16, **148**
20–21, **148**
21: 1, **178**
8, **102**
22: 12, **95, 116, 186**
15, **136**

Contents

MEDITATIONS AT SUNSET

Prologue 1

Introduction 13

The Healing of the Man Born Blind 19

The Good Shepherd 35

The Resurrection of Lazarus 51

Our First Meeting with The Lord
(Regarding Saint Andrew's Vocation) 81

The Healing of the Blind Man Bartimeus 99

The Feast of Christ the King 127

To Every Man a Penny
(Parable of the Workers sent to the Vineyard) 157

Vocation of Saint Matthew
(The Dance of the Damned) 193

The Rich Young Man
(The Challenge of the Eagles) 249

www.ingramcontent.com/pod-product-compliance
Lightning Source LLC
Chambersburg PA
CBHW060413010526
44107CB00006B/679